CAULDRON OF TURMOIL

AMERICA IN THE MIDDLE EAST

CAULDRON OF TURMOIL

AMERICA IN THE MIDDLE EAST

BARRY RUBIN

HARCOURT   NEW YORK

BRACE   SAN DIEGO

JOVANOVICH   LONDON

HBJ

Copyright © 1992 by Barry Rubin

Requests for permission to make copies of any part of the work should be mailed to: Permissions Department, Harcourt Brace Jovanovich, Publishers, 8th Floor, Orlando, Florida 32887.

Library of Congress Cataloging-in-Publication Data
Rubin, Barry M.
Cauldron of turmoil: America in the Middle East/Barry Rubin.
p.   cm.
Includes bibliographical references (p.   )
ISBN 0-15-116128-3
1. Persian Gulf Region—Foreign relations—United States.
2. United States—Foreign relations—Persian Gulf Region.
· 3. Persian Gulf War, 1991—Causes. I. Title.
DS326.R84   1992
327.73056—dc20   92-12043

Designed by Lisa Peters
Printed in the United States of America

First edition

A B C D E

To Judith Colp

IN THE EARLY MORNING we mounted and started. And then a weird apparition marched forth at the head of the procession . . . a tall Arab [carrying a gun] splendid with silver plating. . . . The sunbeams glinted from a formidable battery of old brass-mounted horse pistols . . . and . . . a crooked, silver-clad scimitar of such awful dimensions and such implacable expression that no man might hope to look upon it and not shudder. . . .

"Who is this? What is this?" That was the trembling inquiry all down the line.

"Our guard! From Galilee to [Bethlehem] the country is infested with fierce Bedouins, whose sole happiness it is, in this life, to cut and stab and mangle and murder unoffending Christians. Allah be with us!"

I rode to the front . . . and got him to show me his lingering eternity of a gun . . . desperately out of the perpendicular. . . . The muzzle was eaten by the rust of centuries into a ragged fili-greework, like the end of a burnt-out stovepipe. I shut one eye and peered within—it was flaked with iron rust like an old steam-boat boiler. . . . The ponderous pistols . . . were rusty inside, too. . . . It came out then. . . . The Sheik imposed guards upon travellers and charged them for it. . . .

We reached Tabor safely and considerably in advance of that old iron-clad swindle of a guard. We never saw a human being on the whole route, much less lawless hordes of Bedouin.

—Mark Twain, *The Innocents Abroad*, 1869

THE MOST IMPORTANT GOAL . . . is opening our eyes to the mistakes and disasters of the past so that we can avoid them and prevent anyone else from repeating them. The major task for the person who wields his pen and thinks is to expose the face of the truth.

—Tawfiq al-Hakim, *The Return of Consciousness*

BAGHDAD 1989

A human body with a lion's head,
anti-sphinx of the riddle-waved Tigris
flowing over its secret dead; where a man's
form is more frightening than a cat's,
a lion's face over French suits or
Bedouin burnoose.

where Manna from Heaven is the favorite
pastry, where wobbling Abu Nuwass, poet and
libertine, stands, lost in statuary, lifting
his emptied cup of wine; and the taxis' song
under the marshbirds at dawn, after the warbling
call to prayer, and the bronzers banging in the
souqs, and soldiers lifting rifles in the
square.

noontime bright in a land without light, where
the stranger is greeted once but not twice,
where meat is not butchered but dies of fright.

an evening deep in a nation of sleep, creeping
in on all fours as the great cat roars, Babylonian
beast boasting all the old names, all of the
titles both rolling and sonorous, among them the
great Nebuchadnezzar's "Victorious."

someday the silt shall lift up the head that a
false human body now raises instead; like
Nebuchadnezzar, victorious, and dead.

—Raymond Stock

CONTENTS

PREFACE

THIS BOOK IS the culmination of fifteen years' study of U.S. policy and Middle East politics. All of my opinions, much of the material, many of the anecdotes, and all of the unattributed quotes are the result of direct observation and private discussions with American and regional policymakers and experts.

In addition, this volume is part of a broader inquiry into the sources of political belief, behavior, and misunderstandings between cultures. In *Paved with Good Intentions* (1980), I described the history of U.S.-Iranian relations and of U.S. involvement in the Persian Gulf up to the 1979 revolution and the hostage crisis. *Secrets of State* (1985) was a detailed history of the U.S. foreign policy–making process and the American way of dealing with the world. *Modern Dictators* (1987) looked at the Third World's prevalent systems of political rule. A number of more specialized studies presented the background to these events (*The Great Powers in the Middle East, 1941–1947* [1981]; *The Arab States and the Palestine Conflict* [1981]) and examined particular issues in Middle East politics (*Islamic Fundamentalists in Egyptian Politics* [1991]; three edited books on terrorism; and the coedited *Israel-Arab Reader* [1984]).

In the present endeavor, I am grateful for the assistance of a number of people and institutions. Even a brief account must mention the textual advice of Judith Colp and the economic consultation of Dr. Patrick Clawson. Professor Amatzia Baram and Ofra Bengio helped in my understanding of Iraq. Silvia Cherbakoff-Rosenberg and Gabi George did indispensable research work. Naomi Landau's attention to detail was invaluable.

Financial support has come from the Fulbright exchange program, the Harry Guggenheim Foundation, the Ford and Bradley foundations, and the U.S. Institute of Peace. Especially acknowledged is the use of facilities so generously offered by the Moshe Dayan Center of Tel Aviv University.

The meticulous, conscientious editing of Claire Wachtel and the help of my agent, Barbara Lowenstein, are also most gratefully acknowledged.

INTRODUCTION

———◆———

In August 1990, America suddenly entered its greatest crisis since the Vietnam War by opposing Iraq's invasion and seizure of Kuwait. Like thunder on a soft spring day, the confrontation could not have been more unexpected. The world was just celebrating an end to the superpowers' Cold War, which had helped inflame the globe's every corner for nearly a half century. The USSR and East European states were dismantling Communist dictatorships and moving toward democracy and national self-determination at astounding speed. A shooting war seemed more unlikely than at any time in recent memory. And until that summer, the U.S. government had regarded Iraq as a friend, despite its brutal regime and militant rhetoric.

Despite the increasing U.S. involvement in the Persian Gulf area over the previous decade, the showdown's location was as remarkable as its timing. Americans still considered Kuwait, Saudi Arabia, and Iraq to be exotic and largely incomprehensible places whose culture and ideas were as far from their own as anywhere on the globe.

The Persian Gulf region, though, had been moving from obscurity to centrality in Americans' minds ever since the early 1970s, when the oil price boom began to transform the area from one of the poorest to one of the richest in the world. This remarkable turnabout was followed by Iran's Islamic fundamentalist revolution, which triumphed in February 1979, then held U.S. diplomats as hostages from November 1979 to January 1981. Iraq invaded Iran in September 1980, expecting a quick, easy victory that would make it master of the Gulf. Instead, the result was the Iran-Iraq war—

Gulf War I—an eight-year, million-casualty battle, which eventually involved U.S. military forces sent to convoy Kuwaiti tankers and combat Iranian attackers.

Tehran lost the war in 1988, and as soon as Iran's bid to dominate the Gulf failed, it was Iraq's turn. Drunk with victory and burning with ambition, Baghdad set off to make the Gulf its empire, starting with the August 1990 takeover of Kuwait. But the United States reacted by forming a coalition to handcuff the aggressor with the first truly global economic embargo in history. The United Nations—usually a bureaucratically inefficient, politically dead-locked organization whose trademark was the stalemate—passed a dozen sharp-toothed resolutions demanding Iraq's immediate and unconditional withdrawal from Kuwait. The ruthless dictator Saddam Hussein swaggered in defiance, rattling his alleged stockpile of germs, poison chemicals, and atomic bombs.

Over 500,000 U.S. troops, alongside about a quarter-million allied soldiers, awaited the signal to go to war in a desert that was about the last place on earth where they expected to be. The twenty-eight-nation military coalition deployed arms so advanced, so bristling with electronic marvels, as to seem designed for a science fiction serial. When Saddam ignored the coalition's January 15, 1991, deadline for his withdrawal from Kuwait, the result was Gulf War II. On January 17, U.S. warplanes attacked Iraq, using their modern, accurate weaponry with devastating effect.

On February 24, after five weeks of bombing and no sign of an Iraqi pullout, U.S.-led forces began circling around the dazed Iraqi army's right flank. Suffering only minimal casualties while inflicting heavy losses on the Iraqis, the allied forces sliced deep into southern Iraq. Tens of thousands of Iraqi soldiers rushed to surrender. The road north from Kuwait City was clogged by a ghostly traffic jam of tanks, trucks, and cars abandoned by the fleeing Iraqis. Finally,

Saddam Hussein entreated for a cease-fire, while trying to disguise the dimensions of the defeat from his home audience and credulous Arab supporters.

The melodrama was so tightly plotted—with a cast of characters including an evil mustachioed dictator; hapless victims; and heroic, clean-cut rescuers—as to appear more the product of a thriller writer's imagination than a real-life event. The generally happy ending included Iraq's defeat, Kuwait's rescue, and minimal allied casualties. There were also tragic results: the flight of almost two million refugees from among Iraq's anti-Saddam ethnic groups; the permanent displacement of hundreds of thousands of foreign workers from Kuwait and Iraq; the death of many Iraqis; and Saddam's survival, which would enable him to inflict more terror on his subjects.

These are the bare facts, presented by endless television coverage and miles of newsprint as vast as the desert during the seven dizzying months of the Kuwait crisis. Cameras showed images to the world with such a surfeit of detail as to obscure the causes and meaning of these truly bizarre events.

It could still be debated whether this had been a great American victory or merely a last-minute escape from a disaster that originated in gross incompetence by U.S. leaders. Certainly, U.S. failures to comprehend the workings of regional politics and the meaning of earlier events had led directly to more than one near disaster. Just as Gulf War II had been the culmination of a long battle for supremacy in the area, the Kuwait crisis had also arisen from a decades-long series of U.S. and Arab errors and miscalculations. And even after winning the war, the United States seemed likely to lose the peace. As always, misreading experience simply invited fresh disasters.

The story of U.S. involvement in the Gulf revealed the same

blend of well-meaning idealism, self-absorbed ignorance, and half-formulated realpolitik that had characterized so much of the country's diplomatic history. In 1980, I wrote a book describing the U.S.-Iran relationship as a road that, though paved with good intentions, had nonetheless led to political disaster. The interaction between the United States and Iraq followed a parallel pattern.

Yet one must also have sympathy for the difficulty of the U.S. policymakers' task. It was hard for a democratic culture to comprehend such dictators' intentions or for a highly pragmatic society to deal with an ideologically doctrinaire one. America had also required some time to understand and respond to challenges from Nazi Germany and Communist Russia, societies with far closer cultural backgrounds.

Those European struggles shaped U.S. politics and diplomacy in the 1940s and 1950s. In fighting the Cold War, the United States had next found itself deeply involved in Southeast Asia, where the Vietnam War became its focus from the early 1960s to the mid-1970s. Almost immediately thereafter, the Persian Gulf became the main region for U.S. foreign policy crises. The reputations of three presidents—Jimmy Carter, Ronald Reagan, and George Bush—were made or broken there. Yet like Dorothy in the mythical land of Oz—whose namesake is a real ancient city near the Gulf—the United States had to discover for itself that the Middle East was not Kansas.

Whatever the failings of the American politicians, their greatest critics in academia and journalism did not do much better. The experts had generated more myth than truth about the region, being too quick to recast the local dictators as moderates and the aggressive regimes as having only modest demands. Too often, they took the noisiness and extremism of states or movements as proof of their strength. If the American sin in some parts of the world had been to act as a bully, in the Middle East the cardinal vice of U.S. policy—and even more of its would-be intellectual advisers—was appeasement.

Still, to assess fairly the U.S. involvement in the Middle East and the Gulf requires praise as well as self-criticism. Despite its bumbling, the United States generally achieved success, and its policy usually—if not always—stood on the side of virtue against the worst aggressors, terrorists, and dictators.

Moreover, if America did not easily understand the region, people there found the United States, its system of government, and its motives equally unfathomable. Middle East dictators feared and hated America because they knew it was objectively strong and assumed that it would use its power—as they would—to dominate the region. Inevitably, the United States stood as a barrier to their ambition for conquest.

At the same time, they took America's yearning to be popular even with its enemies and its obsession with morality and legalism as signs of a spiritual weakness they could exploit. In short, men like Ayatollah Ruhollah Khomeini and Saddam Hussein saw U.S. self-restraint as proof that the United States was a pitiful, helpless giant. When they challenged it, they found out otherwise.

Saddam and Khomeini also discovered that their own Arab and Muslim neighbors were unwilling to act on the political and religious ideas they professed, which American experts likewise took at face value. Saddam promised to give his Arab neighbors what they had so long claimed to want: unity in a single state, Israel's destruction, and the expulsion of Western influence. Staking everything on these ragged yet still potent myths, he assumed that others would side with him or surrender to him.

Saddam's plan did not work. True, Arab states cheered his verbal threats against Israel, his calls for unity, and his growing arsenal.

By invading a fellow Arab state, however, Saddam became so dangerous that he justified his neighbors' breaking the Arab and Islamic code against inviting U.S. troops and joining the West—and even Israel—in an open battle against fellow Arabs.

While Arabs claimed to believe in Arab nationalism, they would not fight for Saddam, just as Muslims spoke favorably about the rule of Islam but would not accept Khomeini as their leader. Khomeini and Saddam, like Hitler and Stalin, had also made the classic mistake of assuming that their almost total control at home could be easily expanded ever outward beyond their borders. As had happened in Europe with the failure of both fascism and communism, totalitarian dictatorships were as unable to impose themselves very long on their region as they were unable to build utopias at home.

The Middle East is still a place where visions of conquest, utopian social transformation, and politically profitable violence are very much alive. Despite the great opportunity offered by their oil money, the region's countries have squandered so much wealth and destroyed so many lives for the sake of intolerant ideas and dictators' lusts that one might well despair of the human race's sanity.

Just as communism and fascism each failed to conquer Europe, neither Arab nationalism, revolutionary terrorism, nor Islamic fundamentalism could triumph in the Middle East. Yet despite this fact, these doctrines were still able to sabotage the very progress they promised to bring. Would a dozen years of crisis lead to a historical turning point, breaking this cycle and teaching Americans and Middle Easterners a better understanding of the region? Perhaps war's futility and fanaticism's high cost would be driven home in a part of the world that had more of both than anywhere else. From the ruins might come a new order for peace and security, both in the Gulf and from a resolution of the Arab-Israeli conflict.

The Gulf crises of the 1970s, 1980s, and 1990s also offered instructive test cases for the social functions of ideology, religion, nationalism, economic development, and cross-cultural understanding—and a testing ground for the post–Cold War world. Thus, this book is meant to be not just the story of what led to the 1990–91 crisis, but also an inquiry into many broader social and political issues in our times.

CHAPTER ONE

INNOCENTS IN THE BAZAAR

Hojja borrowed a neighbor's copper pot and returned it a week later with a smaller one inside.
"What's this?" asked the owner.
"Good news!" Hojja replied. "Your pot had a baby!"
A month later, he again borrowed the pot, but this time he kept it. When the neighbor complained, Hojja sadly told him, "Alas, your pot died."
The enraged man demanded, "How can a pot die?"
"If a pot can have a baby," replied Hojja, "it can die as well."

—*Middle Eastern folktale*

There once was a wealthy American manufacturer of bathroom fixtures named Charles Crane, a well-educated, public-spirited man who became interested in international affairs. In 1919, President Woodrow Wilson asked him to serve on a commission investigating conditions in the Middle East after World War I. An aide to Wilson explained that the President thought the main qualification for men like Crane to be emissaries to the Middle East was that "they knew nothing about it."[1]

For four hundred years, the Ottoman Empire of the Turks, from its capital in Istanbul, had ruled most of the Arab world. But the empire's long-term decline and a fatal decision to join the losing side in World War I had brought it to collapse in 1918. The British and the French were busily carving up the former empire. It was time to create a new order in the Middle East.

After several weeks of travel in the area and meetings with vocal Arab nationalists, the U.S. commission concluded that everyone in the region wanted a single Arab state and it endorsed that goal as the people's will. The commissioners did not realize that the tiny elite that gave them this information had a vested interest in a solution that would create a vast empire for itself to rule.

President Wilson paid no attention to the commission's advice. The United States was still uninterested in playing a political role in the Middle East. Crane himself, however, remained actively interested in the area. A few years later, in a spirit of international brotherhood and tolerance, he decided to build a memorial at the grave of some great Muslim. But whose? To find an appropriate subject for this honor, Crane traveled to Istanbul. There he found a candidate. Jamal al-din al-Afghani, who died in 1897, was a thinker, an intriguer, and an adviser to princes. In the Ottoman sultan's service, al-Afghani had proposed the doctrine that all Muslims should unite politically against the West and its ideas.[2]

Actually, al-Afghani and his ideology were both frauds and failures. His concept of Islamic political unity, disguised as a transnational utopian creed to benefit all Muslims, was really designed for the Ottoman Empire's partisan political advantage. During the nineteenth century, the empire had been gradually losing its European Christian provinces as the new force of nationalism inspired revolts that eventually gave birth to Greece, Romania, Yugoslavia, and Bulgaria.

In contrast, the Ottoman Empire's Muslim subjects had remained loyal because they accepted the empire as their rightful Islamic ruler. For them, the sultan was still God's Shadow on Earth and Commander of the Faithful. Al-Afghani suggested that the ruler manipulate this Islamic legitimacy in order to discourage Muslim citizens from a secular nationalist disaffection. Thus an ideology masquerading as a mass movement was actually a state's imperialistic tool for ruling other peoples. In the end, Islam did not save the Ottoman Empire. In the twentieth century, the Arabs would discover nationalism for themselves. And since each Arab or Iranian ruler would try to use Islam for his own benefit, Muslims could never unite under a single banner.

Theological as well as nationalist disputes also doomed Islamic unity. Al-Afghani's notion of Muslim solidarity was refuted by his need to lie about his own identity. The name al-Afghani—meaning "the Afghan"—was an alias he took to hide his true, Persian, origin. Like most Persians, al-Afghani belonged to the Shia Muslim sect, which was looked down on by the majority Sunni Muslims.

Over a thousand years before, during Islam's early era in the seventh century, the prophet Muhammad's son-in-law Ali and Ali's two sons had been murdered during a struggle for Muslim leadership. A less pious dynasty seized control of the Islamic empire. Ali's defeated partisans became the Shia branch of Islam; the victor's supporters became the Sunni Muslims. Doctrinal differences widened over the centuries. The Shia were more inclined to follow charismatic, independent clerical leaders and were bitter at Sunni oppression; the Sunni often saw the Shia as heretical. In political terms, however, the issue was a struggle between factions that in the course of time became separate communities, each with its own structure and identity.

By posing as an Afghan, al-Afghani was trying to pass as a Sunni, since most Afghans belonged to that group. He knew that the prejudiced Sunni would not accept a Shia as their Islamic leader, a fact that contributed to their rejecting the claim to leadership of Ayatollah Khomeini, another Iranian Shia, a century later.

Al-Afghani's decision to hide his true identity was one more piece of evidence that the concept of Muslim unity was not very effective in an Islamic world that, then as now, was badly split over issues and loyalties. Although twentieth-century Westerners trembled to think that millions of Muslims might launch a holy war, this could never come close to happening. When, for example, the Ottomans followed al-Afghani's earlier advice and called on all good Muslims to fight the British in World War I, most of their Arab subjects ignored them.

On the contrary, small Arab groups, well subsidized by the infidel British, allied with England against their Muslim Ottoman rulers. The British officer T. E. Lawrence—Lawrence of Arabia—was their most famous military adviser and paymaster. This contradiction between theory and reality put no dent in Western credulity about Islam as an international political force.

Ignoring or ignorant of al-Afghani's failure and anti-Western ideas, Crane thought him a good choice as a hero for cross-cultural amity. Even so, the well-intentioned American had a problem. Al-Afghani died in the sultan's prison and was interred secretly. No one knew where in Istanbul he was buried. Persistent inquiries failed to resolve the question.

Then, one day, an apparent miracle happened. A Muslim visitor came to Crane's hotel suite in Istanbul, claiming to have been one of al-Afghani's students. He offered to show Crane where the body was interred. Being sincere and honest, Crane assumed the same of others. Accompanying his guide to an old graveyard, Crane experienced a dramatic moment when at last the man stopped, looked around, thought a moment, and then proclaimed, "Here is the resting place of al-Afghani!"

Crane built a monument on that spot, an unintended symbol of

Americans' recurring naïveté in dealing with the Middle East.[3] It was one more manifestation of an American tendency toward foolish innocence when, a half century later, Saddam Hussein fooled the United States by feigning moderation, then surprised it by seizing Kuwait. The syndrome reappeared yet again when President Bush let the dictator retain power after Iraq's defeat.

The story of Crane and al-Afghani also ends, however, with a symbolic lesson in American power. Once Crane had proclaimed al-Afghani's importance and identified a specific burial spot as belonging to the man, the Afghan government accepted this judgment. If the Americans thought al-Afghani was a hero, that was good enough for the Kabul regime. It disinterred "al-Afghani" and brought him "home," to be buried with honor as a great citizen of their country despite the fact that the corpse was probably the wrong one and the man himself had been no Afghan. The Afghans, like many Arabs and Muslims, still thought Western acceptance was necessary to authenticate their own doctrines—even the anti-Western ones. If the West bowed to Khomeini or Saddam, the region's people were likely to assume that these dictators would win and accept them as patriarchs and power brokers. Given the local penchant for conspiracy theories, even U.S. inaction would have enhanced the dictators' influence, since their neighbors would then have thought these men were acting with Western backing.

Almost every time an Arab leader met with Westerners or made a speech, he ritualistically invoked the inevitability of Arab unity, the centrality of the Arab-Israeli conflict, and the weakness of the U.S. position in the region. American experts, journalists, and government officials often accepted as true the words of the Arab politicians and intellectuals, ignoring the fact that their actions consistently contradicted this party line. Given this chorus of rhetoric,

Arab nationalism, Islamic fundamentalism, radical regimes, terrorist groups, and the Palestinian revolution seemed powerful movements that were riding the wave of history to an inevitable victory.

In their own romance with illusion, Arabs and Iranians inflicted wounds on themselves that were far worse than any inflicted by the West. By blaming America for their own mistakes, Middle Easterners were escaping from responsibility and refusing to face their true inner problems, a pattern of behavior that ensured that they would find no solution. The result of all this activity and struggle was a horrendous loss of life and resources and great suffering in five Arab-Israeli and two Gulf wars, over fifteen years of civil war in Lebanon, numerous coups, Iran's revolution, and many incidents of terrorism and assassination.

For decades, the circus played to a sell-out crowd: Radical dictatorships pledged socialist equality and populist democracy; Arab states warred to destroy Israel; Palestinian and Islamic fundamentalist terrorists machine-gunned civilians; rival ethnic groups fought over Lebanon; Egypt, Libya, and Syria bid to lead the Arab world; Iran strained to spark Islamic revolutions; Iraq tried to conquer its neighbors.

The Arabs and Iranians fell prey to false prophets and ideologies that promised a shortcut to victory yet blocked peace and progress. Khomeini was unable to expand his Islamic empire. The Palestine Liberation Organization could not destroy Israel. Saddam lost the war in Kuwait against an Arab-American alliance. Many Arabs still believed that the militant route could work, but they were also cynical about actually resolving the conflicts that cut so deep and had gone on for so long.

The outlook of Americans came from a very different tradition, a relatively happy history that extolled pragmatism over ideology and claimed that peace and prosperity were inevitable as history's happy ending. The strength of the Middle East's militants was judged to be considerable. But it was expected that they would see the light of reason and make a deal if offered a reasonable compromise by America.

In short, the Middle East's continuing strife, hatred, and terrorism were so "abnormal" by U.S. standards that Americans reasoned that the United States could solve these problems. When this approach did not work, many Americans assumed that it was because U.S. policy had not tried hard enough. Thus many Americans accepted the charges emanating from the Middle East that crises and oppression were their own country's fault. The fact that many Arabs or Iranians hated America was taken as further proof of its culpability. When Lebanese terrorists hijacked a TWA plane to Beirut in 1985, a citizen wrote the Senate Foreign Relations Committee: "We are the most hated nation in the world. And rightly so!"

Having enemies, though, was not necessarily conclusive proof of American guilt or a cause for shame. Extremist politicians like the Ayatollah Khomeini, Saddam Hussein, Libyan dictator Muammar Qaddafi and Syrian dictator Hafez al-Asad—who wanted to rule the Middle East—or PLO leader Yasir Arafat—who spent most of his career trying to destroy Israel—were neither deluded nor crazy to hate the United States. They knew what they wanted and were right to see the United States as blocking their way. And the United States was right to stand in their way. The fact that those opposed to peace, democracy, or freedom reviled America was actually evidence of America's virtues and principles.

Just as Washington did not cause the area's conflicts, it could not easily solve them. Both Washington and Moscow discovered how difficult it was to order around the region's smaller powers. The United States could not end the Iran-Iraq war or Arab-Israeli conflict until the belligerents wished to do so. Nor could America persuade Lebanon's ruling Christians to institute reforms, the Saudis to help the peace process, Israel to give up land to the Arabs in exchange for peace, or Jordan's King Hussein to negotiate with Israel.

The USSR was similarly frustrated with its allies. It wanted the Arabs to unite against the United States. When Syria took advantage of the civil war in Lebanon to occupy most of that country in 1975, or tried to split the PLO in order to seize control of it in 1983, and when Iraq invaded Iran in 1980 and Kuwait in 1990, they were acting against Moscow's wishes. "The Arabs," a Soviet joke admitted, "take everything from us except advice."

Thus, while U.S. policy had faults, it was not to blame for the region's various crises. Such Western self-vilification is really, as the French writer Pascal Bruckner explained, a kind of "perverted boastfulness" to assert that "we are still at the apex of history . . . we are still the master race." Under the guise of sympathy, the Arabs and Iranians are portrayed as having no will or ideas of their own. Such eternal victims are considered to be childlike, objects of history who cannot be held responsible for their own acts. The Third World's disasters, repression, corruption, and stagnation must be Western creations. Torture must be practiced in the prisons of Arab dictators because their police were Western-trained. Terrorism must be a response to mistreatment promoted by Western policies.[4]

Of course, not all Americans thought alike on such matters, but this type of thinking was common among the academics and experts who generated most of the policy debate and the criticisms of U.S. policy in the Kuwait crisis. At a meeting in Cambridge, Massachusetts, where I spoke in late 1990, one audience member after another rose to denounce the evil imperialist United States, which was allegedly using Saddam's invasion of Kuwait as an excuse to seize the Gulf for itself.

While not embracing the anti-Americanism of a considerable minority in the universities, journalists and Middle East experts often shared this perception of American guilt. Some of them, however, mitigated this notion by further suggesting that many of the U.S.-Iran or U.S.-Arab disputes were caused by a lack of communication rather than a clash of interests. If only U.S. policy treated Middle East dictators and radicals fairly and cleared up misunderstandings, they would no longer be antagonistic toward America; if Washington forced its local allies to give ground, enemies would meet them halfway. Yet the real problem was that the two sides had very different visions of life, society, and politics.[5]

The cycle of American misunderstanding was particularly hard to break since every few years a new American president and his appointees came to office with little experience in the region. Each administration in turn thought it would be easy to free hostages in Lebanon, resolve the Arab-Israeli conflict, or establish stability by convincing dictators of America's goodwill. This was how President Carter treated Khomeini until his followers seized the U.S. embassy in Tehran and how President Bush handled Saddam before the invasion of Kuwait. U.S. leaders expected others to be as eager for peace and cooperation as they were. They thought problems too easy to solve and concessions too likely to defuse grievances. Repeatedly expecting their proposals for bilateral cooperation or Arab-Israeli negotiations to win quick acceptance from various Middle East dictators, Presidents Carter, Reagan, and Bush were left looking foolish when this did not happen.

In 1986, I accompanied Senator Gary Hart on a Middle East trip. At breakfast with the director-general of Israel's foreign ministry, the senator inquired, "What would you do if King Hussein invited Prime Minister Shimon Peres to Amman?"

The diplomat showed his professionalism by not missing a beat

17

as he took another bite of omelet. "I think I can say, Senator, that if King Hussein invited him for tomorrow, we would have his bags packed tonight."

The senator smiled and added confidently, "I believe he is ready to invite Peres."

Taking another forkful of omelet and giving a polite little smile, the official asked, "What makes you say that, Senator?"

"That's what he told me," answered Hart, referring to their meeting a few days earlier. King Hussein had indeed given Hart a Bedouin banquet in a tent and during conversation made polite assurances of his moderation and friendship for America, but he had never indicated any willingness to go further in making peace.

Hart had heard what he expected to hear rather than what he was told. Convinced now that he was going to bring peace to the Middle East, the senator undertook a secret mission back to Jordan. He believed that it was really a simple matter to solve the Arab-Israeli conflict, Hart told his staff, since all the parties said they wanted peace. The main thing lacking, he concluded, was someone as smart or persuasive as himself to bring the warring parties together. When Hart secretly returned to Amman, however, the king denied having made any offer to meet Peres. The senator had been one more victim of the Middle East's tendency to make Americans confuse wishful thinking with reality.

Such expectations proved consistently wrong. The extremists were both more irreconcilable and more feeble than most American observers expected. Arabs and Muslims were divided, and the moderates wanted the United States to protect them from their brothers. The demagogues' threats to set off earthquakes and volcanoes in the region were hot air, but only if the United States acted to counter them.

An Arab politician once accurately noted that Russians want to be feared, the British crave respect, and Americans yearn to be liked. No Americans wanted more desperately to be liked than those in government, academia, and journalism who dealt with the Middle East. It is a natural human trait to seek acceptance by and develop empathy with the people one studies. There were also occasional threats, particularly from Syria, to Western journalists who were critical. A high-ranking Iraqi official told a British reporter visiting Baghdad, "In politics we have enemies, and sometimes we have to kill them. Perhaps someday you'll be an enemy and we will have to kill you."

To make matters worse, the study of the Middle East became the first academic discipline to be intimidated by standards of political correctness. Edward Said, the radical Palestinian-American literature professor, charged in his 1978 book, *Orientalism*, that Western scholars who criticized Arab states or political cultures—following scholarly methods that were standard in studying other parts of the world—were tools of imperialism and Zionism. At public meetings, Said read lists of scholars whom he deemed enemies of the Arabs.

The accusation that Middle East experts were prejudiced against Arabs could not be more inaccurate: the opposite was true. The prevailing approach to understanding the Middle East among American experts has been called Arabism, a word that implies a good understanding of Arab culture, history, and politics. Many of those holding such views had no such knowledge. "All you need to be an expert," a State Department official accurately observed, "is an atlas and a copy of the *New York Times*."

Direct observation bore out such cynicism. Those who set themselves up as guides to the Middle East were often the most disoriented of all. The expert most featured on American television during the Kuwait crisis spoke no regional language and had neither done serious research nor ever produced an in-depth study. Another oft-televised "specialist" and ex–government official told a conscientious subordinate, uncertain of her qualifications to speak on the Middle East, "Why don't you fake it? That's what I always do."[6]

Instead of indicating a high level of wisdom, "Arabism" came to have a political meaning: identification and agreement with the Arabs' views and self-image as conveyed by their official spokesmen. In effect, the Arabists argued that the Arabs can be understood only by their admirers and unconditional supporters.[7]

Those in government, seeing their task as smoothing U.S. relations with the Arab states, frequently became advocates representing Arab grievances or, more accurately, the claims of Arab dictators. U.S. ambassadors to Jordan, Syria, and Iraq became, in effect, the ambassadors from Jordan, Syria, and Iraq. Once retired, the envoys and officials often became these states' lobbyists in Washington or made their livelihood in major commercial deals that depended on the rulers' goodwill.

The academics specializing in the Middle East saw themselves as courageously fighting an uphill battle on behalf of a misunderstood, mistreated people. Personal friendships, lavish hospitality, and years spent in that part of the world could make one see its residents as personal "clients." Understanding easily could slide into sympathy, which could quickly become uncritical partisanship. Voicing support for Arab causes seemed the best way to obtain visas, invitations, information, audiences with Arab leaders, and lucrative jobs from regimes or from companies doing business with them.

At a scholarly conference I attended in 1981 at Britain's Exeter University, for example, the meeting's chairman sent Baghdad a telegram of support for Saddam Hussein, which, the surprised participants were told, they had supposedly unanimously endorsed. Also, an Arab scholar browbeat a British academic, whose paper

cited a work by an author considered too critical
until the professor apologized.

At the same conference, a famous British expert, Peter Mansfield,
gave a talk listing a dozen ways in which Saddam was a great
leader, the equal of Gamal Abdel Nasser. An American professor
named Eric Davis made a slavish speech about the prevalence of
democracy in Iraq, then stated privately that he was only angling
for Iraqi permission to do research there.

This circus atmosphere was broken dramatically by Hanna Batatu, a diminutive, timid-looking Arab scholar, who had the temerity
to mention Iraq's murder of dissidents. A towering young Iraqi
"student" stood up in the audience and growled, "You are not
allowed to say these things!" Batatu replied, "I am a free man and
say what I choose!"

This meeting was an extreme case. Nonetheless, for personal and
professional reasons, these specialists in universities, think tanks, or
government were eager to prove themselves to be pro-Arab. They
blamed their inability to shape U.S. policy on "the unmatched influence of the Israel lobby in American politics [which preempted]
other vital interests in American policy," as one of them said. This
situation, claimed another, made "open and rational discussion of
the issues" almost impossible.[8] In general, though, when the experts'
advice was followed, the results were usually adverse.

Scores of these government officials, journalists, academics, and
analysts make a living by talking and writing about the region,
discussing it endlessly at seminars, conferences, and expense-account
lunches at posh Washington restaurants. It was only a short step
for them to decide that they were the ideal peacemakers. In an
endless round, the experts jetted off on fact-finding expeditions to
the region, where they heard what the local governments and intellectuals said and then came home to repeat it.

Remarkably few of them knew much about the workings of Middle East politics or the social life of the countries, outside the luxury hotels or the salons of the elite who flattered them and seemed to be just like them. Yet to heed the party line of Arab governments, state-controlled media, and intimidated intellectuals was to miss much of what was really happening. It was easy for Westerners to assume that regimes talking so much about the oppressed must be progressive and, since no open dissent was allowed, popular. One reason the United States was unprepared for Iran's Islamic revolution was that the experts and journalists got their information from the shah's offices and wealthy Iranians who themselves were oblivious to the threat.

During the 1980s, many experts and journalists extolled Iraq as the "good guy" in the Iran-Iraq war. American high school texts became apologists for Saddam's regime, ignoring the fact that Iraq had been the aggressor and celebrating the alleged freedom and prosperity there.[9]

One night in 1983, I dined at the popular Philadelphia Restaurant in East Jerusalem with a diplomat from the U.S. embassy in Jordan. After the dozen dishes had been cleared away and the sweet Turkish coffee served, it was time to pose the question I had been aching to ask all evening: Why did the American embassy in Amman keep wrongly assuring the secretary of state that King Hussein would soon negotiate with Israel?

"Well," he explained, "that's what they told us."

"But don't you do more than report conversations? Aren't you supposed to analyze situations as well?" I was genuinely puzzled. If U.S. diplomats were merely to record what Middle East leaders said, a stenographer would qualify for the task. Whatever Saddam or Arafat or Asad wanted the Americans to think became what the U.S. government believed.

Amman, Jordan, is one of the world's most claustrophobic cap-
itals. Its tiny elite of families close to the palace acts as an echo
chamber, intensifying every rumor and conspiracy theory to the
edge of hysteria. U.S. envoys stationed there often fell under this
spell. When I spoke before the Amman World Affairs Council in
1982, the first questioner complained that the Jews controlled U.S.
foreign policy, a claim that would have been less surprising if it
had been made by a Jordanian rather than one of the U.S. embassy's
top diplomats. The U.S. ambassador at the time, Richard Viets,
later became Jordan's main lobbyist in Washington. Arab governments' real intentions and capabilities were lost in this mass of
concealing verbiage, inexperienced listeners, and venal interpreters.

Ironically, by misinforming the Arabs about Western views and
misleading the West about Arab politics, the pro-Arab officials and
experts did far more harm to their friends than did those who
criticized Arab policies. Condemning U.S. support for Israel as
contrary to American interests, Arabists made Arab rulers expect
that this help would decline, as well as persuading them that they
need not make compromises since Washington would pressure Israel
to give them what they wanted.

When Arabists accepted private assurances of moderation from
King Hussein or Saudi rulers, the United States did not require
these leaders to prove their claims. When American experts and
diplomats advocated concessions to radical states, dictators such as
Saddam Hussein concluded that the United States was too frightened to respond if they did something like invade Kuwait.

Strolling into the midst of the region's violent, persistent conflicts,
Americans like Crane and Hart, Carter and Bush, as well as academics and diplomats, often acted like innocents in a bazaar. They
believed what people in the region told them as a shopper might
accept a merchant's description of his carpet's high value. Being

poor bargainers, they declared, "This is the most beautiful rug I've ever seen! How much is it?" Shoddy tourist trinkets were billed as valuable antiques and were eagerly purchased for a high price. In the end, though, like the well-heeled, naive tourists it breeds in such profusion, the United States could afford its follies. American power was at such an advantage that the United States was able to sustain its overall interests quite well.

The years were far less kind to the Arab states. Neither national independence nor radical revolution brought them the power and economic development they desired. It should have been clear that these states badly needed the kind of self-criticism and reform that had been so healthy for Western societies. The persistence of regional problems came from local shortcomings, not foreign conspiracies or American ineptness. Arab nationalism created its own imperialism; Arab inflexibility made it impossible to resolve the Arab-Israeli conflict.

If the Arabs wanted a solution to the region's problems, the Arabs would have to change their own systems and policies. In the words of Lebanese-American professor Fouad Ajami, there were "real limits" to any U.S. ability to shape events: "In the final analysis, all societies must work out their own problems and shape their own destiny. No regime can be propped up forever by outside forces, and no amount of external pressure can remake societies, spare them the agonies of historical change, shelter them from a turbulent world, or immunize them from underlying forces opposing their structures."[10]

No foreign leaders looked at politics more differently from Americans than did Khomeini and Saddam, and no Middle East leaders were greater champions of the traditional outlook than were these two dictators. They tried to fulfill the old Arab and Muslim dreams by demanding unity under themselves, insisting on the centrality of the battle against Israel, and trying to expel Western influence in the region. The very extremism of their ideology, however, would test these Middle East and Arabist myths, just as the extent of their hostility to the United States would challenge the American fable about the possibility of conciliation with the radicals.

CHAPTER TWO

AMERICAN GRAFFITI

The veneration and affection which some of these men felt for the scenes they were speaking of heated their fancies and biased their judgment, but the pleasant falsities they wrote were full of honest sincerity, at any rate. Others wrote as they did because they feared it would be unpopular to write otherwise. Others were hypocrites and deliberately meant to deceive. . . . But why should not the truth be spoken of this region? Is the truth harmful? Has it ever needed to hide its face?

—*Mark Twain,* The Innocents Abroad

It is hardly surprising that Americans find Middle East politics to be frustrating and unfamiliar. How could they easily understand someone so alien in background and behavior as Saddam Hussein or comprehend an Islamic fundamentalist revolution in Iran? U.S. policy, too, has been slow to comprehend these personalities and events. Until Khomeini seized hostages and Saddam seized Kuwait, the U.S. government failed to anticipate their militant deeds.

In no small part, the problem for U.S. policy was compounded by serious flaws in the thinking that often guided it and pointed U.S. policymakers, experts, and journalists—and hence their audiences—in the wrong direction. The root of the difficulty was the pervasiveness in America of four myths about the Middle East: (1) that the U.S. regional position was weak and shaky; (2) that

Arabs—or Muslims—would unite against the United States; (3) that the Arab-Israeli conflict was the area's overwhelming central issue; and (4) that the United States could succeed only by making concessions to dictators rather than by confronting them.

First, the U.S. position in the Middle East was said to be fragile—dependent on Arab goodwill and imperiled by Soviet gains—whereas actually it was quite strong. Malcolm Kerr, the scholarly president of the American University in Beirut, gave the most succinct summary of the views of those who thought the United States was itself to blame for the situation. Kerr wrote in 1980: "The Camp David strategy has led to an Egyptian-Israeli deadlock over the question of Palestinian autonomy, and to a visibly growing irritation elsewhere in the Arab world, as well as in Israel. The Lebanese crisis, always in danger of precipitating a new Arab-Israeli war, is as far as ever from any solution. The Iranian revolution— itself the product of American folly in the past—continues to baffle and dismay Washington policymakers." The Afghanistan and Iran-Iraq wars showed America's "strategic disadvantage vis-à-vis the Soviet Union in the Gulf area. . . . In short, all over the Middle East, signs point both to dangerous situations and to the inability of the U.S. government to control events—or perhaps even to understand them."[1]

"The peoples in the area—even those who have been and still want to be associated with the United States," Edward Said wrote in 1979, "have been losing hope in the credibility, sincerity and willingness of American administrations to act decisively, even in their own long-term best interests. Over the years many Arabs have turned to Moscow, not because they wanted to but because they felt they had been left with no alternative."[2]

Since America supposedly needed them more than they needed it, the Saudis, Egyptians, or others would lose patience with U.S.

policy and turn Marxist or fundamentalist. They were not, Kerr claimed, the "exclusive clients of any great power" but would choose sides based "on who assists them in solving problems that they cannot solve alone."[3]

Author Robert Lacey agreed: "We should not assume that the House of Saud will continue to be as pro-Western as it is at present. When people discuss radical, fundamentalist pressures inside Saudi Arabia, they forget that the House of Saud could very easily shift itself in a more radical direction."[4]

The region was allegedly on the verge of an anti-American earth-quake and the collapse of friendly regimes. But was the sky falling? In fact, these regimes' maneuvering room was limited. The leaders of Saudi Arabia's conservative ruling family were not going to favor becoming a Marxist monarchy that allied itself to Moscow or an ardent ally of Islamic fundamentalists who were eager to destroy them. They needed the United States because they did not trust neighbors who wanted to grab their power and their money. U.S. protection meant the difference between their continuing to enjoy a life of luxury and being murdered by foreign invaders or domestic revolutionaries.

Arabists' predictions that U.S. mistakes would bring major Soviet gains also proved to be wrong. The radicals had turned to Moscow in the 1950s and 1960s not because they were disillusioned with America but because they saw the USSR as a model for statist economic development, an ideological soul mate, a source of arms for aggression, and an ally in their drive to take over the area. Syria, for example, allied itself with Moscow because the United States would never support its ambition to rule Jordan, Israel, Lebanon, and the Palestinians. In contrast, the Soviets were willing to furnish Syria with seven thousand military advisers, plus huge stocks of advanced planes, missiles, and tanks.

Nonetheless, U.S. interests flourished and Soviet influence declined during the 1970s and 1980s. A decade after Kerr's and Said's litanies of woe, Egypt and Israel remained at peace; Arab states fought alongside America against Iraq; the Russians had retreated from Afghanistan; Iran was trying to rebuild relations with the West; and multilateral Arab-Israeli peace talks were taking place under U.S. sponsorship, based on the Camp David accords.

Moreover, the regional upheavals that occurred were largely natural outcomes of the destabilizing birth of nations and the traumas of development, parallel to those in other parts of the Third World. The new Arab states were in disorder until some power balance could be achieved among their factions and communities. Ideas and social innovations—secularism, nationalism, land reform, socialism, women's equality—brought conflict and sometimes revolution. These changes also made it necessary to establish a well-founded regional structure. But this was impossible as long as Iraq, Iran, Syria, and Libya wanted to take over the area, efforts that the United States tried to block.

Ironically, it was Soviet policy, which most closely followed the Western experts' advice, that ended in disaster. The USSR opposed Israel and helped radical regimes and the PLO, only to lose influence in one country after another. Moscow found the radical clients unreliable as allies and constantly threatening to draw it into dangerous confrontations with the United States.

Although the radicals in the Middle East—like those elsewhere in the world—used anti-American demagoguery to muster domestic support, they confronted the United States directly only when they thought it too weak or timid to harm them. In contrast, moderate Arab regimes like Saudi Arabia's preferred to remain on good terms with Washington, recognizing its strategic, military, economic, political, and technological power. The radicals—as Iraq's takeover of Kuwait would show—would be the big losers in challenging America; the moderates became the big winners by soliciting America's help.

The second myth was that the U.S. regional standing was in danger because all Arabs or Muslims were liable to unite against America. When a self-proclaimed Muslim leader (like Khomeini) or a self-declared chief of the Arabs (like Saddam) appeared, it was feared that his influence would sweep the region. In fact, the constant conflicts within Arab and Muslim groups were the usual root cause behind disorder in the area. During the Cold War, the Arab states split between the Soviet and the American camps because they wanted these superpower patrons to aid them in their local disputes. The rise of powerful dictators like Khomeini and Saddam only deepened these regional conflicts, fostering the Iran-Iraq and Kuwait wars, not some cross-national alliance of peoples.

Given their own conflicts, rivalries, and differences, Arabs were incapable of joining together to rule the Middle East or to fight America. While most Arabs agreed in theory that they should unite or at least cooperate, in practice the notion provided an excuse for never-ending battles among countries. No state would subordinate itself to any other state. The only merger among different Arab countries had been the United Arab Republic, created by Egypt and Syria in 1958. In less than three years, the Syrians were so fed up with Egypt's treating them as second-class citizens that they broke up that union.

The same pattern prevailed among the Muslims. In the early decades after their religion spread, seventh-century Muslims had indeed been governed by a single political authority. But it was not long before factions went to war and separate states formed. This was how the Middle East had functioned for well over a thousand years. Even most of the modern Islamic fundamentalist movements were localized and inward-looking, trying to build an Islamic society in their own country rather than to erase national boundaries and create a single state ruling all Muslims.

Arab cooperation was, of course, a more realistic goal than Arab unification. Even here, however, the expectations of Arab intellectuals and Western experts proved to be greatly exaggerated. They frequently argued that U.S. pressure against any Arab country would bring the enmity of all Arabs. What happened was the exact opposite. For example, on April 15, 1986, a U.S. air raid against Libya retaliated for Libyan-sponsored terrorist attacks that had killed Americans at the Rome and Vienna airports and at a West Berlin discotheque. The air strike was wildly popular among Americans.[5]

The private reaction of Arab governments was not very different. Accepting the myth of Arab unity, the magazine *U.S. News & World Report* ran a headline claiming: "Revenge and Anger [against America] Resound in Arab World." Yet most Arab states were privately pleased to see Libyan dictator Qaddafi hurt and embarrassed. No Arab government did anything to help him, refusing even to hold a summit condemning the U.S. attack. The Organization of Petroleum Exporting Countries (OPEC) rejected Qaddafi's call for an oil boycott; Algeria did not postpone sending a high-level delegation to Washington to improve relations. Egypt allowed a U.S. aircraft carrier to sail through the Suez Canal.[6]

This pattern recurred frequently, from the days when Arabs joined Britain in World War I to fight their own Muslim rulers to the 1990–91 Kuwait crisis, when most Arab states aligned themselves with America against Saddam. In the end, nothing contributed more to Arab and Muslim disunity than Arab countries' or Islamic Iran's invoking the idea of unity as a license to undermine their neighbors' sovereignty. And the more the radicals tried to force the moderates into such a shotgun wedding, the more the latter needed the United States to protect them from their militant brethren.

The third myth was that the Arabs were so obsessed with the Palestine question that almost nothing else counted in setting their own policy and attitude toward America. Kerr called the issue "the number one preoccupation of many of the countries of the area throughout the period since World War II." The cost to America, Kerr claimed, included "the radicalization of half a dozen Arab regimes, the strengthening of their ties with Moscow . . . their hostility to the United States, [and] the destruction of Lebanon."[7]

"The Palestine question remains a formidable obstacle and burden to U.S. relations with the Arab world," added another respected scholar, John Campbell. "It undermines the moderates and strengthens the wild men. It plays into the hands of the Soviet Union. It threatens to isolate the United States with Israel as the only friend in the region."[8]

The Arabists' claims were that the United States could win over the Arabs only by concessions on the Arab-Israeli conflict and that unless America quickly resolved the issue on terms satisfactory to the Arab states and the PLO, American interests would be destroyed. If not for Israel, ran these arguments, the Arab world would be wholeheartedly in the Western camp.

Professor Zbigniew Brzezinski wrote in 1975: "It is impossible to seek a resolution to the energy problem without tackling head on—and doing so in an urgent fashion—the Arab-Israeli conflict." But except for a brief oil embargo against the United States during the 1973 Arab-Israeli war, the Arab oil-exporting states never used the "oil weapon" as part of the conflict. The West handled the skyrocketing oil prices and resulting financial problems remarkably smoothly and quickly, and totally apart from the struggle. Western banks and companies sold the Arabs so many products, investments, and arms to recycle their newfound petroleum income that in a little over a decade, the Gulf oil-exporting states were running budget deficits.

Clearly, the conflict was a major issue in the Arab world, but it rarely had the obsessive centrality so often claimed. While the Arab-Israeli dispute was the most highly publicized Middle East issue, there were other, equally or more significant, points of conflict in the region, which had little or no relation to it. These included the struggle between Arab radicals and conservatives for power in each state and in the region, the stress and slow pace of economic development, rivalries among Arab states trying to dominate their neighbors, the fall of Iran's shah, the Iran-Iraq war, the USSR's invasion of Afghanistan, Lebanon's civil war, and Iraq's seizure of Kuwait.

The Arab-Israeli issue preoccupied far more Arab rhetoric than action, in part because it was easier to rail at Israel than to address difficult, divisive problems at home. Moreover, each Arab regime manipulated the matter—often in conflict with other regimes—to promote its own interests, mobilize domestic support, and gain an edge over rivals. Syria defined Israel and the West Bank as its own property, "Southern Syria." Jordan asserted its own claim to the West Bank. Lebanon's Christians tried to win their civil war against the Lebanese Muslims in 1982 by obtaining Israeli assistance. Every Arab country accused the others of being too soft on Israel. Within each state, rulers and opposition forces branded each other as Zionist agents.

Calculated self-interest also determined how Arab rulers acted toward the PLO. They promoted their own puppet Palestinian factions in an effort to seize control of the organization. Jordan fought and expelled the PLO by force in 1970 when it threatened the country's internal stability. Egypt made a unilateral peace with

Israel in 1979 in order to regain the Sinai and its oil fields, which Israel had captured in the 1967 war. Syria's alleged devotion to the Palestinian cause did not stop it from splitting the PLO in a 1983 takeover attempt. The Syrian army chased pro-Arafat forces from Lebanon; Syria's Lebanese clients attacked refugee camps in Lebanon, killing thousands of Palestinians.

As time went on, the Arab states became even less involved with the issue, being unwilling either to wage war or to make peace. By 1980, Egypt and Israel were at peace, while the Jordan–Israel and Syria–Israel borders were quiet. The uprising in the occupied territories after 1987 showed the Palestinians' nationalist fervor. But the Arab states' lack of reaction demonstrated their indifference. And as long as neither side was willing to make major compromises, the United States could not resolve the problem, no matter how hard it tried.

Most important of all, neither the conflict nor U.S. support for Israel kept Arab states from having close relations with the United States when it was in their interests. In fact, the U.S.-Israel relationship made Washington the conflict's inevitable mediator, holding, in Egyptian president Anwar Sadat's words, "99 percent of the cards" for making peace. The U.S.-Egypt alliance began in the mid-1970s when Egypt's desperate economic situation and Sadat's understanding that the effort to defeat Israel was futile led to his decision that the time had come to use Washington's peacemaking services.

Neither the actual behavior of Arab states nor Middle East politics had much effect on the perception of the journalists and experts who continued to insist that the Arab-Israeli conflict was the beginning and the end for all the region's troubles and the factor bringing the imminent collapse of U.S.-Arab relations.

"Arab states which had thrown Egypt out of the Arab League

because Sadat had made peace with Israel with American encouragement and help would not be willing to join Egypt in a new alignment under American sponsorship," explained the American Middle East expert John Campbell in 1981. The Arabs, *Time* magazine claimed in 1986, felt betrayed because America "has moved closer to Israel than ever before, thus endangering U.S. strategic interests and abandoning claims of being an honest broker."[9]

Many Arab and American writers asserted that a shift in U.S. policy away from Israel was the key to safeguarding the Persian Gulf as well. Without a diplomatic settlement "which will correspond approximately to [the Arab states'] views of a 'just' solution—then close cooperation with the United States cannot fail to operate in a destabilizing manner for the states of the [Gulf] region," wrote one expert in 1983. Professor Charles MacDonald claimed that "U.S.-Israel ties are increasingly forcing the Gulf governments to detach themselves from close cooperation with the United States for fear of undermining their own legitimacy."[10]

Yet again, these predictions were all wrong. In the face of Iran's revolution and Iraq's imperial ambition, most of the Arabs did align with the United States, and the Gulf states cooperated closely with Washington throughout the 1980s. They continued to buy American arms and technology, invested heavily in the United States, begged for U.S. convoys of tankers to protect them from Khomeini in 1987, and wanted U.S. troops to save them from Saddam in 1990.

Ironically, Arab refusal to be more anti-American frustrated those Western experts who wanted such a threat to reinforce their argument for changing U.S. policy. Kerr wrote that the Arabs had erred by letting the United States get away with maintaining Israel as a strategic asset. "Certainly," he concluded, "the United States has been far luckier than it deserved in managing to befriend Israel without sacrificing important interests in the Arab world."[11]

History showed, however, that U.S. relations with Israel and the Arabs were no zero-sum game, in which one side's gain was the other's automatic defeat. As Assistant Secretary of State Richard Murphy pointed out in 1986, "Friendship with one party to the Arab-Israeli dispute has not diminished—nor should it—the reliability of U.S. ties to the other. We are the only superpower trusted by both Israel and the Arabs. By establishing friendship and confidence on both sides, we have made it possible to move Arabs and Israelis toward greater peace and security. We have brokered six peace agreements serving Israeli, Arab, and Western interests. In contrast to the role the United States has played, the Soviet Union, without diplomatic relations with Israel and with limited diplomatic ties and bilateral relations in the Arab world, has only a peripheral role to play."[12]

The fourth misconception was that the best way to preserve U.S. interests was for the United States to make concessions in order to get along better with its enemies, endeavoring to convince them that the United States was in fact not their enemy.

Such an effort was both undesirable and futile. It was dangerous in encouraging the dictators to become more aggressive, since they concluded that no one would stop them. The enterprise was futile because it was no accident, after all, that the most anti-American Middle East states—Khomeini's Iran, Syria, Iraq, and Libya—were those that sought to rule the Arab world. Similarly, the region's anti-American groups, like the PLO, Islamic fundamentalists, and Marxist revolutionaries, sought to destroy Israel or the existing Arab states.

These forces hated America because it was the defender of the more moderate or weaker states that were their intended victims. Since the area's countries were in conflict, the United States could never have everyone on its side. U.S. help for Saudi Arabia, for instance, would inevitably anger both Iran and Iraq.

Radicals, Arab nationalists, and Islamic fundamentalists also thought that the United States was inevitably evil and hated American cultural and political influence because it seemed to be the main force Westernizing Arab and Muslim society. Edward Said wrote from his Marxist perspective that America's real priority in the region was to sell "Kentucky Fried Chicken franchises, Coca-Cola, Detroit automobiles, and Marriott hotels."[13] This alleged agenda was seen not merely as a way of making imperialist profits but as a way of dissolving the very foundations of the existing society by substituting other mores.

Unfortunately, no matter how America behaved, its wealth and power inevitably provoked anger and envy. Said claimed that America's aim in the Middle East was "to oppose nationalism and radicalism" and support each "client regime (no matter how oppressive and unpopular) despite the much-touted official interest in human rights."[14]

The underlying point here, of course, was that U.S. policy ran counter to what the radicals wanted to do. The militant nationalists and the Islamic fundamentalists had learned to use the language of human rights, self-determination, and democracy as propaganda, employing them in the same cynical way as did the Communists. The radicals offered America the unpalatable, unacceptable alternative of proving that it respected Arabs by watching—or, even better, helping—Syria, the PLO, or "popular forces" like Saddam while they undermined or overthrew its own tested friends.

After all, Syria, Iraq, and Libya were far more oppressive and antidemocratic than Jordan, Saudi Arabia, or Israel. Even American patronage would not persuade the radicals to abandon their goals of ruling the region but would simply make it easier for them to succeed.

In short, radicals and terrorists attacked America not because the United States was doing wrong by acting oppressively but because it was doing right by opposing them. There was no way that U.S. concessions would satisfy the radicals, since they desired the complete exclusion of U.S. influence from the area. As part of their rivalry, Syria, Iraq, and Iran taunted each other for not being sufficiently militant and for allegedly being American puppets. And when Islamic fundamentalists took American hostages in Iran and Lebanon, their ultimate goal was to force U.S. citizens and institutions to leave those countries.

Radical regimes and forces were not mollified but further antagonized by U.S. efforts to find a peaceful resolution to the Arab-Israeli conflict in the 1970s and 1980s. Syria, Iraq, Islamic Iran, Libya, and the PLO opposed a diplomatic solution because they rightly expected that it would strengthen U.S. regional influence and guarantee Israel's survival. These countries sponsored campaigns of terrorist attacks not as a warning that the United States must strive harder to bring peace but in order to block diplomacy when they feared it might make some progress.

Actually, American attempts to win over the extremists made things worse. In private life, kind words or a turned cheek may avert conflict, but this was not a valid principle for U.S. Middle East policy. The United States had only two choices in the Middle East: either the Iranians and Arabs would see America as a powerful elephant whose interests they would have to respect, or they would view it as a paper tiger that might easily and profitably be defied. This was a case, if there ever was one, to prove the maxim that nice guys finish last.

In the end, though, the Americans would intervene, and Iran and Iraq would be the ones who retreated. The display of U.S. fortitude would not stir fire storms of regionwide outrage and anti-Americanism. America's power did more to attain its goals than American misunderstandings did to sabotage them. Soviet expansionism was turned back and its influence limited in the Middle East many years before the USSR collapsed from internal problems. Anti-American radicalism was contained, commitments to allies were kept, and oil supplies were maintained.

Despite blunders and setbacks, the U.S. position in the region was stronger at the end of the 1980s than it had been years earlier. The United States had better relations with more Arab states than ever before. Regardless of the continued strong U.S. alliance with Israel, they did not turn toward communism or radical Islamic fundamentalism.

Ironically, the American myths about the Middle East promoted by those claiming to be pro-Arab actually depreciated the Arabs. The majority of Arab leaders acted not as blind fanatics but as rather typical politicians who weighed their rational self-interest. They knew that the regional situation put certain constraints on their actions and forced them to give lip service to certain ideas; they also wanted to see which superpower or local state would win before committing themselves too much. But when threatened by their local brothers, the Arab regimes preferred turning to U.S. power rather than being taken over by Iran or Iraq.

Khomeini and Saddam stumbled into disaster in large part because they believed many of the myths prevalent in the United States. Mesmerized by their own propaganda and ignoring overwhelming odds, they believed victory to be inevitable. They underestimated the United States, provoked it, and then had to suffer the high cost of its enmity. They left neighbors no choice but to join a U.S.-led coalition in order to survive. To make sense of the U.S. miscalculations and Gulf crises of the 1980s and 1990s, the following chapters explain the origins of the regimes of Saddam and Khomeini in the 1960s and 1970s.

CHAPTER THREE

THE DISCREET CHARM OF SADDAM: 1959–1979

Hojja dreamed that a man promised him ten gold coins and put nine in his hand. "You promised me ten," complained Hojja. Suddenly he awoke and saw his hand was empty. He quickly shut his eyes again, reached out a hand, and said, "All right, I'll settle for nine."

—*Middle Eastern folktale*

The man who would confront the United States in a war over Kuwait and confound all its expectations about the region had a background and a worldview that were drastically different from those of every one of his American adversaries. At the beginning of his career, Saddam the revolutionary would fire one of a half-dozen guns in an ambush. Twenty years afterward, he would make himself president of Iraq and within a few months order his nation's army to invade Iran, setting off the largest war in Middle East history. Precisely a decade later, he would attack Kuwait, shaking the region and precipitating a full-scale war of Iraq versus the world.

Even the briefest summary of his career shows Saddam's impressive talent and equally remarkable capacity for political iniq-

iniquity—ruthlessness learned in a political system where such behavior was necessary if one was to rise and survive. He was not a
fool or a fanatic but simply, as often happens in Middle East politics,
a man who combined extremist tactics with a pragmatic strategy in
the pursuit of an extremely radical goal.

He took a critical step on that road on October 7, 1959. At
6:30 P.M. that day, a big car pulled out of Iraq's defense ministry
and drove toward Baghdad's eastern gate, taking Iraq's dictator,
Abd al-Karim al-Qasim, to the East German embassy for its
national-day reception. As the auto turned onto Rashid Street,
the city's main boulevard, a lookout gave the signal. Across from
a school and close to Dr. Hasan al-Bakri's clinic, a half-dozen
armed men—one of them a young revolutionary named Saddam
Hussein—hurried down to the street.

Then everything began to go wrong. One of the getaway drivers,
nervously rushing to get the car ready, locked his key inside. An
artist absentmindedly wandered among the fighters, taking notes
for a picture. As the seconds passed, Qasim's car came closer. Should
they attack or wait for another day? One of the assassins, Abd al-
Wahab al-Urayri, settled the matter by running into the street in
front of the car. He opened fire, killing the driver and wounding
Qasim's assistant.

The other gunmen began shooting. Their two machine guns
quickly jammed. One of them threw a grenade at Qasim's car but
missed; a wounded attacker could not pull a grenade from his
pocket. The assassins were in total confusion, though Qasim's en-
tourage had not fired a single shot at them. The car started rolling
down the hill. Al-Urayri ran around it, pushing his gun up against
the window and trying to shoot Qasim at point-blank range. But
one of his own comrades' bullets hit him in the back, and al-Urayri

fell dead. Saddam and another man, standing in front of the others, were also wounded by their friends' fire.

The gunmen ran away without checking to see if Qasim was dead, though they had been ordered to fire into the dictator's head to be certain. They carried the two injured revolutionaries, leaving behind al-Urayri's body, and jumped into a car that drove them to a safe house. Forty-three bullets had hit the dictator's vehicle; three of them had wounded Qasim, who lay bleeding on the car's floor. The stunned bystanders finally approached the battered limousine, pulled out Qasim, and rushed him to the Dar al-Salaam hospital.

The Iraqi dictator was saved in a ninety-minute operation performed by Russian doctors. His bloody, bullet-riddled uniform was publicly exhibited to show how miraculous was his survival. Suspects were rounded up and, under torture, gave away the conspirators. Fifty-six officers and opposition politicians were arrested. A disguised Saddam escaped to Cairo.[1]

Although the assassination attempt had failed, Saddam had shown himself to be no armchair revolutionary. The story of that shootout became a central part of his self-image and his self-made mythology. Saddam later spread the tale that he had dug a bullet out of his own body, though actually a doctor had done it. Still, even if Saddam exaggerated his fearlessness, there could be no doubt of his courage.

The botched attack on Qasim taught Saddam a valuable lesson which would help him become a successful dictator: When you strike an enemy, make sure that he is dead and finished. Saddam would also always put the highest priority on his personal security and on rooting out antigovernment plots.

But for an Iraqi leader to survive, good bodyguards alone were not sufficient. To stay in power, whoever ruled Iraq had to reconcile its local identity as a separate country with its sense of having a mission to rule over the Arab world. Certainly, Iraq's claim to Arab preeminence was as good as that of any other country. Iraq boasted a civilization as old as Egypt's and had been capital of the great Arab Islamic empire far longer than Damascus or Mecca, from 750 until 1258, when the Mongols pillaged it. Much of the golden era of Arab and Islamic history had taken place on its territory. Thereafter, it was considerably reduced in importance, continuing to decline during the centuries of Turkish rule down to the Ottoman Empire's collapse in 1918.

Iraq had never previously existed, however, as a country in its own right. It was split among three Ottoman provinces before 1918. Britain occupied that land during its battle with the Ottoman Empire in World War I. After the empire fell, the British obtained a League of Nations mandate to run the area and, during the 1920s, created Iraq as a state. As king, they installed Prince Faisal from the Hashemite family in western Arabia, one of the leaders of the wartime Arab revolt against the Turks.

Iraq achieved independence in 1932 and accepted the borders with all its neighbors, including Kuwait. The new country's boundaries, like virtually all Middle East frontiers, could be considered artificial. Yet Iraq was far more a beneficiary than a victim of those whimsical map lines. To the north, Iraq was awarded the oil-rich Mosul district, despite Turkey's objections. To the east, Iraq was given the whole Shatt-al-Arab River, to Iran's great disadvantage. Not content with the bounty brought it by colonial borders, Iraq also occasionally asserted its claim to Kuwait, beginning as early as 1937. "Is it possible," asked Saddam many years later, "for a civilization which is 6,000 years old to have been isolated from the sea? A part of Iraq's land was cut off by English scissors."[2]

But after achieving independence, Iraqis did not talk so much about expanding the country's borders—a manifestation of Iraqi nationalism—as they did about becoming the core of a unified Arab state—Arab nationalism. Baghdad soon became an Arab intellectual and political center, a mecca for militant nationalists from Syria, Palestine, and other places still under British or French control.

Many of the émigrés and local activists thought Iraq was destined to play the role Prussia and Piedmont had filled in the previous century by creating and dominating the new states of Germany and Italy. One of the most dynamic of these Arab nationalist ideologues, Sami Shawkat, director-general of Iraq's Ministry of Education, asked, "What is there to prevent Iraq from dreaming to unite all the Arab countries?"[3] Saddam was heir to that dream.

Born on April 28, 1937, in the northern town of Tikrit, Saddam Hussein was named prophetically—Saddam means "one who confronts." Two features of his early life particularly affected his character: his father's death when Saddam was a boy and the influence of a radical nationalist relative. A fatherless boy in Arab society is often the butt of ridicule and bullying. Though his mother remarried, from an early age Saddam was sensitive about his honor and ready to fight in its defense.

His mother's brother, Khayrallah Tulfah, became a formative influence when Saddam went to live with him to attend school in Baghdad. The move brought Saddam from the provinces to the center of Iraqi political life and under the wing of his bitter, politically extremist uncle. Tulfah had been a career army officer who in 1941 supported a quartet of colonels, the so-called golden square, in staging a pro-Nazi coup against King Faisal II, who was pro-British. Iraq was too far away from the German lines for Berlin to offer much help, and the radicals further isolated themselves by mistakenly shooting down the German plane that was flying in a liaison officer to arrange aid.

The British responded quickly, bombing Iraqi bases and marching a column of troops in to capture Baghdad. Iraq's army crumpled, though its supporters first staged a vengeful pogrom, killing over 180 people in Baghdad's Jewish quarter. The British soon restored Iraq's old regime, and the monarchy thoroughly purged the army, including Tulfah, who thereafter hated the West, the British, and Iraq's rulers.

Given such influences at home, Saddam joined the leftist, nationalist Ba'th (the Arab word for "renewal") party—which had begun in Syria as a support group for the 1941 Iraqi coup—while still in school. The party's ideology mixed Communist and Fascist ideas with a strong streak of Pan-Arab nationalism, advocating both socialism and Arab unity. From his teenage years, Saddam was a professional revolutionary, an armed politician fighting for Arab unity and socialism. He spent his time on politics rather than studies, engaging in street fights with rival groups and organizing an underground apparatus to prepare for the king's overthrow.

The revolution came in July 1958, and the monarchy was overthrown. But the leader was General Qasim—not the Ba'th party. The coup-makers seized the city and murdered the royal family. The body of the pro-Western prime minister, Nuri al-Said—himself a veteran of the World War I Arab revolt against the Ottoman Empire—was dragged through Baghdad's streets. Qasim soon began persecuting the rival Ba'th party, and the assassination attempt in October 1959 was the party's unsuccessful retaliation against the dictator.

For the next four years, Saddam was a political refugee in Cairo. For the young Iraqi, to be living in the capital of Arab revolution must have been an intoxicating experience. By overthrowing his own country's monarchy in a 1952 coup, Egyptian president Gamal

Abdel Nasser had achieved precisely what Saddam wanted to accomplish. Nasser eliminated his Islamic fundamentalist, Communist, and moderate opponents by controlling the army and appealing to the masses.

Four years later, Nasser defied Britain by nationalizing the Suez Canal Company. U.S. and Soviet intervention saved him from a British-French-Israeli retaliatory attack, but the Arab world gave Nasser all the credit. Thereafter, until his death in 1970, most Arabs considered Nasser to be the supreme Arab leader. His voice calling for revolt was heard and sometimes heeded in every corner of the region.

During Saddam's time in Cairo, Nasser was in his heyday. To the still-obscure young man, Nasser was an irresistible role model, a hero who had remade Egypt and now called the Arabs to unity, victory, and revenge, including Israel's destruction and the West's expulsion. The dictator enjoyed the masses' veneration of him for making them feel strong, even if these passionate feelings were based on illusions. "We would clap in proud surprise," the great Egyptian writer Tawfiq al-Hakim later recalled with embarrassment. "When he delivered a powerful speech and said about [the United States] which had the atomic bomb that 'if they don't like our conduct, let them drink from the sea,' he filled us with pride."[4]

Regardless of the facts, those glowing images persuaded the people. "We saw ourselves as a major industrial state, a leader of the developing world in agricultural reform, and the strongest striking force in the Middle East," wrote al-Hakim. "No one argued, checked, verified, or commented. We could not help but believe, and burn our hands with applause." The regime's massive rallies—whose participants were transported, fed, and housed at state expense—were scripted in order to seem spontaneous: "Cheer in unison: 'Nasser, Nasser, Nasser!' Cheer by section, 'Long live the victor of Arabism!' Unison: 'Long live the hero of the revolution . . . the leader of the Arab nation!' "[5]

Saddam may well have been buoyed up by the conviction that he, too, would one day be the object of such worship. Indeed, he did not have to wait all that long.

Although Qasim had survived the would-be assassins' gunfire, he was finally overthrown and murdered in 1963 after a coup organized by a coalition of radical officers, including Ba'thists. Saddam quickly returned to Baghdad. For a few months, his Ba'th party had the upper hand in the government, but its leaders were too indecisive and lacked a strong enough base in the army. Nasser, who had his own followers in Iraq, mistrusted the Ba'thists, whom he saw as too independent-minded despite their claim to support him. So the powerful Egyptian dictator threw his considerable weight against the party. Ousted by its even more pro-Nasser rivals, the Ba'th party was again on the run; and Saddam, as one of its rising middle-level cadres, spent some time in prison. But the new rulers made the mistake of not killing him. The young revolutionary would not return such mercy when his own opportunity came.

In July 1968, the Ba'th party finally regained power in its own coup, and Saddam was among the leaders. During his years in underground politics, Saddam had attracted a following, but he was still a relatively junior figure—only 31 years old—and as a civilian, could not be expected to hold the army's loyalty. Knowing that the officers must be won over, the Ba'th party selected as the figurehead president General Hasan al-Bakr, an older, respected military man.

Saddam, understanding the value of organization, stayed in the background during the next few years while he consolidated personal control over the party apparatus and patiently placed his followers in key positions. He and his colleagues outmaneuvered, imprisoned, exiled, or killed all the competing forces, including Nasser's supporters and ambitious military officers. Then he wiped out rival factions and leaders in the Ba'th party. After a series of complex purges and maneuvers, he was soon vice-president and the power behind the throne—the country's real ruler—at an age when most men of political genius are just starting the first steps up the ladder to power.

Like Iraq's political tradition, Saddam's personal experience had been a harsh one. Saddam's predecessors had paid with their lives for being too soft. He had learned that one must kill or be killed, destroy one's enemies or be overthrown by them, and ruthlessly centralize power or face national disintegration. This experience shaped a very different kind of politician from the kind usually found in western societies where power is won or lost in free, peaceful elections. Saddam intended to stay in control, and his rationale was not unlike that attributed to George Patton, the hard-driving American World War II general: The point is not to die for one's own cause but to make the enemy do so.

Achieving power was not the end, but the beginning, of Saddam's struggle. Maintaining peace among Iraq's three communities was an especially urgent task. His own Sunni Muslim group, the traditional ruling elite, constituted only about 20 to 25 percent of the population, albeit the most urbanized and educated segment. The Sunni, who dominated the government, the Ba'th party, and the officer corps, knew that if the regime fell, the other groups might seek revenge against them, and thus the Sunni had a particular incentive to support the government.

The Kurds of the northern mountains, about 20 percent of Iraq's people, were not even Arabs. They spoke their own Indo-European language and still followed tribal chieftains. Though fierce warriors, they were unintegrated into Iraqi society and thus not drafted into the army. In the 1960s, before the Ba'th party came to power, the Kurds had frequently rebelled under the leadership of the Kurdish Democratic party, demanding autonomy. But while troublesome, the Kurds were only a secondary threat, since they wanted not to take over the country but merely to rout the central government from their home territory.

The primary potential threat came from the Shia Muslims of the south, who composed the majority in Iraq. There were relatively few Shia in the Sunni-dominated Ba'th party. Aside from their religious differences with the Sunni, the Shia had some important, potentially dangerous political distinctions. They had close contact with their coreligionists in Iran, and the possibility that Iraqi Shia would join with Iranian Shia was one of Saddam's worst nightmares. In addition, many of Iraq's Shia were loyal to their own clerical hierarchy, which provided an alternative political leadership to Saddam's government and resented the Ba'th regime's secular policies. Finally, the Shia community was unhappy about its poverty and lack of influence relative to the power and affluence enjoyed by the Sunni rulers.

The Ba'th regime used a combination of repression and material incentives in dealing with these communities. It granted autonomy to the Kurds, then reneged on this promise as soon as it felt powerful enough to do so. The Kurds revolted again, with covert Iranian, U.S., and Israeli help. Saddam sent his army into the northern mountains and, in 1975, made a treaty with the Shah, giving up half the Shatt-al-Arab River on their mutual border in exchange for Iran's agreeing to shut off all external aid to the insurgents. The rebellion sputtered out, and government authority was reestablished.

But Saddam did not operate through repression alone. He built a base of support among the masses by encouraging Iraqi nationalism and using Iraq's growing oil income to improve living standards and carry out a concerted development program. The lives of most Iraqis improved. Those Shia and Kurds loyal to the regime faced no discrimination. Everyone in Iraq was heavily indoctrinated with Ba'th party ideology, and young people had a chance to obtain a good education and to rise in the government, the party, and the army. Saddam made sure that Sunnis kept a large majority at the highest levels of these institutions, but there was plenty of opportunity for all communities in the prosperous 1970s.

Although Saddam and the Ba'th party were totally secular in ideology, they knew the importance of securing support from the largely religious masses. The government paid millions of dinars to Shia clerics to win their loyalty and showed its respect for Islam by, for example, enforcing the public observance of such key Muslim tenets as the annual fast during the month of Ramadan. Military units were renamed for historic Shia leaders, and the birthday of the prophet Muhammad's son-in-law Ali, the Shias' particular hero, was made a national holiday.

As important as keeping the communities quiet was the need to maintain control of the army. During the three dozen years of Iraq's history up to 1968, there had been five successful coups and numerous attempted ones. Saddam broke this cycle. The government's tight control over the military, however, was paid for at the cost of greatly reducing the army's effectiveness.

Since Iraq's pre–Ba'th party regimes had always purged the party's supporters from the army, Saddam had few high-ranking career officers on whom he could depend. As long as he kept General al-Bakr as president, the civilian-dominated regime had a respected military figure at the top. But Saddam was also sensitive about his own lack of soldierly credentials and therefore made himself an honorary general and later a field marshal. He constantly wore fancy uniforms and used military phrases in speeches.

Saddam's main technique, however, was to interfere continually in the running of the armed forces. He made senior appointments on the basis of political loyalty rather than skill, constantly shifted officers, and removed generals who became too popular. The regime's intelligence services closely watched the officer corps, sifting for the slightest sign of disloyalty or disaffection.

In governing the society and economy, Saddam followed the Soviet model of ensuring that the party controlled the state and the state dominated all aspects of public life. Young people, for example, were organized into Soviet-style pro-regime groups: the Vanguards, ages ten to fifteen; the Youth, ages fifteen to twenty. By recruiting so many activists through Ba'th party–directed trade unions, women's organizations, and professional associations, Saddam placed his eyes, ears, and supporters throughout the society. As a way of monopolizing power, this method was brilliantly successful.

The regime also controlled the economy—foreign oil companies were nationalized in 1972—and just about everything else. All newspaper articles and radio broadcasts reflected the government line. Everyone's career and even personal survival depended on collaborating with the regime, mouthing its ideas, and rising through its institutions. Compared to other Arab dictatorships, Iraq was severely repressive and tightly controlled. Given the choice between being tortured or rewarded by the regime, most Iraqis backed Saddam or kept their mouths shut.

During his first decade of power, Saddam concentrated on solidifying his rule at home. While never forgetting his ultimate goal of ruling the Gulf and the whole Middle East, he put this dream on the back burner. The Iraqi regime talked a very militant line but acted cautiously in its foreign policy during the 1970s. Saddam's predecessors had broken relations with the United States during the 1967 Arab-Israeli war, and after taking power, the Ba'th party could not appear so unmilitant as to restore them. Iraq ignored the United States except to condemn it verbally or to sponsor terrorists to attack it. Baghdad aligned itself, though never submissively, with the Soviet Union.

In inter-Arab relations, Baghdad's propaganda and intelligence services tried to encourage Ba'thist revolutions in the Gulf Arab states and to increase Iraq's influence in Syria, Jordan, and the Palestinian movement. But Saddam knew that his own country still took a backseat to Egypt and Syria, the main contenders for Arab power.

While at the start of Saddam's rule Iraq spoke in the name of a Pan-Arab nationalist ideal, it moved steadily throughout the 1970s toward an Iraqi nationalism, which had several advantages over Arab nationalism for Saddam. The Kurds were not even Arabs; the Shia were unenthusiastic about Arab nationalism, which they saw as a guise for domination by the Sunni elites who already ruled Iraq and most of the other Arab countries. Together these two groups constituted almost three-quarters of Iraq's people.[6]

To make matters worse, the ethnic majorities had potential foreign allies against Saddam. "When we talk of the great [Arab] homeland," he warned, "we must not push the non-Arabs among our people to look for a country outside Iraq."[7] The Kurds at times looked to Iran, Israel, the United States, and even the USSR—a disproportionately large number of Iraq's Communist party members were Kurds—to help them achieve independence or autonomy. The Shia could seek help in neighboring Iran, ruled by fellow members of their sect and possessing its own large Kurdish minority. To meld these disparate communities into a nation would take more than Arab nationalism.

It was better to build a sense of Iraqi nationhood and a common pride in the people's history. Saddam thus tried to revive the glories of ancient, non-Arab, pre-Muslim civilizations in the land of Iraq—the Babylonians and Chaldeans and Assyrians. He compared himself to the great emperor Nebuchadnezzar, conqueror of Jerusalem some twenty-seven hundred years earlier. Another useful hero was Saladin, vanquisher of the Crusaders, who not only came from Saddam's home town of Tikrit but was a Kurd as well.

Saddam's doctrine maintained that Iraq was part of an Arab nation but also its predestined ruler, and any conquests it made would provide booty that Iraqis would share. Thus, for Saddam, Iraqi unity was more important than Arab unity. Iraq would act opportunistically in its self-interest by allying with Washington or Moscow and defending or attacking neighbors as its interests dictated.

At first, Baghdad inveighed against the "reactionary" Arab monarchies led by Saudi Arabia as being feudal, pro-Western, and doomed. "It is our duty," said President al-Bakr, Saddam's surrogate, "to liberate the Arab people everywhere. . . . We should ignite the Arab revolution in every Arab land." A top party theoretician rejected as criminal the idea of "distracting the masses" by building up individual states instead of merging them by force.[8]

Yet Iraq was strengthening itself rather than struggling for change in the Arab world. Rather than siding with fellow Arab revolutionaries against traditionalists, Iraq pursued its own interests by hypocritically cooperating with conservative Arab regimes like those in Saudi Arabia and Jordan while quarreling with Saddam's radical rival, Syria. In 1970, when Jordan's army fought a civil war with the PLO, an Iraqi army unit stationed there stood passive, not helping its radical Palestinian allies.

By 1975, Saddam was explaining the need for a "balance" between Iraq's interests and those of the Arabs as a whole. In 1979, he went further: A unified Arab state, he admitted, was still only a dream;

Iraq already existed and was its people's real homeland. By 1986, Saddam went even further: "The Arabs are today 22 states, 22 situations, 22 rulers and leaders, 22 economic and social situations and 22 special national situations."[9]

Iraq's role in the conflict with Israel was a good example of this pattern for Iraqi policy. Saddam was violent in his anti-Zionist rhetoric and sponsored Palestinian terrorism against Israel. But since Iraq had no border with Israel, he could talk belligerently while remaining disengaged in practice. Egypt, Syria, and Jordan suffered the losses in war, the Saudis and Kuwaitis paid the bills, and Iraq criticized them for not fighting harder and more often.

Baghdad's view of the issue, like its attitude toward Arab politics, became more openly in favor of Iraqi nationalism over time. In 1970, an Iraqi leader called the Palestine issue "the core and essence" of Arab politics, to which all else must be subordinated. But eleven years later, Saddam complained in a speech that since Iraq fought by itself to liberate land from Iran in the Iran-Iraq war, the Palestinians should defeat Israel by themselves. A Ba'th party resolution at that time made a rare confession of past error: Iraq had spent too much time and effort on "the Palestinian question, in a way that largely exceeded its capacity."[10]

Iraq did send some forces to fight Israel in the 1948, 1967, and 1973 wars, but its army did not perform well. In 1967, Israeli planes crossed Jordan to hit Iraq's totally unprepared air force base at the H-3 oil-pumping station near the Jordanian border. In 1973, Iraq's tank brigade on the Golan Heights took a wrong turn at night on its way to the front. Astonished Israeli soldiers watched as the lost Iraqi tanks, lights ablaze, rolled directly toward them. The Israeli forces finally opened fire and virtually wiped out the unit.

The main mission of Iraq's army, however, was not to fight Israel but to repress the Kurds and block coup attempts by anyone in the regime foolish enough to think he could replace Saddam. In June 1973, Major General Nazim al-Khazar, head of the secret police and one of Vice-President Saddam's right-hand men, invited the defense and interior ministers to visit his new, high-technology investigation center. Instead of feting them, al-Khazar had the two officials stripped and thrown into a cell. He had no particular ideological ax to grind; al-Khazar simply wanted power for himself.

Later that day, President al-Bakr was returning from a visit to Poland, and Saddam was supposed to welcome him at the Baghdad airport. Having earlier ordered his men to blow up the terminal, al-Khazar sat down in front of his television to watch the reception end with Saddam's death. But nothing happened: al-Bakr was delayed, and security was so extensive that al-Khazar's men canceled the attack, thinking their plan had been discovered. Apparently, however, the panic was unnecessary. Saddam was just being typically cautious.

Since their coup had failed, al-Khazar and fifteen accomplices tried to escape over the Iranian border, taking along the defense and interior ministers as hostages. Hunted down by helicopters and trapped just three miles from the frontier, al-Khazar's men killed the defense minister and wounded the interior minister before being captured.

When al-Khazar was brought back to Baghdad barefoot and with a torn shirt, Saddam mocked him. Such a face-to-face meeting was part of Saddam's method, to publicize the personal nature of his victory and the certainty of his vengeance. Al-Khazar and twenty-one others were executed.

Iraq led the Middle East in political executions during the 1970s, averaging a hundred each year. Saddam also used terrorism against opponents who took refuge abroad. Britain expelled eleven members of the Iraqi embassy staff in 1978 after an exiled Iraqi prime minister was shot in London. Other Iraqi dissidents were murdered in South Yemen, Kuwait, and Sudan.[11]

Secret-police units, often headed by Saddam's relatives, used beatings, electric shock, burnings with cigarettes, and sexual abuse against the regime's victims. In this way, opposition in Iraq was crushed. The classic torture was the *falaqa*—burning the soles of the feet—but prisoners were also hung up by handcuffed wrists on hooks. They were told that they were about to be shot and forced to stand in front of firing squads, then they were whisked back to their cells.[12]

Saddam cultivated a fearsome image to deter other would-be self-nominated successors. Videotapes of executions were sent to the leaders of the Gulf Arab states to show them the price of defying Saddam. An American journalist interviewing the dictator once asked Saddam about some of the Shia leaders he had shot as opponents, estimating the number at seven.

Saddam yelled, "Seven!"

The journalist, thinking he had angered Saddam by overestimating his repression, said, "Well, maybe five."

"I'll have you know," said Saddam proudly, "that I shot six hundred of those traitors, and they all deserved it." Westerners never easily grasped that Arab dictators prize ferocity above felicity.

Gradually, Saddam reshuffled party and government leaders to install more of his associates. Step by step, he purged party veterans, accusing some of trying to unseat him, perhaps in conjunction with Saddam's next-door rival, Syria. When he caught Iraq's Communist party recruiting in his army in 1978, Saddam executed twenty-one of its leaders and banned the party, calling it "a rotten, atheistic, yellow storm which has plagued Iraq." He reduced Iraq's dependence on Moscow, criticizing the 1979 Soviet invasion of Afghanistan and buying more Western arms and goods.[13]

By the late 1970s, Saddam was also becoming interested, for the first time, in rebuilding relations with the United States, where there was a growing fascination with Iraq's commercial potential. American magazines like *Business Week* and *Newsweek* ran headlines proclaiming "The Dramatic Turnaround in U.S.-Iraq Trade," "Iraq Starts to Thaw," and "New Scramble for $8 Billion in Contracts."[14]

In May 1977, President Jimmy Carter, announcing a plan to "aggressively challenge" Moscow for influence in radical states, sent a high-ranking State Department official to Baghdad, offering conciliation. Carter and the Commerce Department were eager to let General Electric sell engines to Iraq's navy for its four new Italian-built frigates; but Congress stopped delivery as "contrary to common sense," given Iraq's extremism. National Security Adviser Zbigniew Brzezinski announced, in April 1980, "We see no fundamental incompatibility of interests between the United States and Iraq." The United States and Iraq, Brzezinski said, wanted the same thing, "a secure Persian Gulf." Whatever his intention, Baghdad took such statements as an encouragement to attack Iran.[15]

Saddam was certainly not the saint described by his son Uday: a benefactor of "widows, orphans, families of martyrs and the needy," who hated money, feared God, and enjoyed "fishing and looking after sheep."[16] Nonetheless, he was a strong and pragmatic leader, who had made Iraq powerful and prosperous. In Iraqi politics, it was more important to be feared, respected, and secure than to be popular—or, perhaps more accurately, having such attributes was the only way to be popular.

By July 1979, Saddam's control of Iraq was so complete that he sent sixty-eight-year-old President al-Bakr, who had suffered a heart attack, into retirement and made himself president. "I will be a commander among commanders and not the only commander," Saddam said in his inaugural speech. But he immediately began ensuring his monopoly on power with a new purge. Scores of party leaders were accused of planning a coup in cahoots with the United States, Israel, and "the powers of darkness." Five members of the top-level Revolutionary Command Council and sixteen others were executed by firing squad.[17] Saddam's timing was understandable: Dramatic changes in the Gulf and a revolution in Iran were offering him what seemed to be the best possible chance to conquer the region.

CHAPTER FOUR

IRAN'S REVOLUTION AND GULF WAR I:
1979–1985

Hojja tried to save money by feeding his donkey less and less hay. One day, the donkey died. "Oh, no!" Hojja explained. "And just when I had it used to living on nothing."

—*Middle Eastern folktale*

While Saddam was consolidating power in Iraq, the Persian Gulf area was making a dramatic leap forward: A backward backwater was becoming one of the world's most strategically significant, financially powerful regions. The main countries along the Gulf's shores—Iran, Iraq, Saudi Arabia, Kuwait, and the United Arab Emirates—were all major oil producers and contained most of the world's petroleum reserves. The combination of extraordinary wealth, rapid change, and so many old conflicts and dictators made this a very rough, dangerous neighborhood.

The genie of oil brought many riches to the area. The fact that oil was the Gulf's sole resource made it all the more precious. By 1973, all of the Gulf regimes had nationalized petroleum production, having wrested management from Western companies, and had pushed up prices quickly. At first, the Gulf states' rising oil income seemed a pure blessing. But petrodollars unleashed a tidal wave of modernity, which threatened to unglue the traditional Gulf Arab way of life—based on merchants, caravans, and nomadic livestock raising—with its strict adherence to Islam, its family and tribal loyalties, and its suspicion of change. In a single generation, the Gulf's peoples were catapulted from camels to jets, from tents to skyscrapers; poor herders became cosmopolitan businessmen who dwelt amid luxury.

Alongside these internal changes was red-hot political ferment. The first place to feel this danger was Kuwait, a particularly vulnerable, tiny country whose very name, meaning "little fortress," was a reminder of a long history of defending itself from tribal raids and conquests. Before the oil boom, Kuwait was a center for fishing, trading, and pearl diving, the place where caravan routes from Iraq and the Saudi desert met picturesque dhows at the water's edge. The ruling al-Sabah family was already reigning there in the eighteenth century, when the United States was still a British colony.

Mutual interests brought Kuwait and Britain together in 1899. To escape from the domination of the Ottoman Empire, which then ruled the lands that would later become Iraq, the al-Sabah family accepted British protection. London intervened to block the efforts of its rivals Germany and Russia to extend their influence into the area. In 1913, the British and the Ottomans drew Kuwait's boundaries, which Iraq would accept when it became independent in 1932.

Nonetheless, just after London gave Kuwait full independence in 1961, Iraq claimed that territory as its own, coveting the country's oil wealth and 120 miles of Gulf shoreline. In self-defense, Kuwait invited back British troops for a few months and then replaced them with an Arab League peacekeeping force—including soldiers from Egypt, Jordan, Saudi Arabia, and Sudan—which stayed two years, until the danger dissipated. Kuwait also paid Iraq a bribe to leave it alone.[1]

Britain had become the protector of other small states on the Gulf's Arab coast: Bahrain, Qatar, Oman, and the half-dozen tiny sheikhdoms that would band together as the United Arab Emirates. London's administrators and soldiers had fended off the covetous ambitions of Iran, Iraq, and Nasser's Egypt. But this era came to an end in 1971 when Britain called home its ten thousand soldiers in the Gulf as an economy measure.

Britain's departure had some advantage for the Gulf monarchs; the local Iraq-sponsored radicals could no longer demand that the area be liberated from the British military presence.[2] But these little states—plus Saudi Arabia and Kuwait—worried about who might try to take over next, since they could not defend themselves against Arab brothers who would gladly loot their treasure and their sovereignty. Iraq was the most immediate threat, since it was allied to Moscow, advocated antimonarchical revolution, and periodically revived its claim to Kuwait.

The Gulf monarchs, then, were eager to establish new security arrangements. Ironically, the fact that Arab nationalism posed the greatest menace made non-Arab help more appealing to them. Any Arab advisers or soldiers brought in might turn out to be subversives. Thus the Gulf states preferred to import British advisers and Pakistani soldiers and to obtain U.S. and Iranian security guarantees.

As a conservative king, the Shah of Iran, Mohammed Reza Pahlavi, was a reliable ally for his fellow monarchs on the Arab side of the Gulf. Although he wanted to be the leading power in the region, the Shah—unlike Iraq—was not interested in taking over the Arab states. The Gulf Arab monarchies did not object, therefore, when Iran strengthened its strategic position by occupying three of their small islands near the Gulf's mouth in November 1970. When a Marxist insurgency broke out in southern Oman, that country's government turned to Tehran for troops—and British officers serving as counterinsurgency consultants—to defeat the rebels.[3]

Since Iran and Iraq were the two most powerful and populous states bordering the Gulf, it was not surprising that they were geopolitical rivals for primacy there. But the conflict went far into history and deep into their societies. Over a dozen centuries earlier, at the battle of Qadisiyya in 637, Arab armies destroyed the Persian empire and spread their own rule and new religion. Almost all Persians became Muslims. But while the Arabs triumphed militarily, theologically, and politically, Persia remained a distinct civilization, whose more advanced culture dominated the great medieval Islamic states. Religious differences intensified national distinctions: While Iraq was generally ruled by Sunni Muslims, Iran was a center for Shia Islam. And the Iranian empire often fought its neighbor to the west for control of the fertile lands near today's Iran–Iraq border.

Thus the modern power struggle between Saddam and the Shah—and later between Saddam and Khomeini—was simultaneously a battle between two religious sects (Sunni and Shia), two nations (Arab and Persian), and two philosophies (radical Arab nationalism and the Shah's conservatism, later replaced by Islamic fundamentalism), each seeking to control the Gulf and the Middle East. This web of rivalries was compounded in the 1960s and 1970s by the Cold War between the Shah's pro-Western stand and Iraq's alliance with the USSR.

The United States was another protector for the Gulf monarchies as it gradually became involved in this area. A U.S.-Iran relationship was already well established. When a nationalist prime minister in Iran challenged the shah's power back in 1953, the U.S. government became convinced that this anti-shah movement would turn toward

Moscow. The CIA helped organize a coup to restore the monarch to power.

On the Arab side of the Gulf, the Americans had always taken a backseat to the British. Still, a consortium of U.S. oil companies controlled Saudi oil, and a U.S. air base operated in Dhahran until 1961. A tiny U.S. naval force, docked in a corner of Britain's Bahrain base, stayed after the British left.

The emerging power vacuum and the region's growing significance engaged U.S. attention in the 1970s, but Washington was not eager to play a bigger role there. The Gulf was far from America's shores or bases; U.S. policy was preoccupied with the Vietnam War. The shah was lobbying for American support so that he could guard his weaker neighbors from radical Iraq, and this idea struck the Nixon administration as a good solution to the problem of regional security.

In May 1972, President Richard Nixon visited Tehran and agreed to back Iran as the Gulf's policeman—to preserve stability and block revolution there—promising Iran huge arms sales, military training, and technical help. This U.S. strategy was referred to as the two-pillar policy, making Iran and Saudi Arabia the foundations for regional stability, though Iran was the real strongpoint.

In less than a decade, however, Iran itself would prove to be the weak link among the local states. The main causes of unrest were internal. The massive oil income pouring into Iran after prices and profits shot up in 1973 brought social disruption. Economic development, modern education, urban migration, and other innovations created large, impatient expectations for a better life, which the shah's government could not satisfy.

This same modernization process undermined the society's historic foundation and the regime's traditional base of support. Millions of peasants, who had been politically passive in their isolated villages, were attracted to the cities by the lure of jobs and higher living standards. Their hopes were often disappointed in the rapidly expanding slums of south Tehran and other cities. The move from countryside to town was in itself quite disorienting, plunging the migrants into a totally unfamiliar style of life, one that seemed more influenced by Western than by Iranian customs. Islam was one of the few guideposts left to them from their former lives.

The old middle class of craftsmen and bazaar merchants was also shaken up. Competition from Western manufactured goods and the monopolies of the shah's privileged courtiers threatened their economic security and status. This culturally conservative class disapproved of the new, Westernized middle class of professionals and government bureaucrats. The Islamic clergy, closely allied to the old middle class, feared a tidal wave of atheism from imported Western ideas and growing secularism.

The new Western-educated middle class should have been a pillar of support for the shah, since it was the main beneficiary of his politics. But its members, too, felt little loyalty toward the regime. Torn between their cultural roots and a yearning for more Western-style freedom, this well-educated group resented the stifling atmosphere of fear and repression maintained by the shah's omnipresent secret police.

The most active dissident groups came from among the growing number of students at Iranian schools or those returning from studies in the West, which had been financed by government scholarships. They formed antishah groups, advocating Marxism, Islamic fundamentalism, or some blend of the two ideologies.[4]

The spark that set off the explosion was a demonstration by Islamic theology students in January 1978, violently put down by Iranian authorities. A wave of antigovernment demonstrations began popping up all over the country and escalated month after month as it became clear that the government could not cope with the crisis. Strikes, marches, and increasingly vocal criticism mounted throughout the year. The shah was weak and uncertain; his army's sporadic use of force created martyrs without suppressing the disturbances. By September 1978, the heterogeneous opposition rallied around the leadership of Ayatollah Khomeini, an old enemy of the Shah, who had been exiled for over a decade.

Khomeini had been imprisoned for attacking the Shah's policies, then allowed to leave Iran in the mid-1960s. He took refuge at the Shia seminaries in Iraq. When the Shah requested his expulsion in 1978, Baghdad complied, wanting to ensure that Khomeini's ideas did not spread further among its own Shia minority. The ayatollah went to France, where, from his rented villa outside Paris, he waged an effective propaganda war against the Shah through the international news media and by tapes of sermons smuggled into Iran. Within Iran, Khomeini's talented lieutenants—many of them his former students—established a well-organized network of agents and supporters.

Rejecting any compromise with the Shah, Khomeini demanded a total Islamic revolution that would completely destroy the monarchy and expel U.S. influence. The Western-educated middle class and the Marxist-oriented left went along with Khomeini, believing that they would outmaneuver the elderly cleric once the Shah was gone. Their analysis of the situation was wrong, but Khomeini's overwhelming popularity left the liberals and leftists with little choice but to join his united front.

By the time the Shah appointed a moderate opposition cabinet in December, it was too late to save the regime. The next month, he fled Iran. In February 1979, Khomeini's forces took power, and amid massive rejoicing, the ayatollah returned to Tehran.

For Khomeini, taking power in Iran was only the first step in making the whole Gulf an Islamic empire, which would bring, in his words, "absolute perfection and infinite glory and beauty." Iran's revolution turned the Gulf's whole security system upside down. Instead of Iraq and its puppet Arab nationalist groups subverting the Gulf monarchies, the threat now came from Iran and its Islamic fundamentalist followers. Iran, the Gulf's defender and the West's ally in the 1970s, was now the villain; Iraq had switched from playing a hostile role to being the shield of Saudi Arabia and Kuwait and the West's great hope.

Khomeini was no impractical fanatic. He had outmaneuvered all rivals and proved himself a man of action, among the century's most successful politicians in mobilizing millions of people with his vision through demagoguery, ideology, and organization. In addition, the ayatollah was blessed with a number of shrewd, capable lieutenants, who immediately started building institutions to ensure that the revolutionary government stayed in power.

His ideas were as seamless in internal logic as they were horrifying in their unremitting paranoia and hatred, a paradigm of movements begun to build heaven on earth that degenerate into systems obsessed with selecting enemies to be killed. "You the meek of the world, you the Islamic countries and world Muslims," Khomeini urged, "rise up! Grab what is yours by right through nails and teeth! Do not fear the propaganda of the superpowers and their sworn stooges. Drive out the criminal rulers! . . . March towards an Islamic government!" If only all Muslims cooperated, they would be "the greatest power on earth."[5]

But if Khomeini was so clearly right, why had Muslims not embraced his ideas already? Why didn't the Islamic masses rise up elsewhere? Some creeds would blame humanity's intrinsic fallibility or argue that people must wait for God to choose his own time. Khomeini's answer was that "despotic rulers and wicked clerics misused Islam to create oppressive, corrupt regimes at odds with its principles." Only a popular leader could force people to reject these temptations; only Western agents would resist this virtuous effort.

Thus Khomeini insisted that his enemies had to be enemies of God and humanity as well. To him, the pious Saudis—themselves Sunni Muslim fundamentalists—were heretics, and the radical Iraqis were merely U.S. stooges. America was a satanic force, preventing utopia on earth, deliberately keeping most of the world backward. Many Muslims followed this ideology, but its intolerance toward its coreligionists alienated millions more.

Yet Khomeini's thinking addressed a central problem for the Third World in general and the Gulf in particular: the need to explain why some states are more developed than others. If relative backwardness was due to the shortcomings of local cultural or political traditions, these must be changed according to Western models in order to achieve modernization. The road to development would be long and hard. If, however, the essential problem was external, this would validate Arab and Muslim pride and mean that progress would be more easily attained by overthrowing a reactionary regime and ejecting U.S. influence.

One of the Shah's main crimes, according to Khomeini, was linking progress to Westernization. In prerevolutionary Iran, as elsewhere in the Middle East, tradition was becoming unfashionable, while things Western were seen as representing progress. Indifference to religion, Khomeini charged, was taken to be a symbol of civilization, while piety was a sign of backwardness to an elite that would rather be tourists in Europe than pilgrims in Mecca.

To make matters worse, from Khomeini's standpoint, this Western cultural invasion was popular in many ways. People wanted cheaper, better-quality goods and liberating ideas. Assertions of defiance barely concealed a nagging conviction that Western ascendancy was inevitable and that one might as well join the winning side.

If, as Khomeini claimed, all governments during fourteen hundred years of Islam had failed, why should his experiment be different? Human nature did not change so easily. In Khomeini's Iran, too, there were self-seeking leaders, bitter factionalism, and differences of opinion. This fragility made Khomeini all the more determined to stop America from blocking the thoroughgoing Iranian and regional revolution he had in mind.

Khomeini had good reason to consider Washington to be his most dangerous enemy. The United States, of course, had been a mainstay for the Shah. Yet Khomeini's problem was that Iranians liked or feared America so much that they did not want to fight against its influence. Even many of his top aides wanted to compromise with Washington, following an Iranian tradition of appeasing the strongest foreign power. They publicly denounced America, then secretly asked it for money, support, and favors.

The ayatollah feared that this U.S. leverage might temper his revolution by supporting moderate factions against militant ones— or might overthrow it altogether. And he knew that Washington would do everything in its power to prevent the spread of Islamic revolution to Saudi Arabia and the other Gulf monarchies. Thus Khomeini and his most radical followers wanted a decisive break with the United States, to eliminate its influence and show Iran's people that it could not defeat the Islamic revolution. Anti-Americanism would then be a useful device to rally the masses around the new regime.

In this situation, President Carter did precisely the wrong thing by seeking rapprochement during the revolution's first months in power in 1979. Carter wanted to show Iran that America was benevolent, but he merely made the radicals even more suspicious about whether Washington might subvert them with kindness.

These, then, are the reasons Iranian militants stormed the U.S. embassy in November 1979, kidnapped its staff, and held most of them hostage until January 1981. Khomeini called this a "second revolution," which would banish forever Iranians' servility toward America. "For centuries," said Khomeini, Western propaganda "made all of us believe that it is impossible to resist." Now he rejected compromise, because he wanted to show that America could do nothing against Iran, that America's strength was an illusion.[6]

The revolution could be made safe only by cutting contacts with the United States, "the center for world imperialism," as Iran's ambassador to the UN called it, which "can under no circumstances" be trusted. Ali Akbar Hashemi Rafsanjani, the powerful speaker of parliament, boasted, "Today we don't make any decisions, great or small, under the influence of foreign powers [including] a blasphemous country like the Soviet Union or an imperialist aggressive country like America."[7]

Thus Iran's rulers saw the crisis in practical terms. The radicals used it to displace moderates in the regime and unite the country around themselves. At first, the imbroglio cost Iran almost nothing. It did not need the United States. Iran could still sell oil to other nations. Khomeini correctly calculated that Iran could thumb its nose at both the United States and the USSR: the superpower rivals would prevent each other from attacking him.

But Khomeini was not interested in merely being on the defensive. He thought the hostage crisis was an Iranian victory over America which would inspire a Muslim revolt against the West. Each day the hostages were held, Washington's credibility would fall among Iran's people and the Gulf Arabs. Iran was in no hurry to make a deal. Negotiations went slowly, intermediaries made no progress, and the Western media counted off the number of days of "America held hostage."

For America, then, a successful rescue of the hostages was as much a strategic as a humanitarian goal, to show Iran and the whole Middle East that U.S. power must be taken seriously. If such an attempt was to be made in 1980, however, it could not wait beyond April, because of the coming hot temperatures, short nights, and wild summer winds—the same barriers that U.S. forces would face a decade later in the Kuwait crisis. The U.S. military prepared a necessarily complex rescue plan, since Tehran, near the USSR and far from U.S. bases, was one of the most difficult places in the world in which to undertake such an operation.

According to the plan, eight U.S. RH-53D "Sea-Stallion" helicopters took off from the aircraft carrier *Nimitz,* and C-130 transports flew from Egypt across Saudi Arabia. They were to traverse Iran's desert and meet at a flat, isolated expanse of sand (designated as Desert One) in Iran's Dashit-e-Kavir desert. The helicopters would refuel and then fly two hundred miles to a site near Tehran. They would be met there by U.S. undercover agents, who would put the ninety-man rescue team into trucks and take them to a rented garage, where they would hide during the next day.

The following midnight, a five-truck convoy was to take the unit downtown to Amjadieh Stadium, across the road from the U.S. embassy where almost all the Americans were held. Using folding ladders, the commandos were to climb the embassy walls, kill the guards, and take the hostages to the stadium. A smaller unit would rescue the three diplomats who were detained at Iran's foreign ministry. The helicopters would sweep down into the stadium: four to pick up hostages and rescuers, two to fly air cover, and two in reserve. They would rendezvous with the C-130s and leave Iran, with U.S. fighter planes riding shotgun.

But everything went wrong, due to a combination of bureaucratic mismanagement, the misuse of technology, and bad luck. Two hours after takeoff, on a dark, moonless night in April 1980, one helicopter developed a serious mechanical problem and had to go back. An unexpected dust storm engulfed the formation, and a second helicopter turned around with a broken navigation system.

On landing at Desert One, a third helicopter had a bad leak in its hydraulic system. With fewer than the requisite six helicopters left, the mission commander, Colonel Charles Beckwith of the elite Blue Light counterterrorism unit, recommended that the mission be aborted and the aircraft return to base. President Carter agreed.

A few minutes later, one of the helicopters rose fifteen or twenty feet off the ground to start the flight home. It was a little too low, and that slight miscalculation sent it crashing into a C-130 cargo plane on the ground, slicing a deep gash just behind the cockpit. The commandos in the C-130's passenger cabin pulled an injured crew member from the wreck and ran out the rear door as both plane and helicopter burst into flames, killing eight soldiers. Five other men were badly burned.

Quickly abandoning the site on the remaining five C-130 transport planes, the survivors left behind the other five helicopters and many secret documents, which Iran's army would recover the next day.

The Iranians, who had detected none of these activities, were able to reach the scene so quickly because the overearnest Carter, eager to take personal blame, broke the cardinal rule of never acknowledging covert operations and announced the failure on television. This broadcast was made before the equipment left behind at Desert One could be destroyed or American agents in Tehran safely whisked away.

Tehran claimed the U.S. rescue mission was blatant aggression against a country that had done nothing to deserve it. Nothing, that is, except hold fifty-three Americans hostage. The documents the Iranians recovered at Desert One apparently showed that some of their air force commanders had helped the rescue mission by over-looking its presence. While Iranian soldiers were searching the site, Iranian planes mysteriously bombed it—killing one of the soldiers and injuring two others—probably in an attempt to destroy this evidence. Several high-ranking Iranian air force officers were ex-ecuted shortly thereafter.

The darkness and confusion of the grim, cool night when the rescue mission failed symbolized the shame congealing around a seemingly incompetent U.S. political and military establishment from fifteen years of debacle abroad and at home. Vietnam had brought down Lyndon Johnson; Watergate had wrecked Richard Nixon; the sight of Americans being held hostage in Iran helped derail Carter. It was a low point in U.S. history.

Vietnam, where a bloated U.S. military was defeated despite all its falsely optimistic reports, had already divided America and dam-aged its international prestige. Over fifty thousand Americans died there for no good result; Americans had fled Saigon in humiliating disorder as the victorious Communist armies entered the city in 1975. At home, John and Robert Kennedy and Martin Luther King had been assassinated in the 1960s; President Richard Nixon, caught in a welter of crimes and misdemeanors, had resigned in disgrace in 1974.

Carter had been elected in 1976 as a supposed antidote to this mess. His moralism, uncertainty, and diffidence seemed virtues com-pared to his predecessors' arrogance of power. But then Iran's rev-olution displayed bound-and-gagged U.S. diplomats as booty in a calculated spit in America's face. Carter's last hope of vindication went crashing with that helicopter in the Iranian desert.

Senator Mark Hatfield of Oregon complained that the rescue

attempt "was fraught with elements of the gamble. The risks were far greater than any possibility of success." Congressman Jim Wright of Texas called the failure "an almost unbelievable . . . chain of bad luck." Yet this failure exposed incompetence at the highest levels. The key problem was the breakdown of three helicopters, which—the official military inquiry determined—had been poorly chosen and maintained. Helicopters and pilots unsuited for such a long flight had been included for bureaucratic reasons: the U.S. Navy demanded a share in the operation.

As if this were not enough, Secretary of State Cyrus Vance resigned from office over the rescue attempt because he could not morally countenance a resort to violence, although the United States had exhausted every peaceful procedure in five months of fruitless negotiations. Having previously told European allies that the United States would not use force, Vance did not want even the appearance of having misled them.

All these aspects of the affair raised a chilling question: Was it really immoral for the United States to employ force to free its diplomats kidnapped and tortured for many months?

If the United States could not free its own diplomats held hostage, it could hardly protect Gulf monarchs. Such U.S. restraint was interpreted by Iran and Iraq in 1980—and by Iraq in 1990—as weakness to be exploited by aggression.

The knowledge that the United States would not interfere was a major factor in encouraging Saddam to attack Iran in 1980. On the one hand, he saw that country as weak. Having gone through so much disorder and having purged its own army, Iran might crumble before an Iraqi invasion. Iranian political exiles who opposed Khomeini whispered to Saddam that the Iranian regime was on its last legs. "If the door of a derelict house is kicked in," an Iraqi officer said, "the house will collapse." And since Tehran had expelled its American protector and so totally isolated itself, Saddam reasoned, it could expect no help from anyone else.

On the other hand, Saddam was prompted to attack Iran because Khomeini was staking his own claim—in the name of Islamic fundamentalism—to the Gulf and Iraq. Saddam had no intention of letting Iran rule the Gulf, since he saw that as his own destiny. Most immediately, he was motivated to strike at Iran because Khomeini's call for Islamic revolt threatened Saddam's own survival. Tehran was doing its best to foment an Iraqi Shia uprising, sponsoring an assassination attempt on Iraq's foreign minister as well as other terrorist acts. Iraq's already restive Shia majority might respond by rebelling against the ruling Sunni minority.

Even before Iran's revolution, Iraqi Shia had been organizing revolutionary cells. Underground groups ambushed government officials and bombed offices. Demonstrations broke out in the Shia holy cities at the annual processions marking Hussein's martyrdom twelve hundred years earlier at the hands of the Sunni ruler Yazid, to whom Iranian propaganda was comparing Saddam. The crowds chanted, "Saddam, remove your hand! The people of Iraq do not want you!" A popular young Shia cleric, Baqr al-Sadr, was a prime candidate to be Iraq's Khomeini. The regime struck back with ferocious repression. About six hundred clerics and activists were executed, including al-Sadr and his sister. Iraq also deported over two hundred thousand ethnic Persians, who might conceivably be supportive of Iran.

While repressing the Shia opposition, Saddam also wooed Iraq's Shia, promoting more of them to top posts in the government, party, and army. They were, he reminded them in speech after speech, Iraqis by citizenship and Arabs by ethnicity. "God destined the Arabs to play a vanguard role in Islam," he ingeniously explained, so "any contradiction between a revolution which calls itself Islamic and the Arab revolution means that the revolution is not Islamic." Tehran's real ideological inspirations were Zionism, "Persianism," and the reactionary concepts of "the Khomeini gang."[8]

Saddam also went on the offensive with his own ethnic subversion, encouraging rebellions among Iran's Kurdish and Arab minorities. Tensions rose steadily, and there were artillery duels along the frontier during the summer of 1980.

The war's immediate cause was a border dispute over a small but strategic area. An important part of the Iran–Iraq border is formed by the Shatt-al-Arab River. While most boundaries run along a river's midpoint, Iraq's then-ally Great Britain had helped Iraq gain the whole waterway in a 1937 treaty with Iran. This situation placed Iran in a tenuous strategic position, since Iraq controlled the approaches to its main oil port, Abadan. In 1975, when Iraq was fighting a strong, Iran-backed Kurdish revolt, Saddam made his deal with the Shah to split the river down the middle in exchange for Tehran cutting off aid to the Kurds. Now that the balance of forces was again in his favor, Saddam renounced the 1975 treaty and demanded the whole waterway.

On September 22, 1980, Saddam ordered his army to march into Iran, expecting a quick, easy victory to make him master of the Gulf and the Arab world. Instead, it was the start of a long, bloody war that would set back his ambitions by a decade.

The battle would seesaw for eight years, reducing the two prosperous states to near bankruptcy. The results were heaps of bodies, hundreds of thousands of refugees, the black smoke of burning oil, tons of noxious rhetoric, and undreamed-of political challenges for the United States. For the first time since World War II, missiles were fired at cities. Iraqi chemical weapons brought horrifying deaths to thousands of civilians and soldiers.

The conflict would be a struggle for supremacy and survival

between two dictators who were indifferent to casualties and two systems—radical Arab nationalism and revolutionary Islamic fundamentalism—that were determined to destroy each other. In the end, no one would gain anything from all the suffering and sacrifice of this thoroughly unnecessary conflagration.

During its early years, though, the war was popular on both sides. "I may have the power to stop Iraqi citizens from demonstrating against Saddam Hussein in Baghdad," commented Saddam, "but I do not have the power to make these same citizens fight" so bravely inside Iran.[9] Iraqis fought eagerly, out of patriotism and hatred for Iran.

Most Iraqis did not want their country to be conquered by Khomeini. Saddam's effort to rally Iraq's Shia Muslims largely succeeded in keeping them in line, either from fear or because they identified themselves as Arabs. Having made more progress in Iraq than in practically any other Arab country, urban middle-class women did not want to don the full-length black cloaks forced on their counterparts in Tehran. The Baghdad statue of the great medieval poet Abu Nuwas—himself of Persian descent—holding aloft a wine cup displayed another popular Iraqi custom opposed by Iranian fundamentalists, who banned all alcohol.

Although the war intensified patriotism among most Iraqis, Saddam took no one's loyalty for granted. As always, he used material incentives as well as fear to control Iraq's people. Families who lost sons were given cars, and the regime imported more and better food than Iraqis had enjoyed in peacetime.

One of the main growth items in Iraq was posters of Saddam. His picture was everywhere, showing him dressed in battle fatigues and commando beret, with a pistol holstered on his hip, or depicting him as a peasant, a Kurd, or an heir to ancient Babylon's glories. This campaign arose from Saddam's megalomania and his toadies' ingenuity at finding new ways to glorify him, but it also made sense. Iraqis, like Iranians, wanted a strong leader, whose wisdom and ruthlessness would lead them to victory.

Iran had its own propaganda assets. Tehran played its Muslim card, pointing out that Michel Aflaq, the founder of Iraq's ruling party, was a Christian, as was Foreign Minister Tariq Aziz. Iran's radio referred to the former as "the Jew and criminal Begin's ally" and the latter as "Hanna" Aziz, using a typical Middle Eastern Christian first name. "Revolution by the Arabs," declared Iran's foreign minister Ibrahim Yazdi, "can never triumph unless it is through Islam." In the eyes of Islam, said Ayatollah Hussein Montazeri, Khomeini's designated successor, all Muslims should live under a single government.

This plan for forcible unification also applied to the Gulf Arab monarchs. "Brothers in struggle!" Radio Tehran addressed Arab listeners, "vengeance against the enemies of Islam, unbelievers, hypocrites, and tyrants may be delayed. However, God gives respite but does not forget!" As for the Saudi and Kuwaiti rulers, "It is necessary to rob them of their wealth by all available means; the simplest is to burgle them and take by force their money and jewelry." Western influence must be thrown out and every Arab regime destroyed to establish "the government of Islam on its ruins."[10]

The small, oil-rich Gulf Arab states all trembled at such words. The Saudis and Kuwaitis knew, of course, that Iraq was their first line of defense against Khomeini. Still, to be defended by Iraq was like having a hungry lion as a bodyguard: Saddam had to be constantly fed, lest he devour his clients. The Gulf monarchies nourished Iraq by secretly shipping its goods through their ports and donating around $30 billion to its war effort. In addition, the Saudis and

Kuwaitis gave Iraq the profit from a million barrels of their own oil each day.

Saddam insisted that he was doing them a favor by accepting their money. "The glory of the Arabs," he said, "stems from the glory of Iraq." In short, what was good for Iraq was good for the Arabs. To which one might have added, "Or else!"[11]

Officially, the Gulf monarchies insisted on defending themselves. Their efforts to do so, however, were feeble. Saudi Arabia, Kuwait, the United Arab Emirates, Bahrain, Qatar, and Oman formed the Gulf Cooperation Council (GCC) in 1981 and put a token unified force in Saudi Arabia. This was little more than a joke. They were banking on Iraq to stop Iran's armies. And if that did not work— as Iran's battlefield successes in the mid-1980s would make questionable—only the United States could save them.

Victory for either side in the war scared the Gulf monarchies, since the winner would claim the small states as prizes. Who would protect them if Iraq collapsed, and who could preserve them if Saddam won? They would call on America only in their real hour of need—a U.S. military presence would upset Iran, Iraq, and domestic opinion—but they would not hesitate to do so if the alternative was suicide or surrender.

The war confronted the United States, too, with a difficult dilemma, which Washington also resolved in favor of backing Iraq while displaying an apparent neutrality. The United States did not want Iran to win a victory that would let Khomeini control the world's main oil fields. But while it was imperative to keep Iran from destabilizing the Gulf Arab states, the United States also did not want to push Iran into the Soviet camp.

President Jimmy Carter warned in January 1981 that the United States would fight any "outside force" trying to control the Gulf "by any means necessary, including military force."[12] This "Carter Doctrine" was ostensibly aimed at deterring a Soviet invasion of Iran while also putting Khomeini on notice that the United States would, if necessary, defend the Arab monarchies against him. To back up this warning, the United States set up a "Rapid Deployment Force" to move troops quickly to the Gulf and fight there if necessary. The U.S. government also sold huge amounts of arms to Saudi Arabia. Almost unnoticed in the rush of events, America had entered into an unofficial defensive alliance with the Gulf monarchs.

Like the U.S.-USSR alliance against Hitler in World War II, the U.S. association with Iraq was wrought by necessity. As in the pact with Stalin, though, Americans quickly forgot their temporary friend's true nature. The *Wall Street Journal* insisted in 1981 that Saddam's "rhetoric shouldn't obscure the fact that Iraq, probably more than any other Mideast nation except Israel, is embracing Western values and technology." It was becoming an advanced secular society, "with a car in every garage, a television set in every living room, universal education, and chic French fashions for emancipated Iraqi women. Such a society should eventually become congenial to the West."[13]

Assistant Secretary of Defense Richard Perl took a more skeptical and ultimately accurate view: "It is foolish to think that a pro-Marxist, pro-Soviet Ba'thist regime, the leader of Arab radicalism and rejectionism, is about to become an American ally or even a tacit partner without exacting an enormous price." Especially dangerous, he warned, was encouraging Iraq's "imperial ambitions" to dominate the Gulf.[14]

Nonetheless, Secretary of State Alexander Haig claimed that Iraq showed "a greater sense of concern about the behavior of Soviet imperialism in the Middle Eastern area," and he sent a delegation to Baghdad in April 1981 to test the waters for improving relations. Trade increased, and the U.S. government cleared the sale of International Harvester dump trucks and five Boeing transport planes. The number of Iraqi students in America tripled to 2,500.

Among the evidence ignored by the United States was Iraq's drive for nuclear weapons and its threats against Israel. France had helped Iraq build reactors and provided a three-year supply of uranium, sufficient for three bombs; Italy was reportedly ready to train Iraqis to handle radioactive substances that could be used to make plutonium. In August 1980, Saddam urged the Arabs to destroy Tel Aviv, Israel's largest city, with bombs as soon as possible. Saddam also said he would use nuclear weapons against Israel when they were available.[15]

Israel took his threat seriously. On June 7, 1981, just as the nuclear reactor near Baghdad was about to begin operation, Israel destroyed it in a daring bombing raid, with its planes flying low, fast, and undetected across Saudi territory. Although Iraq—as Saddam liked to remind everyone—was in a state of war with Israel, the raid was widely criticized. President Reagan condemned Israel's attack, though noting its "reason for concern in view of the past history of Iraq." Vice-President George Bush was more categorical in castigating Jerusalem's action as "not in keeping with international standards"; he urged suspending U.S. aid to Israel and endorsed a UN resolution against it.

Yet while U.S. leaders assumed the Arab world wanted them to condemn Israel, the Arabs themselves did nothing in retaliation, rejecting Saddam's request to use the "oil weapon" against the United States and withdraw funds from U.S. banks. They were not especially enthusiastic about Iraq's having nuclear weapons that might someday be used to threaten or attack them. And if Israel had not destroyed the installation, Baghdad might have had a bomb in time to use against Iran or, certainly, to intimidate any opposition to its occupation of Kuwait.[16]

At first, even the Iran-Iraq war did not break the ice between Baghdad and Washington. Iraq feared that once the hostage crisis was over, the old U.S.-Iran alliance would be restored. But when Washington and Tehran remained at odds after the return of the fifty-two remaining hostages in January 1981, Baghdad saw its own opportunity. Assisted by Saudi and Kuwaiti lobbying, Iraq launched a multimedia campaign to court the United States.

During the first months of the war with Iraq, Iran seemed closer to collapse than to triumph. With the advantage of surprise, Iraq advanced against a disorganized defense and captured a large slice of Iranian land. Appearances were, however, deceptive. Baghdad had no strategic plan to force Tehran's surrender. Trained in clumsy Soviet steamroller tactics, the Iraqis advanced slowly. There were no Iraqi pincer moves to cut off and encircle Iranian units, no daring raids to seize crossroads in the enemy's rear and block reinforcements.

Saddam's military ignorance handicapped Iraq. His commanders were inflexible, afraid to take the initiative without the dictator's direct orders. Politics also imposed restrictions: The army's Shia units were not considered completely reliable, and Saddam wanted to keep casualties low lest heavy losses or the depletion of loyal Sunni units endanger the regime. Thus Iraq fumbled its advantage, and the advance faltered, giving the Iranians time to regroup and dig in.

Rather than begging for peace, Iran rallied in a war of national defense. Younger, more competent, U.S.-trained officers had replaced the shah's inept favorites. Determined volunteers from the new Islamic Revolutionary Guards Corps, eager to be martyrs,

rushed forward in human-wave attacks. Iran encouraged its warriors to seek martyrdom. "The path of jihad [holy war] is the path
to heaven," said Radio Tehran. Afraid to retreat lest Saddam execute
them, tens of thousands of Iraqi troops stayed in place, to be surrounded and captured by Iran. Baghdad's armies were pushed back
toward the border.[17]

Iran also gradually gained the economic and strategic advantage
over its enemy. By releasing the U.S. hostages, Iran recovered $8.5
billion of its financial assets, which had been frozen by the United
States.[18] It was also able to continue shipping oil through the Gulf
while its navy blockaded Iraq's short coastline and cut off Baghdad's
petroleum exports. Iran closed another major Iraqi export route by
bribing Syria to close a pipeline that ran across its territory to the
Mediterranean. Thus Iran was able to sell abroad over two million
barrels of oil a day, while holding the exports of money-starved
Iraq to about one-third that level.

On July 14, 1982, Iranian troops had so reversed the initial phase
of the war that they advanced across the border into Iraq. The
possibility that Iran might seize Baghdad gave many Arabs nightmares. If Khomeini won the war, his troops might turn toward
Jordan or Saudi Arabia. A fundamentalist triumph could set off
rebellions in a half-dozen countries. Since Israel's army was at that
time simultaneously invading Lebanon and besieging Beirut, panic
increased. Arab headlines screamed: "Khomeini and Zionism Are
Two Bayonets in Conflict with Arab Nationalism."[19]

Iran's leaders now faced a major decision. Having driven Iraqi
troops off their own soil, should they end the war or fight on to
topple the Baghdad government? Khomeini did not hesitate to
choose total victory over Iraq as his goal, thinking it only a matter
of time until Iraq collapsed from bankruptcy or Iran's army broke
through to Baghdad. Success would be the ultimate proof of the

Islamic system's superiority, and Khomeini believed that Saddam's fall would make the Gulf states erupt in revolution like a row of volcanoes.

While Khomeini believed victory to be inevitable, his lieutenants hoped it was possible. Each military advance or claimed triumph in battle encouraged them. Meanwhile, the war helped maintain Iran's internal unity and kept otherwise unemployable youths and the army busy. Any Iranian politician who urged peace was branded a traitor, as happened to President Abolhassan Bani-Sadr, who had fled to exile in Paris in 1981. When Moscow and Iran's Communist party criticized the continuation of the war in 1982 as a distraction from fighting the United States and Israel, Iran's government banned the party and arrested its leaders. To Soviet statements that the war was "mindless," Iran angrily replied that such a word better described Soviet aggression in Afghanistan.[20]

The battlefront was now a three-hundred-mile-long line from the Zagros Mountains' foothills down to the Gulf. In the mountainous north, Iran aided insurgent Iraqi Kurds while Iraq helped rebellious Iranian Kurds. Most of the fighting took place in the swampy center and south, where trench warfare came to resemble the futile, endless, and bloody campaigns of World War I. Indeed, Iraq's survival did hang by a thread. Unless it held the vital road connecting Baghdad and Basra, just west of the front line, Iran would cut the country in two and be only a few miles away from these two main cities. Iran's leaders predicted that the next campaign would be the "final offensive."

Still, Iraq did not crumble. Its economy and morale survived, thanks to Western credits, Saudi-Kuwaiti aid, and two oil pipelines, which bypassed the Iran-patrolled Gulf by traversing Turkey and Saudi Arabia. The Iranian human-wave assaults that had worked so well against demoralized Iraqi forces on Iran's territory now

suffered heavy losses, inflicted by well-entrenched Iraqi forces defending their own soil. The offensives of October–November 1982, February and November 1983, and February 1984 all failed miserably.

The Gulf monarchies, however, were not persuaded that the danger was over. As the tide had turned in Iran's favor by 1982, the Kuwaitis, who literally could hear the sounds of battle across the border, became increasingly nervous. They tried to buy peace by offering to pay Iran huge reparations, a proposal that made Iraq very nervous. Tehran refused, demanding that Kuwait pressure Saddam to resign. Iran's prime minister accused the Gulf monarchies of being collaborators with America and sneered, "Do you not realize that you are facing a revolution that has roots in all countries, and that the populations of your countries are less than that of Tehran alone?"[21]

Thus, just as Iraq hoped, Iran's radicalism and aggressiveness, the endless war, and the fear of a wider Gulf conflagration were pushing together a loose alignment of neutrals—the United States, Gulf Arab monarchies, and the USSR—all wanting to prevent an Iranian victory and a consequent spread of Islamic fundamentalism. The threat forced this triad to cooperate among themselves for the first time in history and to help Iraq. The United States, the only country able to break the deadlocked war, was about to become the protector of last resort for Kuwait, Saudi Arabia, Iraq, and even Iran itself.

CHAPTER FIVE

IRAQ'S VICTORY: 1985-1988

"Why are you digging a hole?" Hojja's neighbors asked him.
"To bury all the dirt in that pile."
"But what will you do with the dirt from the new hole?"
"I can't deal with all the details!"

—*Middle Eastern folktale*

In 1985, the Iran-Iraq war was still raging after five years of bloody fighting. Thousands of men were dying during sporadic offensives in the frontline on mountains, sunbaked plains, and marshes to gain a few yards of territory at best. With the battle deadlocked, Baghdad and Tehran desperately sought another road to victory. They both saw the United States as the key to success.

This was a remarkable situation. The world's two most radical, anti-American states were competing to auction their souls to the American devil to get it on their side. Iran secretly negotiated with America for arms; Iraq escalated attacks on Iran's tankers and oil facilities to force U.S. diplomatic intercession to end the war and protect neutral oil shipping. The Kuwaitis and Saudis, too, would seek U.S. protection, disregarding their own years of complaints against its intervention in the area. Anti-American, Arab nationalist, and Islamic rhetoric were all meaningless. Everyone wanted to win the strongest superpower's favor.

In its earlier days, the war had made Khomeini's regime more popular as the masses rushed to defend the revolution and the motherland. But by 1985, Iran was in serious trouble. Casualty lists grew ever longer; the promised victory was nowhere in sight. Iraqi planes made psychologically devastating attacks on Iran's cities, and many people fled Tehran. Even strict laws and vigilant patrols could not stop draft-dodging. The army command and Khomeini's aides began to realize the fight was hopeless but could do nothing against the ayatollah's stubborn insistence on destroying Saddam.

Iran still hoped that either Iraq would collapse or its own forces would break through. But Saddam continued to survive—as he had done so many times before—by resourceful innovation. Baghdad's defense lines held, and Iraq bought all the modern arms it wanted. The unending war seemed to be a pyre consuming Iran and Iraq whose fire might easily spread outward, enflaming the whole Gulf.

With the war deadlocked in the field, Baghdad had counterattacked in 1984 by striking against Iran's economy. Saddam had purchased French-built Super-Étendard fighter-bombers and Exocet antiship missiles to attack Iran's tankers and the main oil terminal at Kharg Island. By not even objecting to these sales, the United States became Iraq's accomplice in expanding the war.

As a result of this escalation, Iran's economy was in bad shape. Low oil prices, world overproduction, and Iraqi attacks on tankers reduced its income from $23 billion in 1983 to only $6 billion in 1986, by which time Iran could sustain its spending levels for only two more years. There was inflation, unemployment, shortages, and signs of growing domestic unrest. Khomeini himself admitted that Iran must escape its isolation. When the huge crowd at a March 1985 Persian new year rally chanted, "War! War until victory!" Khomeini replied with a shocking fatalism: "Victory and defeat lose all meaning because service to God and obedience to his orders is what matters."[1]

Khomeini fell into Saddam's trap by retaliating to the tanker war in kind. Iranian speedboats shot at tankers carrying Kuwaiti and Saudi oil or stopped freighters thought to be carrying goods to Iraq. The world oil glut kept the international energy market from disruption; the fact that there were more ships for hire than cargoes to fill them encouraged owners to continue risking the Gulf route. But this new phase of the war unnerved Kuwait and Saudi Arabia, while it drew Western attention to the danger this fighting posed for an oil-dependent world economy.

As President Reagan began his second term, in January 1985, the war and its dangers were much on his advisers' minds. At a time when Tehran was generally thought to be winning the war, they rightly expected it might lose. They also worried, unnecessarily, that the Soviets might take over Iran. The long border between Iran and the USSR and the presence of a hundred thousand invading Soviet troops in neighboring Afghanistan were geopolitical realities. But the Soviet troops were too badly bogged down in Afghanistan to consider attacking Iran, whose rugged terrain and hostile population made it a much tougher target. The Soviet regime was also increasingly preoccupied by the internal problems that would cause its own collapse a few years later. Further, any Soviet move into Iran could bring on a military confrontation with the United States. Nonetheless, many high-ranking U.S. officials could not be shaken from a belief that the Soviets were about to try to gain power in Iran.

At the same time, the White House was frustrated and humiliated by its inability to free American hostages in Lebanon, held by Iran-backed terrorists. Reagan turned resolution of this emotional issue—kept in the public's mind by frequent media interviews with grieving relatives—into a personal crusade.

Up to that point, the administration had taken a consistent position on the war: neutral in theory, tilting toward Iraq in practice. By not openly taking sides, it avoided entangling itself in the fighting or pushing Iran into an alliance with Moscow. Yet by leaning toward Iraq, Washington ensured that Iran would not win a victory which might transform the Gulf into an anti-American inferno of radical fundamentalism.

The United States and Iraq grew steadily closer in the first half of the 1980s. In 1982, Iraq expelled its terrorist protégé, Abu Nidal, whose anti-PLO Palestinian group had staged many attacks on American and other civilians. Abu Nidal's colleagues continued to operate from Baghdad, but the State Department dropped Iraq from the list of states sponsoring terrorism and allowed it to buy U.S. civilian planes.

The next year, 1983, U.S. envoy Donald Rumsfeld visited Baghdad. The Reagan administration granted Iraq huge credits to buy grain and offered intelligence based on satellite photographs of Iran's military deployments. Meanwhile, Operation Staunch was launched to block arms sales to Iran, while U.S. allies were encouraged to sell weapons to Iraq. The United States and Iraq restored full diplomatic relations in 1984. In many ways Iraq was treated as a U.S. ally, and it was never censured for having invaded Iran or starting the tanker war.[2]

Given this U.S.-Iraq rapprochement and the fact that Islamic Iran and the United States already thought each other to be the world's most evil country, a U.S.-Iran rapprochement seemed about the least likely possible event in the mid-1980s, as ridiculous a notion as the Berlin Wall coming down or the USSR ceasing to be Communist. Iran's UN ambassador, Said Rajai Khorasani, wittily explained that Iran's relations with the United States were exactly what Iranians wanted—none whatsoever—and said he hoped that "the situation will remain the same."

It was U.S. intelligence's assumption that this pattern would not soon change. A CIA–State Department report in late 1984 argued that Iran's virulent anti-American, anti-Soviet policy would continue as long as Khomeini lived. Some officials in the National Security Council (NSC) were more worried about Soviet influence. George Cave, a retired CIA official, met regularly with Iranian émigrés who purveyed wild tales of Khomeini's imminent fall and the alleged Communist leanings of Iran's clerical leaders. Cave passed these claims on to credulous White House officials.

Both Israel and the Gulf Arab states, each for its own reasons, hoped Washington could persuade Iran to be more moderate. Israel sought to weaken Iraq—an enemy still at war with the Jewish state, sponsoring terrorism and daily threatening its extinction—and rebuild its alliance with Tehran, which had flourished under the Shah. To keep communications open and to secure the emigration of Iranian Jews, Israel had sporadically sold a small amount of military equipment to the Islamic regime. Obviously, Iran was not about to reestablish relations with Israel, but there were hopes of a behind-the-scenes understanding.

The Saudis and Kuwaitis wanted Iran to end the war, which was being fought on their borders, as their oil tankers were attacked and terrorists operated in their territory. Conscious of the many threats around them, the Saudis and Kuwaitis kept almost $200 billion in assets abroad and imported huge amounts of arms. Their oil income had declined from almost $150 billion in 1981 to only

$45 billion in 1985. To circumvent the tumultuous Gulf, the Saudis had built a pipeline to the Red Sea.[3]

In the spring of 1985, there suddenly appeared an opportunity for change. Manouchir Ghorbanifar, an Iranian broker who sold everything from carpets to guns to political access, approached Israel, claiming to represent Iranian moderates who wanted to reestablish good relations with the West. Although the Israelis did not know it, he was acting on behalf of the Rafsanjani faction, which wanted U.S. help to win control over Iran.

This faction was one of three political blocs in Iran—the other two were led by Ayatollah Hussein Montazeri, Khomeini's designated successor but a weak leader, and President Ali Khamenehi—that were competing for power, without ideological motives. Ghorbanifar's mission was to portray Rafsanjani's faction to the Americans as moderate and to paint its rival Montazeri group as pro-Moscow extremists.

It is unclear how much, if anything, Khomeini knew about his followers' dealings with the Americans. Given Khomeini's advanced age and lack of involvement in day-to-day affairs, however, the factional battle had already raged out of his control, and the combatants largely ignored his repeated calls to stop it.

The Americans dealing with Ghorbanifar never fully understood the Iranian politics behind his approach. They did, however, appreciate that if Ghorbanifar genuinely represented someone in Tehran, this was a significant opportunity. It meant that the Islamic Republic of Iran, which had kidnapped U.S. diplomats and daily denounced the United States as the "Great Satan," was now talking about détente. Tehran's propaganda had blamed the United States for Iraq's ability to continue fighting so effectively. Yet if America was so powerful, it was all the more urgent for Iran's leaders to reduce U.S. hostility.

The first task for the Israelis and Americans was to verify Ghorbanifar's credentials. He was a questionable character who once reportedly worked for SAVAK, the Shah's secret police, and later became a double agent involved in conspiracies that were complex even by Iranian standards. Sometimes he acted for the Khomeini regime; at other times he helped its enemies. Apparently, he had supplied arms for a plot to kill Khomeini, then betrayed it to Iran's authorities, who executed those involved.

To prove that this time he was on the level, Ghorbanifar provided in 1985 a detailed, credible account of the captivity of William Buckley, the CIA station chief in Beirut kidnapped by pro-Iranian terrorists and the hostage the U.S. government most wanted back. (Unbeknownst to Washington, Buckley had been tortured to death.) Ghorbanifar's information was forwarded to National Security Adviser Robert McFarlane. The Americans approved Israel's dealing with Ghorbanifar.

Next, Ghorbanifar worked with Adnan Khashoggi, the controversial billionaire and Saudi agent, to prepare a thirty-five-page memo in July 1985 analyzing Iran's inner workings for the U.S. government. This report gave the NSC a rationale for bypassing the CIA, the agency usually charged with covert operations. The argument was ironic, given what would happen later: "None of the Iranians whose help we need," it said, "would consent to work with the CIA [because they] don't want to wake up one morning to read their names in the *New York Times*."

Labeled "Strictly confidential, for your eyes only," the Ghorbanifar–Khashoggi paper described Rafsanjani's faction as pro-Western moderates, Montazeri's faction as pro-Soviet leftists, and Khamenehi's faction as neutral. Ghorbanifar asked the Americans to help the moderates win and end "Iran's destructive capacity."

This characterization of Montazeri was quite false. He was more conservative than radical, favoring a free-enterprise economy and not being especially militant in urging the spread of revolution abroad. He was certainly not pro-Soviet. The real issue was that Khomeini had chosen Montazeri to replace him when he died, and thus, for Rafsanjani, Montazeri was the man to eliminate. By posing as a moderate fighting Soviet puppets, Rafsanjani was playing the old Iranian game—despite all Khomeini's teachings—of persuading foreigners to put him into power.[4]

Developments in Iran made U.S. officials more willing to believe that the situation there was ripe for change. In March 1985, Iran had lost its last real chance for victory against Saddam, as still another massive offensive bogged down in southern Iraq's swamps. Iran's dead there, suffocated by Iraqi poison gas, lay heaped in no-man's-land. Baghdad had made good on its boast to "turn the Huwaiza Marshes into a floating graveyard."

Iraq also carried the war into the heart of Iran. At a nationally broadcast Friday prayer meeting in Tehran University, a man detonated a bomb strapped to his waist, killing himself and five others. "We will retaliate for this savage act with the utmost strength and power," asserted President Khamenehi a few minutes later. "Every punch will be answered by a harder punch." But Iraq was punching hardest. Its missile attacks and air raids on twenty-four Iranian towns left seven hundred dead and twelve hundred wounded. Between March 6 and 19, Iraqi planes bombed Tehran seven times. Hundreds of thousands fled to the mountains north of the city. In poor south Tehran, hitherto a regime stronghold, demoralized slum-dwellers rioted for two days in mid-April. Between late May and mid-June, there were a dozen more air attacks on Iran's capital.[5]

On July 7, Ghorbanifar hosted a meeting at a hotel in Hamburg, Germany, dramatically introducing the Americans to a genuine Iranian leader, Ayatollah Hasan Karoubi, a close associate of

Rafsanjani and friend of Khomeini's son. Karoubi said he was representing Iranian moderates who wanted to defeat the "pro-terrorist, pro-Soviet" forces in power. Iranians knew that the easiest way to persuade America was to manipulate its fear of Soviet expansion. Unless the United States helped "restore Iran to the West," Karoubi claimed, it would blow up in civil war, and "in a few months—two years at the most—it will turn into a satellite of Communist Russia."[6]

A week later, Karoubi sent a letter to the U.S. government from Qom, Khomeini's headquarters, with "Top Secret, please destroy after reading" written across the top. It listed dozens of groups, politicians, military commanders, and officials—a widely disparate collection of moderates and militants—allegedly ready to support a pro-U.S., moderate line. Karoubi asserted that an Iranian leader would publicly confirm his offer of conciliation with the West. As promised, a few days later Rafsanjani stated that Iran would be willing to renew diplomatic relations with the United States if America "took the initiative and redressed its past wrongs to Iran."[7]

How could the United States do this? Tehran was uninterested in a U.S. apology for supporting the Shah or in a change in U.S. policy toward Israel. In the best realpolitik fashion, Iran's leaders were quite willing to go against their own ideology and public statements to obtain weapons through Israel.

Despite Khomeini's verbal thunderbolts, the officials running Iran's government and its war effort were neither fools nor fanatics. They had to worry about such mundane matters as paying the bills and counting the casualties. Since Iraq's defense lines depended on well-entrenched tanks acting as massed artillery, Iran needed anti-tank weapons to break through. Since Iraq's bombing attacks on Iran's cities sowed panic and opposition to the war and the regime, Iran needed antiaircraft missiles to shoot them down. Iran's president, seeing off a hundred thousand more troops to the front, admitted to them that human-wave attacks could not defeat modern weapons. Obtaining missiles to blow up Iraqi tanks and Hawks to shoot down Iraqi planes was Iran's highest military priority, important enough to justify dealing with the Great Satan itself.

Equally, despite its own arms embargo against Iran, the U.S. government was ready to supply the weapons—albeit indirectly at first—by letting Israel sell Iran over five hundred U.S.-made anti-tank missiles from its own stockpiles. On the day this delivery was completed, September 14, 1985, an American hostage, Reverend Benjamin Weir, was freed in Lebanon.

Hoping to win release for all the hostages, Washington next approved a shipment of 120 Hawk antiaircraft missiles; Israel sent the first 18 in November, but the Iranians returned them because they were not the latest model. On October 27, Ghorbanifar, Karoubi, the Israelis, and U.S. representative Michael Ledeen (an NSC consultant, unfamiliar with Iranian politics) met in Geneva, Switzerland. The basic deal was that the United States would supply weapons in exchange for the release of all the Americans held hostage in Lebanon.

With such sensitive issues at stake, the U.S. government put the negotiations and logistics into the hands of top officials. The key operational man was Lieutenant Colonel Oliver North, an energetic NSC staffer with a strong personal commitment to the Nicaraguan contras. North and his superiors—first, National Security Adviser McFarlane and, later, McFarlane's replacement, Admiral John Poindexter—had little experience with diplomacy or the Middle East. Having been given the task of freeing hostages, they acted in the best military tradition of doing anything necessary to fulfill this designated mission. Instead, the situation required a longer-term, strategic view of U.S.-Iran relations and Gulf politics. Ironically, the Reagan administration had followed the example of the much-criticized President Carter by giving hostages such a high priority as to make U.S. policy itself hostage to the terrorists and their sponsors.

The American negotiators also did not understand what they were doing in terms of Iranian and Gulf politics. They subverted Kuwait's position by promising to press for the release of seventeen Shia terrorists from an Iranian-backed group imprisoned for a series of 1983 attacks in Kuwait.[8] North and retired general Richard Secord, who handled the operation's logistics for a profit, took the remarkable liberty of telling Iran that the United States would help remove Saddam, a commitment Reagan had never approved.

By the end of 1985, the Reagan administration was split over whether or not to keep trying the arms-for-hostages effort. Secretary of State George Shultz and Secretary of Defense Caspar Weinberger opposed further sales, preferring to maintain the pro-Iraq approach; Poindexter and CIA director William Casey supported the secret deal. Reagan agreed with the latter and gave Poindexter control of the operation. In February 1986, the United States sold Iran one thousand U.S.-made antitank missiles. Casey and North used some of the funds generated by these sales to buy arms for the Nicaraguan contras, despite Congress's ban on direct aid.

Although Iran had not kept its end of the deal by obtaining the release of all the American hostages in Lebanon, in May the Americans again offered Iran Hawk missile parts if all American hostages were set free. Retired national security adviser McFarlane returned to government service in order to travel to Tehran secretly on a Southern Air Transport plane. The Iranians seemed unprepared for his arrival, and only low-level Iranian officials met him. His interlocutors in Tehran did not want their dealings to be so open. After four days in the Tehran Hilton, he left, bitterly disappointed.

Hopes were reignited on July 26, when a second American hostage, Reverend Lawrence Jenco, was released. Although McFarlane had warned Iran that no further arms would be forthcoming, the administration again sent more Hawk parts.

The American connection was now such a poorly kept secret, and so financially and politically lucrative, that Khamenehi's faction joined the negotiations in September. The Rafsanjani and Khamenehi factions were now aligned against Montazeri, and the United States found itself an instrument in this struggle.

Five hundred more antitank missiles were sold in late October 1986, and a third hostage, David Jacobsen, was released in November, just before all these arrangements were made public by Montazeri's supporters, published in a Lebanese magazine, and quickly reported in the American media. At that point, the whole enterprise collapsed.[9]

The prevalent interpretation of the U.S.-Iran affair was that Iran's leaders had conned Washington into providing arms by pretending to be moderates. The Reagan administration was said to be so eager to free hostages, gain a diplomatic success, and finance the contras that it was tricked into helping Iran.

The Iranians did exaggerate the Communist threat to Iran and their own moderation. Still, Rafsanjani's men were basically telling the truth. They did want to follow a more moderate policy than Khomeini's, escape from the ruinous war with Iraq, rebuild relations with the West, resolve the hostage issue, and downplay support for Islamic revolution or terrorism. Rafsanjani's later behavior would show that he was not bluffing, because he knew that détente with the West was necessary for his regime's survival.

Reagan once told McFarlane, "The key element is whether or not these people are indeed devoted to change and not just simply opportunists, self-serving radicals." This was a typically American misreading of the Middle East and one that the operation's critics would later repeat by ridiculing the idea that Iran's leaders were moderate. But this was beside the point. These politicians needed American help because they wanted power. Selling arms to free hostages was a mistake; using Iran's weakness to force it to change policy was not.[10]

Alongside the politics of survival and factional maneuvering, the Iranians' third motive was personal greed. Rafsanjani's men paid for the arms with funds they took from the Swiss bank accounts of Iran's state-owned oil company, then they pocketed a sizable percentage as commissions. To subsidize their Iranian collaborators, the United States and Israel agreed to inflate the weapons' prices, which also meant more money for the American and Israeli arms merchants involved and for North to use to buy weapons for the Nicaraguan rebels.

When Iran paid \$5.1 million for antitank missiles in 1985, \$500,000 went to Ghorbanifar and \$600,000 (in \$100 bills) was passed in an attaché case to Karoubi in Switzerland. On the Hawk deal, \$6.7 million was to go to Ghorbanifar and the Iranian politicians. Iran's regime, Karoubi chortled at one secret meeting, "will be overthrown with its own money." An Israeli participant later commented, "This Iranian government is more corrupt than in the days of the shah."

North was especially naive about Gulf politics. The hostage issue, he wrote in a memo to Poindexter, was a necessary first step and arms sales a "confidence-building" measure to handle a "primitive, unsophisticated group who are extraordinarily distrustful of the West."[11]

In fact, the fundamental American error was not to bargain with Iran but to bargain so badly. Three times Iranian interlocutors pledged to deliver the hostages from captivity, three times the United

States sent arms, and three times the Iranians were unable to fulfill their promise. Rafsanjani's faction was handicapped because it could not control the Lebanese terrorists, whose links were to more extremist circles in Iran's government.

Yet the administration remained willing to try again, while the number of American hostages in Lebanon actually increased as more kidnappings took place. As had happened during Carter's earlier Iranian crisis, the more Washington played up the hostages' importance, the more Iran raised the price and the harder it became to win their freedom.

Although Washington had Tehran over a barrel, the administration acted as if the situation were reversed. Iran was in terrible shape, unable to obtain new arms or keep its economy going while stuck in an unwinnable war. America held all the cards: It could threaten to intervene against Iran, subvert the regime, or help selected politicians gain power. By emphasizing the hostage issue, America's weakest bargaining point, the Reagan White House put itself into the position of begging for their release.

The relatively small amounts of arms supplied by the United States and Israel had no effect on the war and were apparently never even used on the battlefield. The real impact in Tehran was political. Rafsanjani turned the whole intrigue to his advantage as he consolidated his mastery over Iranian domestic politics. When pro-Montazeri activists revealed his secret dealings with the Great Satan, Rafsanjani denounced them as liars and traitors. Some of Montazeri's supporters were arrested. By controlling access to Khomeini, Rafsanjani and his allies persuaded the ayatollah to change his mind about having Montazeri as his successor.

Ironically, the exposure of the U.S.-Iran tryst had far more negative fallout in the United States than in the supposedly fanatically anti-American Islamic republic. The White House forced North and Poindexter to resign following disclosure of the financial diversions, and the president's chief of staff, Donald Regan, quit a few weeks later. Critical investigations were made by a special commission, a congressional committee, and an independent prosecutor. The public overwhelmingly condemned the administration's inconstancy in breaking its own embargo on Iran and betraying its policy of not paying ransom for hostages. Constitutional objections were raised on the failure to inform Congress. Legal questions were raised about the misuse of U.S. funds and weapons, enrichment of private individuals, and destruction of official documents, as well as the whole controversy of arms sales to the contras despite the Congress's opposition.

Yet many of the critics among the media and the public also bore some responsibility for having made the hostage issue too high a priority. The strong reaction against the Iran affair reversed public opinion, turning it so decisively against making deals with kidnappers that when Saddam seized hostages in 1990, no one advocated concessions to gain their release.

Despite the greater embarrassment and controversy in the United States, the secret negotiations showed up Iran's weakness. Rafsanjani put the best face on things, claiming that Iran was "so powerful that [the Americans] come and beg . . . to arouse our sense of pity."[12] But the Iranian leaders' eagerness to make deals with America showed that the revolution had failed to transform Iran's political culture and strategic circumstances.

Without admitting so openly, Tehran was retreating, accepting defeat in the war, reopening contacts with the West, and giving up serious efforts to spread revolution. Islam's triumph had brought neither prosperity nor a new utopian order. Although Rafsanjani claimed that Khomeini had vanquished Iranians' fear that the superpowers "were demons who could destroy everything any time they roared," Rafsanjani's own behavior belied these words. By inventing such a fearsome, omnipotent America, Khomeini had made the United States seem so frightfully powerful that Iranian politicians like Rafsanjani were more careful in trying to avoid its vengeance and win its favor.

Nor did the affair do the United States any lasting harm. The congressional investigation asserted that "the United States undermined its credibility with friends and allies, including moderate Arab states, by its public stance of opposing arms sales to Iran while undertaking such arms sales in secret."[13] This assumption was wrong: There was no loss of U.S. credibility with Kuwait or Saudi Arabia. After all, such secret maneuvering and preference for real-politik over ideology was precisely the way they played the political game themselves.

In fact, the Gulf war's deadlock and escalation was making the Saudis and Kuwaitis more trusting of and dependent on the United States than ever before. At the very moment in 1985 when Iran approached the United States for arms, Iraq was escalating the war to encourage U.S. intervention and Iran was avenging itself on Iraq's ally Kuwait. One morning in May 1985, as Kuwait's ruler was being driven to the al-Sif palace, a terrorist from the Iran-backed Islamic Jihad group drove a bomb-laden car into the motorcade, killing himself and two bodyguards. The royal limousine sped directly to a hospital, where the emir was treated for cuts and bruises from flying glass. Kuwait, the crown prince said, "will not give in to any threats or blackmail."[14]

There were many other acts of sabotage and terrorism in 1985 and 1986. Two Kuwaiti Shia were killed trying to plant bombs in a Kuwait City shopping center. The saboteurs had disappeared months earlier while fishing in the Gulf and claimed upon their return to have been prisoners of Iran's navy. Actually, they had been training as terrorists. Iran mined Kuwait's offshore waters, fired missiles at oil installations, and stopped Kuwait-bound neutral ships it suspected of carrying military supplies for Iraq. Iran's surrogate terrorists attacked two Kuwaiti oil refineries. Iran's last advance, in February 1986, resulted in its seizing Iraq's Faw Peninsula on the border, a few miles from Kuwait City.[15]

Kuwait was understandably frightened of becoming the war's main battlefield. As Iran and Iraq had already done, Saudi Arabia and Kuwait dealt with this dangerous situation by trying to arrange U.S. intervention on their side.

In November 1986, at the very moment the U.S.-Iran arms deal came to light, Kuwait began a quest to gain U.S. protection for its tankers in the Gulf by trying—as Iran had done—to frighten America by threatening to turn to Moscow for help. Even the Kuwaitis were bemused by how eagerly and totally the United States swallowed their bait: A Kuwaiti foreign ministry official attributed America's dramatic response to a "Hollywood mentality." Soviet tankers, he said, "have been quietly sailing in the Gulf for some time. So what has changed?"[16]

What had changed was Kuwait's urgent desire to reregister its ships as American, to run the Stars and Stripes up the flagpoles so that U.S. Navy convoys would guard them. Once that happened, Kuwaiti leaders explained, protecting the tankers would be a U.S. problem for which Kuwait had no responsibility. After all, Kuwait's foreign minister insisted, that was why Kuwaiti-owned companies paid taxes in the United States.

The Reagan administration argued that America must rush in to prove itself the guarantor of Gulf security. If the United States did not act, said National Security Adviser Frank Carlucci, its allies would have to choose between "giving in to Iranian intimidation or accepting Soviet offers of protection, and not just for shipping."

Secretary of State Shultz spoke in apocalyptic terms: "The worst thing that can happen to the United States is to be sort of pushed out of the Persian Gulf [and] find the Soviet Union astride the supplies of oil to the free world." President Reagan said, "In a word, if we don't do the job, the Soviets will."[17]

The administration had a hard time convincing Congress—especially the Democrats—to accept the convoying plan. Experience in Vietnam made many of the legislators worry about entering a new quagmire, just as they later feared U.S. intervention during the 1990 Kuwait crisis. In the colorful words of Representative Toby Roth of Wisconsin, "At best the Persian Gulf is a snakepit and we're going to be bit again." Senator Dale Bumpers of Arkansas said, "We're courting disaster . . . a lot of sons aren't going to come back from the Persian Gulf." Even the usually hawkish Senator Sam Nunn of Georgia warned that there were "substantial risks" of violent confrontation with Iran.[18]

If Reagan did send ships, the Democrats wanted to invoke the War Powers Act, requiring the president to remove the soldiers unless Congress approved the operation within ninety days. The Republicans had to filibuster for several weeks before the Senate finally defeated this proposal by a 50–41 vote. In the end, the majority in Congress respected the president's role as chief executive and feared appearing indifferent to a Soviet advance in such a critical region.[19]

Yet while reflagging and convoying Kuwaiti tankers did make strategic sense for preserving Gulf security, it had little rationale in the Cold War context of a Soviet threat or an immediate danger to the oil supply. "The odd aspect of the crisis is that nothing significantly new has happened," former secretary of state Henry Kissinger wrote in an op-ed article. America was risking "an expanded military role that cannot be decisive."[20]

Of course, the importance and the potential vulnerability of Gulf oil were beyond question, since the area yielded 66 percent of Japan's and 40 percent of Western Europe's imports. The Gulf's entrance, the Strait of Hormuz, was barely twenty miles across at its widest point, bringing ships in sight of Iran's Larak Island. Through this chokepoint flowed seven to eight million barrels of oil a day. Yet oil was continuing to flow freely to consumers. Actually, so much petroleum was being successfully shipped from the Gulf that prices had declined and producing states were desperately trying to hold down the supply. Iran and Iraq were selling every possible barrel to finance the war. Further, the tanker war was hurting Iran more than its enemies. Most of the three hundred attacks on shipping and the two hundred seamen deaths were due to attacks by Iraqi planes on ships carrying Iran's oil. The U.S. reflagging and convoying, of course, had no effect on this situation.

The real purpose of U.S. intervention was to show Saudi Arabia and Kuwait that it was willing and able to protect them and their oil exports. Otherwise, these states would quickly bow to the anti-American dictators in Iran or Iraq, who sought to dominate the Gulf. Their most serious fear was that Iran would attack or subvert them. And while Iran made only a limited effort to foment revolution in practice, its rhetoric was quite frightening.

To minimize U.S. intervention, Iran tried even harder to intimidate the Gulf Arabs and Washington by appearing bellicose. President Khamenehi put it bluntly: Iran would first "send Saddam to hell" and then do the same to his collaborators, the Gulf monarchs who "supported unbelief against Islam."

"However long the United States may linger in the Gulf," another Iranian leader explained, "it will eventually pull out . . . and let those states bear the consequences." Iran's Revolutionary Guard commander Mohsen Rezai claimed that Muslims all over the world wrote Tehran, asking permission to attack U.S. embassies. "We do not take decisions in haste," he threatened, "but when we do, hurricanes and earthquakes erupt." He predicted that the Americans would run away. An Iranian diplomat jokingly referred to a gift dessert McFarlane had brought on his trip to Tehran, saying, "One day [the United States] sends us cake and another day it threatens us with bombs and missiles."[21]

More solemnly, the Tehran daily *Kayhan* said: "The very possibility, though faint, that [Iran's forces] will get an opportunity to encounter American troops in the Persian Gulf is drawing huge crowds to the recruitment centers."[22] Why was the chance of confrontation "faint"? Because Iran was bluffing. It had no intention of starting an unwinnable fight with the much stronger United States. Tehran's mistake—like Saddam's a little later—was not in expecting to defeat America but in thinking that the Americans would be frightened away by words.

In fact, despite the militant rhetoric, Iran was already backing down. Rafsanjani explained, "We do not wish to get into a conflict with the United States and we say so explicitly."[23] Iran's actions mirrored Rafsanjani's caution. The first U.S. convoy entered the Gulf on July 22, 1987, and arrived safely at Kuwait's oil terminal two days later. The Iranians stayed away from the convoys, each of which consisted of two to four reflagged tankers and two or three warships. To ensure the operation's success, the U.S. Navy was present in overwhelming force: eleven warships and seventeen supply, patrol, and minesweeping craft, staffed by about four thousand sailors, in the Gulf; just outside were sixteen more ships, including an aircraft carrier and a battleship, with twelve thousand crew members. The mission, which would last a little over a year, cost U.S. taxpayers $15 to $20 million a month.[24]

As Iraq and Kuwait had hoped, this show of strength was accompanied by U.S. diplomatic efforts to push Iran into a cease-fire. On July 20, 1987, the UN Security Council passed Resolution 598, demanding an end to the war. But Tehran blocked U.S. efforts to impose UN sanctions against it by persuading Moscow to oppose the plan and offering to accept a cease-fire if the UN first found Iraq guilty of aggression.

Generally, though, the Iraqi and Kuwaiti strategies of bringing U.S. intervention worked quite well. Iran was steadily pushed onto the defensive in 1987 and 1988 by three factors: First, the United States assembled a multinational coalition—including Britain, France, and Italy—to convoy tankers. Second, the readiness of U.S. forces to fight any Iranian interference with Gulf Arab shipping persuaded Iran that the United States might enter the war against it. Third, Iraq launched successful offensives on the southern front.

On September 21, 1987, for example, night-flying U.S. helicopters using infrared sensors spotted an Iranian ship dropping mines in international waters. The Americans attacked, setting the ship on fire and capturing twenty-six crew members. The mines still aboard were shown to reporters as proof of the ship's activities before the vessel was scuttled and the crew returned to Iran. On October 8, U.S. helicopters sank three Iranian gunboats that had opened fire on them. Afterward, the Iranians were even more careful to keep their distance from U.S. convoys, though they continued to attack unprotected tankers.[25]

The United States even extended its coverage. The original U.S. position had been that the tankers would not be protected while docked in Kuwait. But when an Iranian missile by chance hit the reflagged tanker *Sea Isle City* in Kuwait's harbor on October 17, wounding the American captain, U.S. forces ordered Iranian personnel off an oil platform they used as a communications station and destroyed it in retaliation.

The Gulf Arabs were unconcerned about calling on the infidel Americans to smash a fellow Muslim country, while they themselves stayed on the sidelines. "It would be easy to enter into battles with Iran," explained Kuwait's ambassador to Washington, Saud Nasir al-Sabah, "and hard to bring those battles to an end." A Saudi official commented, "The American military presence, in order to be justified by us, must ensure our total security by ensuring [Iran's] total paralysis."[26] The United States must so intimidate Iran that it would not dare seek revenge later.

Obsessed with gaining U.S. help, the Gulf Arab states were also more openly disinterested in the Arab-Israeli conflict. The November 1987 Arab summit ignored the issue while implicitly endorsing the U.S. presence in the Gulf. The Gulf, it said, was the priority, the place where the real life-or-death confrontation was going on.[27]

While wishing for a U.S. triumph, however, the Gulf monarchies gave only limited help, behaving almost as if they were doing the United States a favor by letting it defend them. Saudi-based AWACS and P-3 reconnaissance planes from Kuwait provided intelligence, but Kuwait sought to preserve its "neutral" stance by refusing to let U.S. minesweeping helicopters take off from its territory. In private conversations, U.S. officials and officers voiced dissatisfaction with the level of assistance. Following its usual way of doing business with the region, Washington accepted this brazen posture and exacted no political price for helping the monarchies.

Still, the war would end only when Khomeini himself could be persuaded to agree. A step in this direction was Khomeini's appointment of Rafsanjani, the architect of secret contacts with America, who believed the war to be unwinnable, as commander in chief of Iran's military. Rafsanjani released hostages to rebuild relations with Britain and France, as had been tried with the United States. France, for instance, repaid $330 million of a loan left over from the Shah's era, allowed an Iranian embassy official suspected of involvement in terrorism to leave, and expelled anti-Khomeini activists. In exchange, Iran quickly arranged for two French hostages to be released in Lebanon.[28]

Iraq's military offenses made ending the war even more urgent for Rafsanjani. In March and April 1988, Iraq fired about two hundred missiles at Iranian cities. When Iraq advanced in the south in April, Iranian forces, fearing Iraq's chemical weapons, broke and ran. The Iranians were short of willpower and equipment, while Iraq had recaptured all its territory up to the prewar boundary.

At 10:10 A.M. on the morning of July 3, 1988, several small Iranian gunboats opened fire on a helicopter from the 9,600-ton cruiser USS *Vincennes*. The warship, equipped with the latest computerized systems and sensors, gave chase and a half hour later sank two Iranian boats and damaged a third.

In the midst of battle, the *Vincennes* detected an aircraft taking off from Iran's Bandar Abbas field—an airport used by both civilian and military planes—and approaching at high speed. Three times the *Vincennes* warned the plane to turn away. But the mysterious plane did not respond, nor did it carry a device electronically identifying civilian aircraft. Instead, it seemed to be descending and accelerating, as an attacker would do. The American commander was not inclined to let the plane come closer. A year earlier, the frigate USS *Stark* had been approached by an Iraqi Mirage fighter, which fired an Exocet missile that killed thirty-seven Americans. Iraq claimed this was a mistake but offered no proof.

Having only seconds to make a decision, the *Vincennes*'s captain concluded at 10:51 that the plane was an American-built Iranian Air Force F-14, such as U.S. Intelligence had reported were being operated from Bandar Abbas. He ordered two missiles to be fired at the intruder.

Three minutes later, they scored a direct hit on the plane nine miles away, and it crashed into the sea. The misidentified plane, however, was an Iran Airlines passenger flight from Bandar Abbas to Dubai in the United Arab Emirates. None of the 290 passengers survived.

"The United States is responsible for the consequences of its barbaric massacre of innocent passengers," roared Foreign Minister Ali Akbar Velayati. "We will not have the crimes of America unanswered," said an Iranian radio commentary. "We will resist the plots of the Great Satan and avenge the blood of our martyrs from criminal mercenaries!"

Iran did seek revenge, hiring a Palestinian terrorist group, the Popular Front for the Liberation of Palestine–General Command, to bomb U.S.-bound passenger planes in Europe. One such operation may have helped blow up a December 1988 Pan American Airlines flight from London to New York over Lockerbie, Scotland, causing the deaths of 270 people. Terrorists hired by Iran were arrested in Germany while trying to place several bombs on other planes.

But Iran's political reaction was to retreat. As his faction had promised the Americans, Rafsanjani did stop the war with Iraq, keep Iran out of the Soviet orbit, and restrain Iran's most militant revolutionaries. He did so not out of moderation but in his own and Iran's interests. Arguing that the United States had now entered the war on Iraq's side and might attack Iran directly, Rafsanjani urged Khomeini to stop the war immediately. Rather than defy America, Khomeini buckled under to end a war he now believed was endangering the Islamic regime, though he described the decision as being akin to drinking poison. On July 20, 1988, he regretfully told his fifty million subjects that a cease-fire would take effect in one month.

Iran had learned the cost of trying to conquer the Gulf or challenge the Americans. In 1979, Khomeini argued that America could do nothing to free the hostages held by Iran; in 1988, he ended the war because he feared U.S. intervention. In the eyes of Tehran's leaders, America had changed from an object for insults to a power that had to be respected.

Khomeini's death in June 1989 began an era of reduced revolutionary zeal. Rafsanjani became president and openly rated pragmatism more important than Islamic ideology, a pattern close to that of China, where the utilitarianism of Deng Xiaoping triumphed after Mao died. "It doesn't matter if a cat is black or white," said Deng, "as long as it catches mice." In his first sermon after Khomeini's funeral, Rafsanjani announced: "We do not have anything against having good relations with the East and the West." For all his might, Khomeini—like Mao—could not ensure that his policies would outlive him by a single day.

As for Iraq, when the cease-fire came into effect on August 20, 1989, its people celebrated as they had never done before. Tens of thousands of people filled the roads and parks; workers came out of offices and factories to cheer the end of their long ordeal. The women sang songs and uttered their high-pitched trilling sound of joy. There was dancing in the streets. Onlookers pounded on drums and waved olive branches from the sidewalks. Teenagers leaned out of cars decorated with Iraqi flags and colored ribbons; drivers honked their horns and flashed their lights to the beat. Loudspeakers blasted out patriotic songs. Although shots fired into the air in celebration killed a number of people during the three-day festival, everyone agreed that the war and Iraq's troubles were now over. The soldiers would come home and life would be better. Wouldn't it?[29]

Saudi Arabia and Kuwait were also hopeful. They had narrowly avoided being swallowed by Iran or engulfed in war. Ironically,

Iran's revolution had pushed most Arab countries closer to America, contrary to Khomeini's predictions. The Reagan administration had been correct in its policy of reflagging and convoying the Kuwaiti tankers. Even the arms deal with Iran—mistaken as it was—had ultimately caused no problem with the Gulf monarchies.

Despite many experts' warnings, the Gulf states did not let Arab nationalism, Islam, or the Palestine question stand in the way when they needed U.S. help. They were increasingly preoccupied with their own neighborhood.

Many observers also expected Iraq to become more moderate. Its wartime financial and political needs had pushed Iraq into an alliance with Saudi Arabia, Kuwait, and Egypt. Yet this was only a tactical move. Saddam was still the same man who had begun and escalated the war. By defeating Iran, Baghdad thought it had become the natural ruler over the region, Saddam's goal when he started the war. Saddam had helped save Saudi Arabia and Kuwait from Iran in order to devour them himself. The United States would only understand Saddam's intentions when the Iraqi leader had gone so far that America would be able to save the Gulf a second time by only the barest of margins.

CHAPTER SIX

THE EVIL GENIES OF HISTORY

The Sultan insisted on taking the reluctant Hojja bear hunting. When Hojja returned, a neighbor asked what had happened.
"It was perfect," replied Hojja.
"How many bears did you kill?"
"None."
"How many did you chase?"
"None."
"How many did you see?"
"None."
"Then how was it so perfect?"
"When hunting bears, it's always best not to find one."

—*Middle Eastern folktale*

If Americans found it hard to understand the politics of the Middle East, this shortcoming was matched by the Arabs' difficulty in explaining events there in light of their own expectations. The Arab political predicament and the U.S. difficulty in handling it would be major factors behind the Kuwait crisis.

Although the Iran-Iraq war had finally ended in 1988, the Arab world was still in disarray. The region's states were as mutually belligerent as ever; the individual citizen's rights were totally insecure. Arab nationalism and Islamic fundamentalism continued to reject the status quo, Iran and Israel were feared as dangerous rivals, Soviet support for the Arabs had disappeared, and the economic outlook was bleak.

Judging from their acts and statements, Arab leaders and intel-lectuals were not convinced by these problems of any need to change the political system or philosophy that had been guiding them for many years. They denied responsibility for the region's lack of peace and surplus of suffering. Just because their concepts had not worked did not mean that they were wrong. After all, argued the Arab writer Hassan Nafan in 1983, Marxism was not proved to be a bad system simply because "it failed to unify the workers of the world."[1]

The analogy to communism was more accurate than Nafan in-tended: The political ideas dominating the Middle East had a great deal in common with that system, which, as events were about to show, was on the verge of collapse. Arab nationalism and Islamic fundamentalism, like Marxism, claimed to be scientific analyses of the world—that is, objectively true—as well as practical guides for solving existing problems and creating a utopian society. In all these cases, however, the concept that claimed to be liberating was actually oppressive, a rationale for dictators to seize and abuse power.

The mythology that undermined American understanding of the Middle East suggested that fundamentalism, Arab nationalism, rad-ical regimes, and terrorist movements could win over the populace, and so U.S. policy had to conciliate them or make concessions to reduce their appeal. The truth was the exact opposite. The most important regional development was—as in the USSR—the sys-tem's failure, which produced a series of disastrous crises for the Arabs, culminating in the 1980–88 Iran-Iraq and 1991 Kuwait wars.

The central problem of Arab and Muslim political thought was to explain and remedy the fact that their supposedly morally and spiritually superior civilization was so weak while the West was so strong. Modern Arab history was largely a parade of unsatisfactory solutions and destabilizing ripostes on this issue.

Marxism, claiming that society was based on capitalist exploitation, called on the workers to unite, overthrow it, and create socialism. Arab nationalists like Saddam and Islamic fundamentalists like Khomeini attributed the Middle East's ills to Western domination but then criticized America from opposite directions: fundamentalists attacked it for undermining traditional society; radical nationalists complained that it preserved conservative forces and ways.

As the historian Hisham Sharabi put it, the Arabs made the West their scapegoat, blaming it for their own repressive societies, separate states, faltering modernization, communal conflicts, and the self-serving rule of small elites.[2] In its Islamic fundamentalist version, as expressed by Egypt's Muslim Brotherhood, the villain was an "alliance of united enemies (Zionism, Christianity, Marxism, Buddhism and cow worshippers [Hindus])" that sought the "breaking, subjugating and smashing" of Muslim and Arab societies.[3]

The nationalists insisted that the solution was for Arabs to unite, expel Western influence, and create a single Arab state. The fundamentalists replied that the answer was for Muslims to unite, expel Western influence, and build an Islamic republic. Every few years, a new version of these arguments arose to cause political upheaval. In the 1950s, Egyptian dictator Gamal Abdel Nasser urged Arabs to rebel against conservative Arab regimes and the West in the name of radical nationalism and socialism; the resulting series of coups brought men like Saddam to power in the 1960s. By the 1970s, new groups—especially among Palestinians and in Lebanon—tried to adopt the revolutionary innovations of China and Cuba to Arab conditions, ridiculing the existing military regimes as too cautious. In the 1980s, Khomeini's Iran called for Muslim uprisings. At the dawn of the 1990s, Saddam made his bid to lead the Arabs into a showdown with the West.[4]

None of these movements fulfilled its aspirations. Each failure only deepened what Sharabi called a "sense of impotence and fear . . . inferiority and frustration which often expressed itself in nihilism and despair."[5] By the close of the 1980s, the Arabs faced a choice between abandoning the effort to achieve these goals or—the option Saddam favored—working even harder to accomplish them. An examination of these three key Arab aims reveals why their pursuit was so self-destructive and, contrary to what Saddam and most American Middle East experts thought, doomed to failure.

First, if Arab unity was so appealing, and so many leaders proclaimed this was their goal, why could it not overcome the existence of separate nation-states with conflicting interests? The answer is that none of the states wanted to merge. Everyone agreed that a Pan-Arab brotherhood should be established; no one agreed who would be Big Brother. Each country and every ideology—radicals and conservatives; Nasserists, Ba'thists, Communists, and Islamic fundamentalists—saw itself as the proper one to run the region. Within states, communal groups struggled for control: Alawite (a composite religion closest to Shia Islam), Druze, and Sunni Muslims in Syria; Christians and Sunni and Shia Muslims in Lebanon; Sunni and Shia Muslims and Kurds in Iraq.

Disputes among different groups of Arabs and Muslims were not so easily settled. In the mid-1970s, Arab and Iranian dissidents organized a solidarity rally in New York to show that conflicts among their countries were merely illusions promoted by reactionary regimes. An Iraqi student lambasted the Shah, to the audience's delight, but when he listed among the monarch's misdeeds the seizure of three small Gulf islands, one of the Iranian hosts went onstage. The Iranian radical whispered in the speaker's ear that his group believed the territory belonged to Iran. The speaker had to withdraw his words or step down. The student stalked off angrily, and the meeting almost turned into a brawl. Several years later, the

Iranian revolution did overthrow the Shah, kept the islands, and began subverting neighboring Arab governments. Before long, the anti-imperialist Iranian and Iraqi brothers in Islam were fighting each other in an extraordinarily vicious war.

Dictators gave lip service to Arab interests and real attention only to their own. This passage from universalist philosophies to nation-state patriotism in the Middle East produced more, not less, instability. As had happened in nineteenth-century Europe, the biggest wars and greatest imperial expansion took place in an age of growing patriotism for individual countries. Syria, Iraq, and Libya tried to build empires in, respectively, Lebanon, the Gulf, and North Africa. Arab nationalism gave each country a license to subvert the others.

The failure of the second goal, to expel foreign influence from the region, was partly due to the Arabs' concurrent endeavors to recruit the outsiders. Fantasies of easy, total victory over the West alternated with a cynical competition among those seeking to cut the best deal with it. The Lebanese-American scholar Fouad Ajami called this behavior "alternating between a search for foreign patrons and an equally frenzied search for foreign scapegoats and demons."[6] During their war, Iraq and Iran both epitomized that principle by trying to persuade the United States to help them. Even the politicians who most loudly proclaimed their passionate opposition to Western intervention avidly solicited such intercession—as long as it was on their side.

This hypocrisy was nothing new. The early Arab nationalists sought British or French subsidies; Britain armed, financed, and directed the 1915 Arab revolt against the ruling Turks. The conservative monarchies that emerged in Egypt, Iraq, Jordan, and the Gulf Arab states during the 1920s and 1930s were British clients. Radical Arab nationalists in the opposition turned to Nazi Germany and Fascist Italy in the 1940s; Nasser's Egypt from the 1950s and then Ba'th party regimes that came to power in Iraq and Syria in the 1960s were Soviet clients, as was the PLO during the 1970s and 1980s. When Iran threatened the Gulf in the 1980s, Iraq and the monarchies turned to the United States; when Saddam invaded Kuwait, most of the other Arab rulers quickly summoned the Americans to save them.[7]

Ironically, by making the West seem so powerful, Arab nationalist and Islamic fundamentalist doctrine intensified the feeling of inferiority and weakness already paralyzing their people. The Arab belief that regional politics was just "a game being played by the Great Powers," wrote the Nobel Prize–winning Egyptian novelist Naguib Mahfouz, made him ask, "Are we rubbish? Have we no minds? . . . Have we Arabs become a kind of toy or plaything? Is there humiliation greater than this?"[8]

If Western power always seemed to overwhelm the helpless Arabs, this gave them an incentive to join the inevitably winning side. Whenever the West was deferential to any self-proclaimed regional leader, the Arab world was far more willing to follow him. For example, when Nasser nationalized the Suez Canal Company in 1956, Prime Minister Nuri al-Said, leader of Iraq's conservative regime, urged the West to overthrow Nasser, warning that unless it stopped him, he would overthrow the moderate Arab rulers to make himself the Arab world's chief.

Heeding this advice, Britain, France, and Israel attacked Egypt and pushed Nasser's regime to the brink of defeat. The United States, however, saw this assault as a renewal of colonialism, which would antagonize the Arabs, and pressured its allies to withdraw. Having survived, Nasser became the political victor. Within a few months, his pro-Soviet, anti-American policy made the U.S. government realize that its mercy had been misplaced. Two years later, as the call of radical nationalism echoed in the region, a coup overthrew Iraq's monarchy and al-Said's government. Nuri al-Said's prophecy was fulfilled when a pro-Nasser mob killed him and dragged his body through Baghdad's streets.

In 1967, however, Nasser miscalculated. By constantly threatening Israel in his speeches and actions, he provoked a war in which he and the other Arab states were decisively beaten in only six days. To excuse his own defeat, Nasser exaggerated U.S. help for Israel. Still, defeat and the fact that U.S. opposition for the first time materially damaged Egypt tarnished Nasser's reputation. The radical wave was dammed.

The Kuwait crisis could only follow the 1956 or the 1967 pattern. If the West allowed Saddam to keep Kuwait, Arabs—convinced that he was the wave of the future—would leap on his bandwagon. Otherwise, they would side with the West, ignoring their own professed ideology.

In pursuit of the third goal, the Arab states' wars against Israel also tested and proved the inadequacy of their ideas and political systems. The Arab scholar Constantine Zurayk wrote of this contrast between confident expectations and dismal truth in the 1948 war, when Israel gained its independence: "Seven Arab states declare war on Zionism in Palestine, stop impotent before it and turn on their heels. The representatives of the Arabs deliver fiery speeches in the highest international forums, warning what the Arab states and peoples will do if this or that decision be enacted. Declarations fall like bombs from the mouths of officials at the meetings of the Arab League, but when action becomes necessary, the fire is still and quiet, and steel and iron are rusted and twisted, quick to bend and disintegrate."[9]

Israel's very existence symbolized the painful hollowness of Arab and Islamic political hopes as well as the emptiness of the dictators' boasts. This fact could neither be wished away with words nor washed away in a sea of blood. Making peace with Israel would force a reexamination of the basic Arab political tenets. By portraying the Arab-Israeli conflict as the main factor of modern Middle East history—"the great alibi," in Ajami's words—Arab rulers and intellectuals had avoided reexamining their own ideology, which did not accord with reality.[10] All the Arab states and factions tried to exploit this self-deception about the issue's centrality. Conservative Arabs asked domestic revolutionaries and radical neighbors to stop attacking them in order to cooperate against Israel. Radical nationalists insisted that the battle with Israel could be won only if the "reactionary regimes" were overthrown and Western influence was extirpated.

Aside from being impossible to implement, however, the Arabs' effort to fight the West was the wrong answer for their problems. After all, Arab society was not a creation of Western imperialism but the product of the very heritage that the nationalists and the Islamic fundamentalists celebrated. "It was hard," Ajami explained, "for the Arab nationalists to acknowledge the simple facts of post-colonial life: that men beget the history they deserve, that Arab life is what the Arabs have made of it."[11]

The real answer to the riddle of weakness was for the Arabs and the Muslims to admit that their own societies, ideas, and political institutions required profound change, a long constructive process rather than overnight and violent solutions. Arab defeats had arisen from excessive radicalism and an inability to compromise, not from too much moderation; internecine conflict instead of cooperation; and strong rhetoric that could not be matched by successful action. Every time the Arabs went to war with Israel or the Palestinians refused diplomatic offers, they worsened their situation.

There could be little progress as long as tyranny blocked democracy, repression choked intellectual and cultural life, arms purchases used up all the available money, war disrupted normal life, and corrupt bureaucracies stifled economic productivity. Yet the power of demagoguery, conformism, and wishful thinking periodically overcame the Arabs' better judgment as they hailed some new hero, until his crashing defeat renewed their pessimism and intensified their inferiority complex.

But for many years it was too politically dangerous and psychologically difficult to admit all this and challenge the absolutist doctrines that inevitably fostered undemocratic systems. Instead, Asad, Qaddafi, Khomeini, and Saddam sought to excuse their own tyranny at home and expand their empires by working even harder to pin the blame for the region's ills on U.S. imperialism, Zionism, and traitorous Arabs.[12]

As Sharabi noted, "Power-holders throughout the Arab world seem to have found it fairly easy to get away with the contradiction between their verbal and actual behavior."[13] Arabs and Iranians were being victimized not by America but by their own rulers, who—like their Soviet counterparts—papered over their crimes and avarice with "progressive" rhetoric.

Like communism—and fascism—the dominant Arab ideologies preached that only dictatorship could impose progress and reform, a process best foreseen by the Egyptian Islamic reformer Muhammad Abdu, who called in the early 1900s for "a despot who would force . . . parents to be charitable, neighbors to be fairminded, and people generally to adopt his view of their interests, be it by intimidation or by joyful consent." Within fifteen years, "their souls will be purified by the most efficacious means available, by amputation and cauterization if need be."[14]

Arab despots found it easier to obtain "popular consent" and carry out "cauterization" than they did to deliver real benefits. "Freedom ran on the tongues in speeches, songs and anthems," complained the Egyptian writer Tawfiq al-Hakim, "at a time when no single free word which the ruler did not want could be expressed without its author entering prison." Despite populist slogans, crowds waited long hours in line at stores "for a piece of meat to be thrown to them." Political revolutions that spoke of progress and populism brought only subversion and strife, "inducing Arab to kill Arab, and Arab to use burning napalm and poison gas against Arab!" "Are the people made happy," al-Hakim asked, "because they hear socialist songs although they are submerged in misery which everyone sees?"[15]

The Arab dictators used three main techniques to hold on to power at home. First, they amassed a large group of active supporters. The monarchs had alliances with tribal leaders and Islamic clerics. The Ba'th party regimes in Baghdad and Damascus built disciplined political organizations based on communal solidarity within, respectively, the Sunni Muslim and Alawite minorities in their countries. For the dictator, socialism meant that the economy was in the hands of his regime, ensuring his complete control and the ability to distribute wealth among his supporters. Aside from career and financial benefits, followers of the regime were motivated by a fear that its fall would expose their community and families to revenge from those they had subjugated.[16]

Second, the regime showed the people that opposition would be punished by ferocious repression. Modern technology, Professor Adeed Dawisha explained, "placed in the hands of the rulers methods of social and coercive suppression that made earlier means of . . . control pale into insignificance."[17]

Few citizens would say that the emperor was naked when he had a machine gun pointed at them. Violence was the foundation for this type of rule. Iran's ambassador to the United Nations smiled as he told heckling Iranian exiles in New York, "Our enemies can try to kill us but we will kill them instead!" Explaining why he closed his shop during West Bank strikes, a Palestinian shopkeeper said, "The [Israeli] police can only arrest you, but your own people will kill you." The PLO ensured its credentials as sole Palestinian representative by murdering any critics in its community. Syria's government assassinated independent-minded Lebanese leaders and journalists as well as thousands of its own citizens. After the death of Egypt's beloved dictator Nasser in 1970, former political prisoners came forward with horrifying accounts of his torture chambers and concentration camps; yet his good name was little tarnished.

Third, the ruler persuaded the masses through his ideology and charisma that they should support him, not only putting "fear in people's hearts," noted Dawisha, but also trying "to win their support, no matter how grudgingly given."[18] Promising Arab unity, Islamic justice, and victory over Israel, while distributing land, jobs, offices, and rewards, he generated enthusiasm. Aside from employing the modern techniques of rallies, radio broadcasts, and propaganda, all the region's dictatorships benefited from historic ideas and social structures that justified their type of government. "For centuries," explained Dawisha, "the pattern of political loyalty in the tribal and village communities was hierarchical," while Islam gave legitimacy to "the centralized structure of political authority."[19]

This cultural background helped even the most secular dictatorships by encouraging popular passivity. The French and American revolutions had proclaimed the people's sovereignty as the foundation of liberal democracy. In the words of the French philosopher Jean-Jacques Rousseau, the people's voice is the voice of God. But this notion was unacceptable to Islamic society, where only the voice of God—as presented in Islamic law—is the voice of God.

The people must follow, an Islamic philosopher wrote, "a regime and a set of laws imposed by God, which they cannot change or modify in any case." A Lebanese fundamentalist explained, "The state in Islam obeys Divine Law, not the people."[20] God's law was determined by the clergy, which among the Sunni Muslims—contrary to Iran's example—was usually controlled by the government. At any rate, this foundation of absolutism made open debate and criticism less acceptable.

Another force strengthening the hand of dictatorship was the popular fear that democracy brought instability. Pluralism was dangerous, an Egyptian intellectual explained: "Dialogue is the beginning of altercation. Altercation is the beginning of internal war and disunity."[21] The idea that tyranny is better than anarchy has deep roots in the Middle East, where life in Iran and the Arab lands alternated between eras of high centralization and those in which rulers lost control of the provinces, leading to anarchy and decline. Having a weak leader usually meant the country would suffer bloodshed, war, and economic collapse.

According to the American view, free speech eases tensions and concessions bring peace, while repression only breeds revolt. But this is not how Middle East politics worked. Concessions were taken as signs of weakness, which provoked more demands and turmoil. With both government and opposition composed of antidemocratic forces, the former's enfeeblement—as Iran's revolution and Lebanon's civil war showed—brought not pluralism but chaos. Each faction's belief that it possessed absolute truth entitled it to crush enemies, who were considered traitors and foreign agents. A paranoid, intolerant style resulted from this pressure-cooker environment.

The rulers also preserved their power by manipulating slogans of radicalism, Arab nationalism, socialism, anti-imperialism, and anti-Zionism within each country. As often happened with Marxism in the West, the intellectuals fell in love with totalitarianism, arguing that a dictatorship based on these correct ideas was better than democracy. People of all classes cheered the self-proclaimed nationalist or Islamic messiahs, many—perhaps most—of them still believing that utopian doctrines and extremist policies were the solution, not the cause, of disorder and disaster.

To be considered moderate in America is a political necessity, since no one seen as an extremist seems to be able to win elections. Ronald Reagan had to demonstrate that he was safely nonradical in order to be elected president; Barry Goldwater and George McGovern, unable to do so, lost by landslides. But in the Arab-Islamic world, the means of seizing or losing political power are radical in themselves. Flexibility is considered more sinful than zeal, since it hinders the pursuit of absolute righteousness and virtue. "That Saddam was a murderer at home," notes Ajami about the Iraqi dictator's rising reputation in the late 1980s, "was of little concern to the Arab intelligentsia who saw him as an answer for the ills and weaknesses of his world." His "two decades of cruel deeds" were unimportant for those who believed that "the end— some dream of national power—justified the means."[22]

Charismatic dictators claimed to reduce the two great threats to stability: factionalized domestic politics and vulnerability to foreign influence. Only someone invested with tremendous legitimacy and authority could enforce discipline on his highly individualistic countrymen. An Iranian politician explained, "We need a focus for the people's emotions." One-man rule was a necessity, an ayatollah insisted, because only a single leader could inspire intense devotion. Iranians rallied in huge numbers to chant, "We are your soldiers, O Khomeini!" They would hardly shout, "We are your soldiers, O Leadership Council!"[23]

How did this system perform for the Arabs during the forty years leading up to the Kuwait crisis? It was a disaster. The taboos blocking an unflinching self-examination made the myths of Arab politics a constant danger to the Arabs themselves, since, at any time, a dictator like Khomeini or Saddam could nominate himself to unite the region, try to destroy Israel, and expel America. After meeting the flamboyant Libyan dictator Qaddafi for the first time, Egyptian journalist Muhammad Heikal warned, "It's a catastrophe!" Qaddafi would cause trouble because he really believed all the propaganda about revolution and Arab unity and intended to implement it.

Through ambition, belief, or both, Arab dictators were prone to take—in al-Hakim's words—"foolhardy gambles" and provoke unwinnable conflicts like Arab-Israeli wars, the Iran-Iraq conflict, or Iraq's invasion of Kuwait. Their contempt for democracy also made them underestimate America. Once the dictators realized that the United States was reluctant to act or unable to manipulate events—being less ruthless and expansionist than themselves—they quickly concluded that it must be too decadent to stop them.[24]

During the two decades between 1967 and 1988, the Arab states and Iran suffered from four major sets of disasters, each bringing instability, bloodshed, defeat, and wasted resources.

The first disaster was the 1967 Arab-Israel war. Egypt, Syria, and Jordan threatened to attack Israel, but their bluster backfired when Israel launched a preemptive strike and destroyed the Arab armies in six days. These regimes were so badly defeated that Ajami called the event "the Waterloo of Pan-Arabism."[25] The Arab states' refusal to make peace left Israel in control of the West Bank, the Gaza Strip, the Golan Heights, and the Sinai peninsula.

In 1973, Egyptian President Anwar Sadat joined with Syria to try to break the deadlock by attacking Israel. Although Israel won in the end, Arab hopes rose on the basis of their improved military performance. In addition, spiraling oil income seemed to promise rapid development and a favorable shift in the balance of power between the Arabs and the West. "The dreams that had for some time tantalized the minds of politically conscious Arabs appeared to be coming true," Ajami later wrote. "A traditionally divided Arab world was acting in unison and Arab armies were finally getting a chance to redeem their honor in a sharp break with a humiliating record of defeats. . . . It seemed as though wrongs were beginning to be righted, that the Arab world had managed to find its place in the sun."[26]

But these hopes were soon dashed in a second series of plagues, between 1975 and 1982. The regional and internal situations did not improve. Egypt was overpopulated, poor, and near economic collapse, while 40 percent of its resources went to finance the army. Unevenly distributed oil wealth split the Arabs between wealthy states, like Saudi Arabia and Kuwait, and those much poorer, like Syria, Egypt, and Jordan. Radicals worried that the region would become too conservative because the balance of power was shifting, in the words of Egyptian Marxist Muhammad Sid Ahmad, from the forces of *thawra* (revolution) to those of *thrawa* (fortune).[27]

In fact, the forces of disorder were still ascendant. A more apt metaphor would be that instead of bringing an Arab *nahda* (renaissance), each year brought a new *nakhba* (disaster). The Lebanese civil war broke out in 1975; Syrian intervention there followed in 1976. Sadat went to Jerusalem to make peace with Israel in 1977 and signed the U.S.-mediated Camp David accords in 1978, splitting the Arab world. Khomeini came to power in Iran and the USSR occupied Afghanistan in 1979; the Iran-Iraq war began in 1980; Israel destroyed Iraq's nuclear reactor in 1981.

Nowhere in the region could one "find two neighboring countries which have amicable relationships untarnished by some historical dispute or rivalry over a host of issues," was the Arab writer Muhammad Anis Salem's pessimistically realistic assessment of the situation in early 1982. There was no leader with the charisma and credentials, no country with the wealth and achievements, to bring the Arabs together.[28] Egypt was a pariah for making peace with Israel. Not only had the Arabs failed to destroy Israel, but the effort had damaged them more than it had the intended victim. Libya launched troublesome subversive campaigns against other regimes. Arab oil revenues declined. The Iran-Iraq war raged on, with Arab Syria supporting non-Arab Iran and the fighting threatening to expand into Kuwait.

That year of 1982 would bring a third, even worse, series of disasters that contradicted Arab ideology and its reflected version among American experts: Syria's massacre of dissidents, Israel's invasion of Lebanon, and fear of Iran's winning the Gulf war.

In February, Syria drowned in blood the myth of the progressive Arab regime by destroying one of its own cities. The predominantly Sunni town of Hama was a center for fundamentalist groups opposing the regime's secular, socialist policies and domination by the minority Alawite sect. After a gun battle between the army and fundamentalists escalated into an uprising, President Asad ordered a three-week, all-out military assault on Hama.

Syria's army looted and destroyed mosques, churches, and historic buildings. Scores of women were raped, hundreds of prisoners were shot. The city's center was wrecked, and between ten thousand and thirty thousand people—mainly women and children—were slain by their own government, more casualties in a few days than a decade of fighting would inflict on Beirut. The regime built a row of new buildings to hide the destruction from the main road. No Arab state protested the massacre of Arabs; Iran, Syria's ally, said nothing about the killing of fellow fundamentalists. These events bared the brutality, torture, and terrorism that lurked behind populist slogans.[29]

In June, Israel invaded Lebanon, where bloody civil war had raged for seven years among Arab communities—Christians, Druze, Shia and Sunni Muslims, Palestinians, and Syrians. Contrary to all Arab propriety, the Christians secretly asked Israel to destroy the PLO's rule in south Lebanon and establish a strong Christian-led regime. Israel quickly defeated PLO and Syrian forces, then laid siege to Beirut. The trapped PLO bargained with American mediators for safe passage to Tunisia, fleeing Lebanon under U.S. protection. Lebanese Arab Christians massacred several hundred Palestinians at the Sabra and Shatila refugee camps.

Beyond verbal protests, Arab countries did nothing to help Syria, the PLO, or Lebanon to fight against Israel. Syria responded by helping rebels angry at their leaders' incompetence and corruption, to split the PLO. Moscow remained passive, proving to be an unreliable ally. The Arabs could take little comfort in Israel's casualties and diplomatic damage: its power, though limited, was still sufficient to defeat them. Arab rulers—if not the masses—knew how risky would be another war with Israel, whose strength deterred Egypt, Syria, and Jordan from military assault or allowing cross-border terrorist attacks from their own soil.

In July, the Iranian army's advance onto Iraqi soil raised the specter of its winning a victory that would inspire new revolutions against Arab rulers. Iran aided fundamentalist groups among Lebanon's and Iraq's Shia communities—"the stepchildren of the Arab world," in Ajami's phrase—for whom Arab nationalism had meant in practice their subordination to Sunni minorities.[30] Iran's soldiers established a foothold in Lebanon, which was dubbed the Iranian Republic of Baalbek.

This high-water mark of Iranian influence coincided with a fourth plague, the rise of Islamic fundamentalism in the Arab world, a doctrine that divided it further and threatened governments with terrorism and revolution. Islam, like Arab nationalism, portrayed itself as a road to unity but became just another area of contention.[31]

Who was the true Muslim and who the traitor? As with Arab nationalism, no one agreed. Conflicts among Persians and Arabs, Sunni and Shia Muslims, Iranians and Iraqis, and even different fundamentalist factions, prevailed over the commonality of Islam. Those disagreeing with him, Khomeini said, were imperialist agents, but few non-Iranian Muslims followed him. Most Arabs did not see revolutionary fundamentalism as Islam's proper incarnation; Iran's defeat in war and its economic stagnation did not encourage emulation.

In theory, all Muslims accepted Islam as the proper organizing principle. Practice was altogether different. Muslims had thought themselves religious for centuries without ever acting as Khomeini prescribed. The great Shia theologians had preached passivity until the messiah returned to put the world right; Muslims usually obeyed their rulers—even impious ones—in accord with other long-standing Islamic teachings. "Islamic Thought in the Last 100 Years Is Largely Un-Islamic," was the paradoxical protest of an Iranian newspaper headline. By so rejecting the way Islam was actually practiced, the radical fundamentalists were turning most Muslims against them.[32]

The fundamentalists were also unable to block the West's alluring, influential onslaught with its movies, love songs, fashions, merchandise and luxuries, science, and education. Most of their compatriots were not quite so eager to boycott Western culture or ideas, and an urgent desire for the West's respect infected even the most militant anti-Western leaders. "The grandeur of the Islamic revolution" was proved, Speaker Rafsanjani of Iran's parliament said proudly, because it impressed the West so much that Iran was now compared to the USSR and France rather than to mere Third World states like Algeria or Vietnam.[33]

Even Islamic Iran preferred to sell oil to the West for hard currency and buy its superior products. Many of the revolution's leaders had Swiss bank accounts, and their taste for modern comforts was the butt of many jokes in Tehran. When a poor women complained about the lack of soap powder, ran one popular anecdote, a pro-Khomeini cleric scolded her by saying, "The Prophet Muhammad's daughter didn't have that."

"Yes," replied the woman, "but Muhammad didn't ride around in a Mercedes limousine."

In Egypt, Iraq, and Syria, though, government repression rather than ridicule crushed the radical fundamentalists. Fundamentalist terrorist groups failed to take over among the Palestinians or Lebanese Shia. The regimes in Jordan and Algeria outmaneuvered and defeated fundamentalist parties that appeared close to winning power through elections.

The Iran-Iraq war was the ultimate confrontation of Arab nationalism and Islamic fundamentalism, yet the combatants had much in common. Indeed, what happened to the Gulf during the twentieth century's second half was surprisingly similar to what befell much of Europe in the first half. The revolutions that put Saddam and Khomeini in power were upheavals as transforming as those fomented by Lenin in Russia and by Hitler in Germany. There were some striking parallels between communism and fascism, Khomeini's fundamentalism and Saddam's radical nationalism.

They were all products of rapid social change that swept away traditional landmarks and made people embrace extreme doctrines to cope with their fear and confusion. Beneath their vastly different trappings, all these movements were based on a modern, Western notion that humanity must shape its own fate rather than wait for divine intervention.

"Miracles are exceptions," Khomeini said. Lenin, Hitler, and Saddam would have agreed with him.[34] History was made by mobilizing the masses for a cause. But first the people had to overcome false consciousness and, since they did not know what was good for them, a dictator had to force them down the right path. This new order could be born only amid a purifying revolutionary bloodshed that wiped out the classes and defeated the foreign conspirators who allegedly blocked progress.

Both Khomeini and Saddam—like Hitler and Stalin, whose nations lost in World War I—were self-made leaders of underdog countries bullied by history and eager for revenge. Willing to use everything the twentieth century could offer, they all created highly centralized states and promised their subjects to expel foreign influence, revive lost pride, repudiate parliamentary democracy for a higher form of community, accelerate economic development, and create a just society. They wanted industrial and scientific progress to underpin their countries' independence and build systems that would last a thousand years.

In foreign policy, the quartet of dictators pledged to join together those—Arabs, Muslims, Germans, workers—who were illegitimately ruled by other regimes. Iranian fundamentalism and Iraqi Arab nationalism, like German fascism and Soviet communism, were presented as universalist ideologies while actually being instruments of empire building. Dreams of glory turned into the reality of ruins. At home, the dictators spilled their countrymen's blood and slowed progress; by subverting neighbors, they brought war and defeat on themselves.

After so many catastrophes under the leadership of such regimes, it was no wonder that Arabs could hardly have been gloomier in the late 1980s. "Today the Arab reality and the Arab dream," wrote Sharabi, "appear separated by an unbridgeable gap. The hope that has animated the past generation's struggle . . . turned into cynicism and despair."[35]

Progress was impossible, King Hussein complained at the 1985 Arab summit, with so much "disintegration instead of congregation, regionalism instead of Pan-Arab solidarity, plotting instead of harmony, hegemony instead of fraternization, destruction instead of construction, and placing obstacles instead of their removal." Egypt's president, Hosni Mubarak, spoke of growing "dismemberment, estrangement, and infighting." Heikal mourned, "All dreams are gone and no dreams are replacing them."[36]

The struggle for preeminence "has ruined us all," noted al-Hakim. Forty years of effort at unity left the Arabs more divided than ever, cooperating among themselves far less effectively than people in any other part of the world. NATO and the Common Market in Europe, the Organization of African Unity, the Association of Southeast Asian Nations, and the Organization of American States were all more effective groups than the Arab League. Ajami summed up the lesson: Arabs desperately needed a whole new political framework. "Pan-Arabism had dominated Arab political life for nearly half a century. It had gripped the young and made life difficult for many rulers. But it was never able to transform the Middle East."[37]

A generation of Arabs had dreamed, and the result was Nasser and the Ba'th party. Just when the seductive fantasies seemed to be vanishing, a new wave of heroes had appeared, promising to realize all their hopes. The perverse genies of history again granted Arab wishes, and the result had been Khomeini and Saddam. The Arab choice was to break the pattern or to repeat it, to turn away from the dead end or again to run headlong into a wall.

Iraq's invasion of Kuwait would be the culmination of this crisis in the Arab ideology and political system. Saddam offered the old-time ideology once more as his answer to the Arabs' dilemma. The Arab world's past ordeals, wrote Ajami, should have made it "immune to another pied piper."[38] But at least up until the invasion of Kuwait, it suffered from an acquired immune deficiency syndrome in this regard. The United States should have learned from the experiences with Nasser and Khomeini. Yet until Saddam launched his invasion, it showed no interest in challenging him. Like Dr. Frankenstein, the Arabs and America created a monster that would eventually turn on them.

CHAPTER SEVEN

AMERICA'S FRIEND SADDAM: 1988–1990

Hojja went to a mill and began taking grain and putting it in his own sacks. The miller saw him and yelled, "What are you doing?"

"I am a fool," Hojja replied. "I just have to do whatever comes into my mind."

"Well, how come you don't take wheat out of your sack and put it into mine?"

"Sir," he replied, "I am just a normal fool, not a complete idiot."

—*Middle Eastern folktale*

"Barring unforeseen circumstances," wrote the Arab journalist Fuad Mattar in a London-based Arab newspaper in July 1989, "1990 and 1991 should be the year of Saddam Hussein in the United States." But he was expecting something far different from a crisis or a war. On the contrary, he predicted that "Americans would love to see him on the television screen." They would find Saddam "as handsome as any star on the 'Dynasty' television series and like the hero of the famous 'Bonanza' television program who is always depicted as a brave man preserving his land and abiding by the law." Indeed, Americans might even ask, "Why should Saddam Hussein not be the region's policeman, given the real vacuum?"[1]

Such expectations were obviously off the mark. Yet it is easy to understand why an Arab writer saw U.S.-Iraq relations as being so amiable at the time. A few days earlier, a delegation of top business executives had come to Baghdad to see Saddam. They were led by A. Robert Abboud of the First City Texas Bank and included ranking executives from General Motors, Westinghouse, Mobil, Amoco, Bankers Trust, Caltex Petroleum, ex-senator Charles Percy, and Alan Stoga of Kissinger Associates. Abboud told Saddam that the group represented companies that were collectively rich enough to form the world's third-greatest economic power, after the United States and Japan. If you plan to start your own country, Saddam joked, Qaddafi might be willing to help you make a revolution.

The businessmen told reporters that they found Saddam pleasant, handsome, charismatic, frank, decisive, and intelligent—in short, everything an executive would see in a foreign leader from whom he wanted billions of dollars in contracts. "In the past," said Abboud, "there were political differences between our countries, but it is possible to overcome them by improving communications and understanding."[2] This kind of wishful thinking was at the root of American ignorance about Iraq, and it was much in evidence during the 1980s in Washington.

On a warm night in November 1984, I walked up the path of a luxurious house in northwest Washington that served as the Iraqi ambassador's mansion. That very day, the two countries had announced the resumption of diplomatic relations, and Iraq's flag flew outside for the first time in many years. The charming, worldly Nizar Hamdoun was promoted from director of Iraq's interest section in Washington to be its ambassador there. To mark the occasion, Iraq's foreign minister, Tariq Aziz, was visiting Washington, and Hamdoun invited a few Middle East specialists to dinner. A call from Hamdoun was one of the hottest tickets in a city where even one's companions at meals is a matter of competition.

As if to illustrate that point, the man standing ahead of me in line to shake Hamdoun's hand tried to score points with the ambassador by warning him that I had written articles critical of Iraq.

Aziz, the dinner's guest of honor, strongly resembled the British actor Peter Sellers, a fact that softened his menacing presence as representative of such a violent regime. With his Cuban cigars and fondness for Johnnie Walker Black Label Scotch, he had an engaging way of hinting at cosmopolitan proclivities and implying that he was more civilized than the tough guys who were his colleagues. Aziz had also perfected one of the great diplomatic skills: He could lie persuasively. "Oh, no," he said, "Iraq has never used chemical weapons," while his eyes conveyed a world-weary, sophisticated regret at being compelled to utter such an obvious falsehood.

Not so long before, the moderator at a Washington think tank where Aziz was giving a lecture paid homage to the foreign minister by refusing to let an Israeli journalist ask the Iraqi any questions. Iraqis must not be assaulted by American norms of free speech. This night, in a newly reopened embassy and at the height of his power and influence, Hamdoun no doubt thought he was providing the foreign minister with an equally friendly forum.

Aziz was visiting Washington to secure additional American help in Iraq's war with Iran. Significantly, the main course included a garnish of bacon and a generous supply of fine wine, a culinary gesture of defiance at Khomeini's fundamentalism, since the Muslim religion dictates that pork and alcohol are forbidden.

Aziz made a strong pitch for the United States to support Iraq in the Gulf. Unfortunately, one of the guests—a senior wire service correspondent—was showing the effects of the liquid refreshments. Suddenly she interrupted Aziz. "Why didn't you retaliate," she asked, "when Israel destroyed your nuclear reactor?" The foreign minister stopped his talk and tried to brush away the question. The wire service reporter did not find the response acceptable. "Just yellow, I guess," she heckled in a slurred voice.

Ambassador Hamdoun looked uncomfortable. Insulting the foreign minister might have been a capital offense in Baghdad, but Aziz soldiered on. He was just explaining why the Iran-Iraq war was the most important issue in the Middle East when another somewhat tipsy writer, Rowland Evans, coauthor of the well-known Evans and Novak column, interrupted him. "You must not talk like that!" he lectured the startled Iraqi foreign minister. The columnist instructed Aziz to tell the U.S. government that the Arab-Israeli conflict was the Middle East's central issue and that the lack of peace was all Israel's fault. Unaccustomed to being attacked for excessive softness on Israel, Aziz looked astonished. Perhaps it was easier to deal with the inner circles of Saddam's regime, where fear bred discipline, than with these wild, unpredictable Americans. It made one better appreciate why Islam banned alcohol.

One of the most intriguing aspects of Baghdad's charm offensive was the role of Ambassador Hamdoun, the articulate and Western-ized son of a general. Hamdoun was the first Arab envoy who really appreciated the distinctive nature of the American political system. He realized that contacts with the State Department alone were insufficient; it was also vital to sway Congress, the media, and public opinion by cultivating journalists, experts, and interest groups. While few people in Washington can be bribed, an ambassador's flattering attentions and confidences over lunch at an expensive restaurant can be far more effective in spreading influence. Those who are personally liked will almost always be believed.

Washington's culture is largely an oral one. A word said in confidence by an official may often have more impact than a hundred analyses of another country's interests and behavior, a thousand hard-line, anti-American speeches in Arabic, or perhaps even ten thousand dead Kurdish civilians.

As Iraq's representative in Washington from 1982 until relations were reestablished in 1984 and then its ambassador until 1987, Hamdoun befriended a wide range of policymakers and opinionmakers, even in the Jewish community, to convince them that Iraq was now moderate and deserved U.S. help. One of his most striking stunts was to send a map, purportedly captured from Iran's army, that showed that Tehran's ultimate target was to be Jerusalem. Hamdoun quoted Khomeini as saying, "Israel must be vanished from the face of the earth." The deliberate, but carefully unstated, implication for Hamdoun's American audience was that, objectively, Iraq was fighting to protect Israel as well as the Gulf monarchies.

When U.S. embassy officials in Baghdad parked on a vacant lot owned by an officers club, Iraqis slashed the tires to send a message. In Washington, however, Iraq could not gain anything from intimidation. For Hamdoun to obtain leverage, he tried to find a way to help important Washington figures advance their own careers. The journalists wanted visas to Iraq and the chance to interview the country's top leaders; the specialists sought access to Hamdoun, free trips to Baghdad, and audiences with Saddam. Such opportunities, and the inside information Hamdoun offered, gave them the chance to write articles and to build their own reputations as Iraq experts. Hamdoun, a master of this game, fed each of them his theme that Iraq was a friend that deserved U.S. support.

Some of Hamdoun's conquests were particularly valuable. There was the former U.S. ambassador who headed the U.S.-Iraq Chamber of Commerce and wrote a letter in the *Washington Post* explaining why sanctions against Iraq for human rights violations were counterproductive. Another ex–State Department official became a paid lobbyist for Iraq who, on one occasion, refused to sign a major study-group report on U.S. policy unless it was brought more in line with Baghdad's interests. Iraq also assisted some young, ambitious "experts" to build their careers by giving them information, trips to Iraq, and audiences with Saddam. Several of them wrote books, subsidized or circulated by Saddam's regime, without a word of criticism about Iraq. One of these people was appointed to a key State Department post, monitoring the proliferation of unconventional weapons to Iraq; others became the leading commentators on Iraq in the media and in academia. It was a superb innovation: Iraq created its own sympathetic American experts on Iraq.

As a result of Ambassador Hamdoun's labors, when the Iran-Iraq war ended, the U.S.-Iraq relationship had enough momentum to sustain itself. Hamdoun was already back in Baghdad as deputy foreign minister, but a fitting testimonial for his achievement was Iraq's July 1988 national day celebration at the Vista International Hotel in Washington, crowded with hundreds of American officials, journalists, socialites, and Middle East experts. By coincidence, it was the very day that Khomeini accepted the cease-fire ending the Iran-Iraq war, which made the event even more of a celebration. There was one notable difference between this party and other embassy affairs in Washington: at the head of the receiving line was a larger-than-life-size cardboard cutout of Saddam himself. I wondered whether protocol required that guests shake hands with it. But the symbolism was clear: Big Brother was always watching. Saddam's ego knew no bounds and Iraqi officials would indulge it to the maximum.

Hamdoun largely succeeded, of course, because U.S. policy was already receptive to his message. Iraq became a large market for U.S. agricultural products, which supplied around 30 percent of its imports, endearing it to farm state legislators like Senator Robert Dole of Kansas. These sales were largely guaranteed by the U.S.

government's Commodity Credit Corporation (CCC), at levels reaching $1 billion a year starting in 1988, while the U.S. Export-Import Bank insured hundreds of millions of dollars in business deals to Iraq. As the second-largest beneficiary of U.S. export loans and the seventh-largest subsidy recipient, Iraq obtained about $4 billion of benefits during the 1980s.[3]

Rather than ask for something in exchange for its help, the White House sought few concessions from Iraq and gained less. It did nothing to discourage Saddam from seeing his war against Iran as a service for which the United States must pay. Instead of using U.S. help as leverage against Iraq, the White House overruled the Commodity Credit Corporation and Export-Import Bank when they complained about Iraqi corruption, violations of U.S. law, and economic unreliability. It was also lenient in granting export licenses for goods that might have military uses and energetic in trying to squelch publicity over Iraq's misdeeds. This policy continued even after the Iran-Iraq war ended and up to the day that Iraq invaded Kuwait. The name for this approach is appeasement.

When the bank suspended its program with Iraq in 1986 because of problems in collecting debts, Vice-President Bush objected, arguing that Iraq's postwar prospects were good and giving priority to building trade relations. Bank officials disagreed, warning correctly that Iraq would continue high military spending and a policy of reneging on debts. Although the Export-Import Bank revived the program, its cautious limits would save hundreds of millions of dollars when Iraq defaulted during the Kuwait crisis.[4]

The Commodity Credit Corporation's dealings with Iraq followed a similar pattern. It reported that U.S. exporters were being forced to pay millions of dollars in kickbacks to Iraqi officials and questioned that country's ability to repay. There were also troublesome reports that the subsidized food bought in the United States was being resold elsewhere and that credits were used for nonfood purchases. In 1989, CCC sought to cut its program from $1.1 billion to less than $500 million until, Under Secretary of Agriculture Richard Crowder wrote National Security Adviser Brent Scowcroft, "the questions concerning program irregularities with sales to Iraq are cleared up."[5]

But on October 6, 1989, Foreign Minister Aziz met Secretary of State James Baker to complain. Iraq, he warned, would not accept a smaller program; the Baghdad regime claimed it showed a lack of confidence. Baker took Baghdad's side and pressed CCC into returning to the full program. In doing so, he ignored an October 13 State Department memo that warned: "If smoke indicates fire, we may be facing a four-alarm blaze in the near future. . . . The integrity of the program is now in question." The Agriculture Department said it found evidence of the diversion of commodities in violation of U.S. law.[6]

The Treasury Department and Office of Management and Budget also urged aid cuts, but a November 8 inter-departmental meeting ended in a victory for the State Department and its ally Saddam. As late as March 1990, Scowcroft was pressing the increasingly reluctant corporation to continue its program with Iraq. U.S. Ambassador April Glaspie, contrary to her later testimony to congressional committees, also lobbied for continued aid, until as late as May 1990.[7]

A major reason for CCC concern, brushed aside by the State Department and the White House, was increasing evidence that Iraq was defrauding American banks and government agencies in its desperate search for funds. The Atlanta branch of the Italian Banca Nazionale del Lavoro (BNL) acted as Iraq's agent to borrow over $4 billion from U.S. banks—$900 million of it guaranteed by the Commodity Credit Corporation—then secretly issued an astounding 2,500 letters of credit to Iraq between February 1988 and July 1989. The office kept two sets of books to conceal the loans. In August 1989, FBI and customs agents raided the bank. The White House thus knew the Commodity Credit Corporation money was being illegally misused when it urged that the program not be cut. The State Department informed Iraq that the United States would not link the BNL scandal to future aid. And it was not until the day the Gulf war ended, in February 1991, that the Justice Department would charge ten bank officials with conspiracy and fraud.[8]

While President Bush later told Congress that no U.S. firms aided Iraq's arms industry, a congressional investigation showed this to be false. About half the BNL loans—partly U.S. government guaranteed—went for military-related projects. Iraq's Ministry of Industry and Military Industrialization, working through the Technical Corps for Special Projects and a Cleveland company, Matrix-Churchill, bought equipment from a dozen U.S. companies, in the guise of constructing a dam, to build its Condor II missile center. The Commerce Department granted export licenses, some of which, a congressional investigation later charged, were altered to conceal a potential military use.[9]

Far from seeking to punish Iraq, President Bush issued National Security Directive 26 in October 1989, defining U.S. policy as seeking improved economic and political ties with Iraq rather than trying to pressure Saddam. This was the self-defeating pattern followed up to the invasion of Kuwait: Iraq was given benefits to keep open dialogue and improve relations, but when Baghdad acted in a contrary manner, the White House argued that withdrawing benefits would reduce dialogue and worsen relations. It was a policy of all carrots and no sticks.[10]

Although the administration's main problem was in its conception of the situation—accepting traditional myths about the region, succumbing to inertia, and misreading events—a number of cases of potential conflicts of interest also appear. Bush's appointee to be U.S. attorney in Atlanta—the man who would be responsible for prosecuting the BNL case—had to disqualify himself because he had represented the Iraqi front company, Matrix-Churchill, which had been a major conduit for BNL funds. Two of the main advocates of the aid programs for Iraq, Scowcroft and Deputy Secretary of State Lawrence Eagleburger, had been officials of Kissinger Associates, which had BNL as a client. A House of Representatives investigation claimed that Scowcroft had worked on the BNL account.[11]

Whatever the origin of American credulity—naïveté, expediency, or commercial greed—Saddam exploited it at every opportunity. The White House allowed forty-five Bell transport helicopters to be sold to Iraq in 1985, on condition that they not be used for military purposes. When Baghdad violated this promise by employing the helicopters to move soldiers, the U.S. government voiced no complaint and permitted Saddam to buy sixty Hughes helicopters. Iraq's Ministry of Industry and Minerals filed fictitious export applications in order to obtain weapons-related technology. An Egyptian-born U.S. citizen working at Aerojet General in California was caught in 1988 while trying to smuggle a material used to make nose cones for the joint Egypt-Iraq Condor II missile project. But the administration worked to keep secret the direct involvement of the Cairo and Baghdad governments.[12]

The U.S. effort to use appeasement to convince Saddam of its friendly intentions was futile. Saddam's career and ideology caused him to view the United States as an enemy blocking his regional ambitions and preferring his overthrow. America, Iraqi leaders and newspapers claimed, kept the Iran-Iraq war going because it wanted

Iraq to be weakened. U.S. influence in the area was inherently against Saddam's interest, since Israel or the Gulf Arab states could seek American help to attack or resist him. The secret U.S. arms deals with Tehran reinforced this existing suspicion, providing a case in which there really was a U.S.-Israel-Iran conspiracy against Iraq.

Since the purpose of U.S. and Gulf Arab support for Iraq was to stop Iranian expansionism, Saddam reasonably expected that these countries would turn away from him as soon as the fighting ended, in September 1988. The irony was that Saddam did not fully appreciate how successful his own wooing of America had been. The friendly U.S. policy toward Iraq did not change, and the same was true for Saudi Arabia and Kuwait, even in the face of mounting Iraqi antagonism toward them.

While the shooting had stopped, UN-mediated negotiations between the two countries bogged down, and the Iran-Iraq cease-fire did not develop into a peace treaty. The reopening of the disputed Shatt-al-Arab river became a complex dispute in its own right, and over 100,000 prisoners of war were still in captivity on both sides. But no one wanted to fight again. At a 1989 regional athletic competition in Kuwait, the Friendship and Peace Games, Iran and Iraq played a soccer match—with a European referee to ensure impartiality—before 25,000 spectators. Baghdad's streets were deserted as Iraqis were glued to their television sets. The final score, 0–0, was a fitting metaphor for the war itself.

But Saddam's ambition to be master of the Gulf only kept growing after the war. He first appeared to be concentrating on reconstruction. "War brings big economic losses, sacrifices and bloodshed," said Iraq's dictator. "Peace is easier than war. Peace is a natural way of life." A new strategy of restraint seemed necessary to maintain good relationships with the Gulf Arab monarchies that held the purse strings. "An Arab," Saddam commented in November 1988, "does not have the right to occupy another Arab country. Instead . . . our relations should be based on dialogue, affection, and interaction." Iraq would not force any special relationship on Kuwait. "How will it be possible for us to live together . . . if the minimum mutual trust is lacking?" Otherwise, with everyone so heavily armed, Arab leaders would be like "Chicago gangsters."[13]

Saddam's talk of brotherhood soon gave way to more sober considerations. For years, Iraq had been insisting that it could have both guns and butter. "The Iraqi economy is stronger than ever before," an Iraqi newspaper claimed. In reality, economic development was at a standstill during the war. Living standards had steadily declined as inflation rose. Iraq had a higher proportion of men in uniform than any other country—triple the Soviet rate and five times that of the United States—and Saddam did not reduce the army's size despite the cease-fire. Iraqis were impatient for some material reward after fighting so hard and suffering so much. Returning soldiers rioted in early 1989 and murdered Egyptian workers whom they accused of stealing their jobs.[14]

The war also left Iraq with gigantic foreign debts. Aside from $30 billion in grants from the Saudis and Kuwaitis, Iraq owed $10 billion to the Soviet bloc, $25 billion to Western and Third World countries, and $5 to $10 billion to banks and companies. Iraq argued that it had earned this money by saving the Gulf from Iran. The creditors disagreed. Saddam's strong-arm methods had their limits. While the banks could not force him to repay Iraq's debts, they would give no more loans. Yet Iraq had to find $30 billion just to repair war damage, and $5 billion of its $14 billion annual earnings was needed for interest payments. Even Iraq's huge oil reserves—virtually its sole source of income—fell short of this challenge, especially since petroleum prices were relatively low.

No amount of cooperation with Jordan, Egypt, or the PLO could resolve Iraq's problems, Saddam realized. "We are all bankrupt," he joked. Iraq's budget deficit was so big that government departments were told to prepare for layoffs of as much as half their staffs. The only way to increase Iraq's income was to sell more oil at higher prices. Yet Iraq could do neither: its OPEC quota limited exports to 2.6 million barrels a day. By agreement of the OPEC member states, each of them was assigned an export quota so as to avoid a glut on the market that would send prices downward. The Saudis raised their own exports at times to hold down prices and keep consumers in industrialized countries from switching to coal, natural gas, and a more efficient use of energy.

This system for balancing prices was a good long-term strategy for states like Kuwait and Saudi Arabia, which had surplus money. But the plan was disastrous for a country like Iraq, which needed a great deal of money immediately and thus wanted to sell as much oil as possible at the highest price. To make matters worse, Kuwait and the United Arab Emirates cheated by exporting more oil than their quotas permitted. Saddam easily convinced himself that Saudi policy and Kuwaiti cheating were bankrupting Iraq.[15]

While not all the problems were its fault, Saddam's regime had effectively taken a rich country and run it into the ground. A balanced reconstruction program might have dug Iraq's way out of this mess. After all, only Saudi Arabia had larger oil reserves than Iraq, which also—unlike the Gulf monarchies—had a large skilled labor force and good farmland along the Tigris and Euphrates rivers. The regime could have cut military spending, but Saddam wanted to maintain his expensive army and high-priority programs to build superweapons. It could have liberalized the economy, but decentralizing authority and expanding free enterprise would have reduced the government's tight control. The fall of the Communist

regimes on which Iraq's government had modeled itself made reform seem frightening, a step likely to produce chaos rather than
prosperity.

Saddam sometimes talked about political changes such as democratic elections, a multiparty system, and more freedom for the
press. In the April 1989 parliamentary elections, only 160 of 900
candidates were party members, yet all contestants were carefully
screened. Saddam explained that reforms were not needed: "We in
Iraq consider ourselves successful . . . and have no problems." Referring to Germany and Japan after World War II, Saddam suggested that since defeated countries—not victorious ones—needed
to become more democratic, Iraq's triumph over Iran proved that
its political order was correct.[16]

Instead of reforming its system, Iraq tried to use the prospect of
lucrative reconstruction contracts to lure foreign investors and lend-
ers, but prospects for Iraqi repayment seemed poor, and few deals
were made. Iraq's demand that companies selling it goods or services
arrange their own financing was particularly unattractive. Egyptian
workers left when the regime broke its promises to send their
earnings home to Egypt. Foreign airlines stopped flying because
Iraq would not let them take their earnings from ticket sales out
of the country. Turkey sharply reduced Iraq's water from the Euphrates River for a month to fill its own reservoirs. The lack of
assistance from other countries in coping with its economic woes
was largely Iraq's fault, but it only further convinced Saddam that
there was an international conspiracy against him.[17]

Meanwhile, he planned too much reconstruction without being
able to pay for it. High-priority projects included rebuilding the
city of Basra and constructing a Baghdad subway system, a Mosul
airport, almost two thousand miles of railway, a highway from Basra
to Turkey, a steelmaking complex, an auto plant in cooperation

with General Motors, fertilizer and petrochemical factories, the Mandawa and Badush dams, a power station, and an oil refinery near Baghdad. Basra, the city most damaged in the war, was to be the showcase. Saddam insisted that it be renovated by May 1989, to show that Iraq was returning to normal. Damage from years of rocket and artillery fire was cleared away, canals were dredged and roads cleared, and a gleaming international airport was reopened. Despite this facade, no new industries were coming there to create jobs and earn money.[18]

In Aesop's fable, the prudent, hardworking ant was well supplied for winter; the spendthrift grasshopper starved. Similarly, Kuwait had wisely invested its $50 billion of income from the 1980s and doubled these holdings to $100 billion, while Iraq had squandered the same amount in war and was left with nothing. But in politics, like nature, a hungry carnivore can prey on fat grazers. Iraq argued that the oil-rich kingdoms had never worked for their wealth, while it had heroically defended them. Baghdad had no better use for its army—which had grown from twelve divisions in 1980 to over seventy-seven divisions at the war's end—than to seize the savings of neighbors it saw as undeservedly rich grasshoppers.[19]

Iraq's leaders, then, were armed and dangerous, drawing confidence from their total control at home, their victory over Iran, and the possession of a huge military machine. Energetic and youthful, Saddam himself was barely fifty years old. The country's rulers believed they had only begun their careers of conquest. A Ba'th party slogan said that it had required twenty years in power, after taking over in July 1968, to ensure its authority in Iraq before uniting the Arabs. This period concluded almost to the day with the end of the Iran-Iraq war, which marked the start of the new era in this glorious history. In tribute to his old idol, who had come closest to winning the mantle of Arab leadership, Saddam put a statue of

Nasser in one of Baghdad's main squares and named a street after the late Egyptian leader.

The Bush administration understood neither that Saddam was about to pursue his ambitions nor that he was ready to sacrifice an effective reconstruction program for political reasons. Most U.S. officials and experts expected Iraq to be sensible, to concentrate on development and reduce military spending. After all, what country would be more likely to follow a pacific course than one that had just barely survived a terrible eight-year war? This seemed logical for those accustomed to democracy but was far from a radical dictator's mentality.

Thus, both the Reagan, then the Bush administrations remained largely passive despite Iraq's crimes against U.S. laws and a State Department report calling Baghdad's human rights record "abysmal" and "unacceptable." The presidents resisted congressional demands to put pressure or sanctions on Iraq for its murderous treatment of the Kurdish minority. Immediately after the war, Saddam forcibly moved as many as 500,000 Kurds to camps and razed 700 villages to create a depopulated security zone along the Iran-Iraq border. Amnesty International reported that hundreds of children had been imprisoned, tortured, or murdered. British and American doctors found that Kurdish refugees displayed symptoms that indicated that chemical weapons had been used against them. Assistant Secretary of State Richard Schifter estimated that chemical attacks on Kurdish towns had killed about 8,000 people.[20]

In September 1988, the House of Representatives voted by a margin of 388 to 16 to invoke economic sanctions against Iraq, at a time when U.S. credits to Iraq were around $1 billion annually. But the White House called sanctions "terribly premature and counterproductive [endangering] billions of dollars" of business for U.S. companies. Senator John Heinz of Pennsylvania said, "Getting tough on the use of chemical weapons by Iraq [was just being] tough on certain U.S. exporters." The administration succeeded in having this proposal so watered down in the Senate that Iraq merely had to promise not to use chemical weapons again in order to obtain Export-Import Bank credits. There were no restrictions on agricultural credits.[21]

And so, in response to Saddam's actions and threats, Washington acted so as to convince Baghdad that the United States was weak. Saddam interpreted U.S. attempts to avoid conflict as proof that America feared confrontation with him. Each act of appeasement only increased Iraq's boldness without persuading its government that the United States wanted to be its friend. The Americans "are out to hurt Iraq," one of that country's top leaders claimed. The problem was not that U.S. actions alienated Iraq but that the nature of Iraq's regime inevitably made it antagonistic to the United States.[22]

Allowing Saddam to threaten the United States without its reacting induced other Arabs to see Baghdad as a winner and further let Iraq think it could get away with seizing Kuwait. No less an expert on this point than Iraqi deputy foreign minister Nizar Hamdoun—albeit in reference to Iran—explained, "Aggressors thrive on appeasement. The world learned that at tremendous cost from the Munich agreement of 1938. . . . How could the German generals oppose Hitler once he had proven himself successful?"[23] If America did not stop Khomeini or Saddam, their neighbors and underlings would certainly not try to do so.

Iran's planning and budget minister, Mas'ud Zanjani, ridiculing U.S. intervention to defend Gulf shipping from Iranian attacks in 1987, expressed the type of thinking that lured Middle East dictators and extremists into more than one confrontation with America. The United States would never fight in the Gulf, explained Zanjani, because its forces were so vulnerable, the American people and their European allies would oppose intervention, and the Americans would quickly retreat if they suffered casualties.[24]

Like the Iranians—and dictators of the past in Japan, Germany, and the USSR—Saddam underestimated America while he played the dangerous game of exaggerating outside menaces to justify his incompetence at home and aggression abroad. The Zionists and other enemies—a category that included Iran, Syria, and the United States—were said to be so frightened and jealous of Iraq's victory that they were conspiring to block its rightful leadership role by economic warfare and military attack.[25]

Iraq's attitude toward Israel was simultaneously paranoid and cynical. Saddam tried to use the Arab-Israeli conflict for his own purposes as a practical tool to unite his people at home and appeal to Arabs abroad. But he probably believed also that Israel was the embodiment of evil and would inevitably attack his country. Although Iraqi intelligence officers met secretly with Israeli counterparts in February 1986—when Iran still seemed able to win the war and Iraq was exploring every alternative—these efforts went nowhere. Iraq remained extremely hostile to Israel. A leading Iraqi poet opened his country's 1989 Babylon cultural festival by proclaiming that Iraq would tear up the Zionists' Torah scrolls as it had destroyed Iran's dreams. Zionism, said Saddam, could not "bear the idea of an Arab victory in battle." He took comfort in the hope that foreign Jews were criticizing and abandoning Israel.[26]

"Direct aggression from Israel is expected," said Saddam repeatedly. Iraq was persuaded that there would soon be a new Israeli air raid to repeat the humiliation of the 1981 destruction of its nuclear reactor. Iraqi gunners were so nervous that they accidentally shot down an Egyptian fighter-bomber arriving for the April 1989 Baghdad air show.[27] Nonetheless, the Iraqis claimed they were not frightened. "The Zionists should realize," said an Iraqi newspaper, "that Iraq in 1989 is different from Iraq in 1981," having become too strong to challenge.[28] Baghdad's arsenal now included arms so terrible—missiles, chemical weapons, and eventually atomic ones—as to deter or possibly destroy Israel.

Further, Iraq was ready to fight a long war, which Israel, an Iraqi journalist asserted, could never survive. During the Iran-Iraq conflict, Iraq had "swum under water for eight years." Iraq's state-run press proclaimed: "Iraq emerged from the war triumphant, familiar with the details of science and technology," so advanced as to break "the myth of Israeli superiority." Now the Arabs could crack the Arab-Israeli deadlock and achieve total victory.[29]

Since the Iraqi regime thought peace was impossible and Arab victory inevitable, it wanted to prevent a negotiated settlement of the conflict. Such a solution, after all, would permanently thwart Iraq's ambitions by strengthening Israel, helping Arab moderates, and intensifying U.S. influence. Thus, as always, Baghdad took a hard line on the conflict. "Assuming the Palestinians agree to take the West Bank and the Gaza Strip to set up a state there," asked First Deputy Prime Minister Taha Yasin Ramadan, "do you think it would in practice lead to a comprehensive and lasting peace, when every Palestinian knows the rest of his country is occupied by Israel, which is there by force of arms?" He doubted it.[30]

One element in Iraq's effort to block diplomacy and seize Arab leadership was to dominate the PLO. The Palestinian cause still had prestige among the Arab masses as the most salient nationalist struggle. Baghdad could not be chief of the Arabs if Egypt, Syria, or Jordan was the Palestinians' patron. With the PLO weakened by the erosion of Soviet support, opposed by Syria, and nagged by Egypt to be more moderate, Arafat needed Saddam even more than the Iraqi dictator needed the PLO leader.

In December 1988, Arafat had promised to accept Israel's existence, endorse UN resolutions calling for a compromise settlement, and end to terrorism. The United States and the PLO opened a dialogue. But Arafat chose to pursue the radical option by working with Iraq; he moved PLO offices and top-level meetings from Tunisia to Baghdad and visited there every few weeks in 1989 and 1990. Baghdad courted Arafat by giving him full honors as a head of state, a huge embassy compound, training facilities for military and terrorist operations, money, and a personal airplane.

While plying Arafat with gifts, Saddam used his power over some PLO groups to push the organization in the direction he wanted. One of the Baghdad-directed factions—the Palestine Liberation Front—launched a big seaborne terrorist attack against Israel in May 1990, using Palestinians recruited in Iraq and rehearsed in Libya. The terrorists, under orders to shoot as many civilians as possible on Israel's beaches, were themselves quickly killed or captured by Israel's navy. Arafat neither condemned the terrorism nor punished the PLO leaders involved. The United States responded to this behavior by suspending talks with the PLO. From Iraq's standpoint, the peace process's breakdown was an achievement that averted the threat of a diplomatic solution.

While Iraq sponsored terrorism and sabotaged peace, it maintained a facade of innocence. Baghdad insisted that reports about its efforts to develop weapons of mass destruction were fictions from Israeli intelligence and were motivated by U.S. imperialism, constituting a propaganda campaign to discredit Iraq and justify a military attack on it. Ironically, though some information about these programs was often ignored in the West because it came from Israel or pro-Israel sources, this material would later prove to have been correct or even to have underestimated Iraq's activities.[31]

Iraq's massive military buildup, however, was a self-fulfilling prophecy, since it increased the very U.S. and Israeli antagonism that Saddam claimed to fear. As an Arab proverb puts it, "He hits me, then he complains." When Iraq bragged about new super-weapons to impress its populace and other Arabs, this publicity sparked more Western news coverage and export controls. "Iraq is building an advanced arms industry to match any in the world," said Hussein Kamil, Saddam's cousin and the minister supervising Iraq's missile and military plants. Kamil had done such a good job that Saddam promoted him to defense minister. At the First International Baghdad Fair for Military Industrialization, Iraq spoke of building two hundred kinds of sophisticated weapons, ranging from cluster bombs to missiles to copies of the advanced Soviet T-72 tank.

Many companies were eager to profit by Iraq's ambitions. For example, Marcel Dassault-Breguet, chairman of the French Dassault Company, was peddling his Mirage 2000 fighters at the fair. "I would answer 'yes' if Iraqi pilots want to use our planes," he said. Moscow, desperate for money, was ready to sell Iraq whatever it could pay for in hard currency, including some of the Soviet arms made available as the Soviets withdrew from Eastern Europe.[32]

German companies, some of which had once contributed greatly to Hitler's war effort, were particularly cooperative with Iraq. A Social Democratic legislator protested to Prime Minister Helmut Kohl that Germany had a special moral responsibility: "The Jews will not forget, the Americans have not forgotten, and the Germans are not allowed to forget."[33] But while the German government intensified investigations, legal charges for violating export laws were filed only after Iraq's invasion of Kuwait.

Of course, Iraq was not the only Middle Eastern country to have a big army, nor was it alone in developing missiles and chemical and nuclear arms. Israel had some nuclear weapons and launched its own experimental rockets in 1987 and 1988. Saudi Arabia was buying Chinese missiles. Libya and Syria were also actively obtaining unconventional weapons. But Iraq's record—it had already fired missiles and chemical weapons against its own Kurdish citizens and Iranian enemies—and rhetoric indicated that it was the country most likely to use them.

By the early 1980s, Iraq's plants were already making a thousand tons of chemical weapons a year. When the West restricted exports to Iraq of the raw materials needed for such products, the country worked to become self-sufficient in producing the needed ingredients and equipment. And items were smuggled by circuitous routes. For example, a Baltimore company shipped chemicals through Jordan before U.S. authorities discovered the real destination and made arrests.

Equipment was purchased from many places, including the United States, for Iraq's Saad-16 missile-building complex near Mosul. A special espionage group reporting to Saddam handled illegal procurement in twenty-two countries. Parts were shipped through third countries—especially Jordan—or dummy companies, many of them in Switzerland. Contraband goods were flown in on Iraqi planes directly from Europe. Iraq also bought shares in European companies to increase its opportunities for buying advanced tools or stealing technological data. As time went on, Iraqi scientists and factories were able to make more of these things at home.[34]

Results were achieved quickly. The Iraqis were preparing typhoid, cholera, and anthrax in underground facilities at Salman Pak, thirty-five miles southeast of Baghdad. Iraq was making rapid progress on developing nuclear weapons too, with reported help coming from China. U.S. intelligence estimated that Baghdad was only a few years away from being able to build an atomic bomb. Whether it could succeed, said the American military expert Anthony Cordesman, would be known only "when one sees a mushroom cloud above northern Iraq."[35]

Most successful of all was Iraq's long-range-missile program. In April 1988, Iraq unveiled a new al-Abbas Scud-B missile. By March 1989, an Iraqi official announced that its missiles had the long-range capacity to hit Tel Aviv. In December, it tested two Tamouz-1 missiles, with a range of 1,200 miles.[36]

While the West was relatively indifferent to these developments, Israel—Iraq's openly declared target—was anxious about the new weapons, about Western companies' eagerness to arm Saddam, and about Western governments' willingness to let it happen. In light of all this information, the United States responded to help Israel defend itself from a missile attack. U.S. aid was already partly funding Israel's own Arrow defensive missile, but this was several years away from deployment. In January 1990, Israel ordered two batteries of U.S. Patriot missiles to be delivered in late 1991, at a cost of $200 million.[37]

The United States and Great Britain also stepped up efforts to block Iraqi smuggling of raw materials and high-technology equipment. This campaign slowed Iraq's progress but had less than enthusiastic support from the U.S. Commerce Department, which freely granted export licenses in order to promote business. For example, only a warning by former Defense Department official Stephen Bryen prevented a proposed sale to Iraq of a high-temperature furnace useful for its nuclear program. Baghdad claimed the device was for medical purposes. Secretary of Commerce Robert Mosbacher, whom George Bush later chose to lead his 1992 presidential campaign, and the department's counselor, Wayne Berman, were ready to approve almost any sale to Iraq.[38]

If Saddam had been more patient, he could have continued developing his unconventional weapons and invaded Kuwait only when he possessed an arsenal—paid for by his intended victims and sold him by democratic states—sufficient to discourage any opposition. But his own miscalculation and Iraq's economic woes would make him act too hastily.[39]

While Iraq's state-controlled media talked about importing American Chevrolets as a "new symbol of affluence," there was rationing and shortages of meat and eggs in Baghdad. The authorities threatened to punish those who stood in the long lines waiting to buy food if they were not more orderly. The minister of trade called bakers into his office to insist that they maintain bread supplies and to warn of stern punishment for selling on the black market. Yet Iraq could not free up enough foreign exchange to import spare parts to replace the bakers' worn-out equipment.[40]

Given Iraq's fiscal weakness, a U.S. threat to cut its huge subsidies and credits would have so undermined the regime's stability as to provide a big incentive for restraint. Instead, Iraq was allowed to go on using U.S. aid to subsidize indirectly its oversize army and its weapons research programs, since this money left Baghdad with more of its own funds to buy arms. Iraq's government remained so sure of American help that it saw no need to make economic reforms by expanding private enterprise, reducing taxes and military spending, or selling off inefficient state companies.

The fact that other Arabs also had economic and political problems encouraged Saddam to think they might rally behind him in a common assault on America, Israel, and the wealthy Gulf Arabs. The general mood of despair was well described by a Jordanian: "The situation is terrible. The whole world is getting democracy except for us. Our economies are a mess, we are weak, we are being left behind. We can't even stop the Russian Jews from immigrating to Israel."[41]

At the same time, Saddam's brotherly rhetoric scarcely concealed the fact that his goal was to isolate Egypt, undermine Syria, dominate Jordan, and milk Saudi Arabia and Kuwait for every possible penny. The Arab states all tried to have it both ways. They sought to stay on Saddam's good side, since it was always good to maintain Arab solidarity for appearance' sake and wise to remember that Iraq might emerge triumphant. Publicly, Egypt, Jordan, Kuwait, Saudi Arabia, and Syria extolled Iraq's reasonableness, pacifism, and good intentions, insisting that Saddam merely wanted to defend himself and concentrate on domestic reconstruction.

Privately, however, they talked in a different way. The Gulf Arab states so feared Iraq as a dominant ally that they wanted to avoid dependence on it. Egyptian leaders called Saddam a "psychotic," and Jordanian officials whispered that they were trying to civilize the crude Iraqi dictator. Moreover, while Iraq's anti-American and anti-Israel rhetoric might score some points among their people, most Arab rulers feared America and Israel enough to prefer avoiding confrontation. If the post–Cold War era was going to be one of U.S. domination, this very fact made it all the more sensible to stay on good terms with the world's sole superpower. The moderates wanted it to protect them from Iraq and Iran; the radicals felt weaker than ever at seeing the collapse of the USSR, which had been their economic and political model as well as their superpower patron.

Arab rulers liked to attack Israel with words or by covertly supporting terrorism, but risking another military defeat by the Jewish state was less appealing. Israel seemed to be growing stronger. Hundreds of thousands of new Soviet Jewish immigrants arrived. The Palestinian intifada achieved nothing material and did not force Israel out of the West Bank and the Gaza Strip.

Poorer Arabs harbored a great deal of resentment toward the rich Gulf monarchies. In the late 1970s, the Saudis and Kuwaitis had committed themselves to a large, ten-year aid program for Syria and Jordan, so that they might confront Israel. Without providing any particular rationale, the donors did not renew these subsidies when they expired in 1988. Less affluent Arabs were bitter that their supposed brothers invested more securely and profitably in the West rather than extending their charity or aid programs.

But most of the needy states preferred to keep good relations with the Gulf monarchs rather than fight them, hoping that honeyed words would persuade them to give more aid. As rivals with Iraq for regional hegemony, Egypt and Syria assumed that Iraqi hegemony over the Gulf would be at their expense. Saudi and Kuwaiti oil riches would flow to Baghdad rather than to Cairo or Damascus.[42] Egypt, as America's closest Arab ally and the only Arab state at peace with Israel, wanted no Arab confrontation with Washington or Jerusalem. Having feuded with its neighbor Saddam for almost twenty years, Syria's regime felt that it would only be victimized if Iraq became stronger.

The situation in Jordan was somewhat different. As Iraq's weakest neighbor, Jordan was intimidated into an alliance with Saddam. But King Hussein thought he could pursue this policy without any cost. He expected to stop short of becoming involved in an Iraq-Israel confrontation. Similarly, the king knew that Jordanian criticism of America would not destroy his old connection with that country. If necessary, he could count on the United States and, indirectly, Israel to save him from Saddam's strangling embrace. It was a dangerous game, but the king had survived many such experiences in his long reign. Jordan's inherently hazardous geopolitical position gave him no choice.

In domestic politics, Jordan's cooperation with Saddam had real advantages for the king. Iraq's radicalism was popular among his Islamic fundamentalist and Palestinian subjects. By cheering

159

Saddam, the monarch sounded like an Arab militant to the mob, and he thus outmaneuvered the local radicals. How could they oppose a government that pursued such a patriotic nationalist policy?

Antagonism against the Saudis and the Kuwaitis was especially high in Jordan and, lacking any leverage over them, King Hussein could only hope to share in loot obtained by Iraqi pressure on the monarchies. Jordan was racked by inflation, unemployment, and a $6 billion foreign debt. In April 1989, riots over rising prices left eight dead and one hundred injured as hitherto loyal citizens attacked banks, burned tires, smashed cars, and battled the police. Crown Prince Hassan blamed the disturbances on Islamic fundamentalists, "the bearded gentlemen." But soon the king was growing his own beard to win their favor.[43]

In practical terms, King Hussein permitted Iraqi reconnaissance flights along his border with Israel and allowed the formation of a joint Jordan-Iraq fighter squadron. Jordan also served as a conduit for shipping weapons technology and strategic materials to Iraq, bypassing Western export restrictions. In response to Israeli warnings, he secretly promised that cooperation would remain limited.[44]

Saudi Arabia and Kuwait were also willing to help Iraq, but they did not want to surrender their sovereignty to Saddam or follow him into a conflict with Israel and America. They offered Baghdad payoffs while continuing to buy large amounts of Western arms and tightening their relations with the United States. Washington was ready to provide these weapons for the profits as well as for the strategic purpose of ensuring Gulf stability. In 1989, the Bush administration proposed to sell Saudi Arabia $850 million in aircraft parts, missiles, and training, plus 315 Abrams tanks for $3 billion.[45]

Asked to approve the sales, members of Congress inquired whom the Saudi arsenal was aimed against, wondering if Israel was the ultimate target. In November 1989, Deputy Assistant Secretary of

State Richard Clarke justified the administration's proposal by explaining, "Saudi Arabia lives in a bad neighborhood. . . . The principal military threat in the region is Iraq."

Congressman Mel Levine asked, "Do you believe that Saudi Arabia could repulse an Iraqi invasion?"

A strong Saudi force, Clarke replied, might deter Baghdad or "slow that attack down until the United States and other friendly forces were able to do something."

Deputy Assistant Secretary Edward Gnehm, about to be named ambassador to Kuwait, leapt into the exchange: "I don't think it is appropriate to focus on Iraq as the principal threat because, in truth, at the present time, Saudi-Iraqi relations are good." The Bush administration rejected the possibility of Iraq's becoming an aggressor. The Saudis made the same mistake in expecting the danger to be defused by appeasement, categorically denying that Iraq was dangerous and praising Saddam.[46]

After evincing no strong reaction to Iraq's use of chemical weapons against the Kurds, threats against Israel, outspoken anti-Americanism, or the ultimatum to Kuwait, the United States had helped convince Saddam that he could get away with occupying and annexing his neighbor. By seeking to avoid any trouble with Iraq, U.S. policy had helped precipitate a much bigger crisis.[47]

CHAPTER EIGHT

BRAVE NEW GULF

*When the call to prayer sounded from the minaret, Hojja
ran away from the mosque.
"Where are you going, Hojja?"
"That was the loudest, most convincing call ever! I am
going to find out how far it can be heard!"*

—*Middle Eastern folktale*

Shigeru Toyoda, the head of the vast Toyota Japanese automotive
empire, listened carefully to a briefing in the Washington conference
room. He was talking to a group of American experts about political
conditions in the Gulf, where Toyota had extensive business dealings. He knew how costly a misreading of the area's future could
be. Another Japanese company, Mitsui, had lost over $1 billion on
a massive Iranian petrochemical project that was disrupted by the
revolution and bombed during the Iran-Iraq war. The Japanese
industrialist also understood that the situation in the Gulf had a
tremendous impact on international business conditions, since most
of Japan's and much of Western Europe's oil came from there.

He listened politely as the experts spoke and their words were translated into Japanese. Then, in his own language, Mr. Toyoda asked a question: "This is all very interesting. But what I really want to know is the date on which the Saudi monarchy will fall."

"We know the date," one of the American consultants joked, "but before telling you, we have to renegotiate our contract for a higher fee."

The revolution in Iran made more than a few foreign observers, and—more important—Iraqi and Iranian leaders, expect that it would be only a matter of time before the Gulf Arab monarchs would go the way of the Shah. The only questions were the timing of their fall and the beneficiaries of their demise.

Those who expected this outcome, however, underestimated the Saudi and Kuwaiti rulers' tenacity and ability. They eventually outmaneuvered Iran and Iraq to succeed in preserving their security. Similarly, Saudi Arabia and Kuwait proved themselves pragmatic rather than fanatic, as prone to self-interest and rational calculation as any other countries in the world. By persuading U.S. policymakers otherwise, however, the Gulf monarchies also managed to obtain what they wanted from America, at the lowest possible political cost.

Just as Iran and Iraq were the predators in the Gulf, which the United States had to block, Saudi Arabia and Kuwait were the potential victims, which America had to protect. These societies— ruled by monarchs and organized by more traditional structures and ideas—were even more difficult for Americans to understand than Iran and Iraq were.

It is not surprising that the myths that so misled American thinking about the region were intensified in the cases of Saudi Arabia and Kuwait. Those regimes used so much Arab nationalist and Islamic rhetoric that it was easy to conclude they believed their utterances. They spoke with such fervor about the Palestinian issue and their hatred of Israel that one might think this was their most passionate concern. Given the cultural gap, it could well appear that the Saudis and Kuwaitis wanted to keep themselves distant from the United States. Their vast oil wealth implied that they were independent of any need for American assistance; their supposed fragility made them seem easy prey for radical ideas and revolutions.

Events in the 1970s and 1980s proved each of these preconceptions to be wrong. Saudi and Kuwaiti behavior belied the claims that the U.S. regional position was shaky, dependent on resolving the Arab-Israeli conflict while foolishly undermining the very moderates it sought to support. Rather than U.S. standing in the area being subject to Saudi kindness, Saudi Arabia's survival was reliant on U.S. goodwill.

Beyond appearances, this reality should have been evident. Saudi and Kuwaiti rhetoric was a substitute for action and a cheap way to buy off radical Arab states and movements. Outside of words and relatively sparse donations, the Saudis and Kuwaitis largely ignored the Arab-Israeli conflict. They were eager to obtain Western goods even if they did not always want to imitate Western culture, and they were badly in need of U.S. protection and arms. The fact that oil wealth was transforming those desert kingdoms at such astounding speed made them more cognizant of their need for American technology and protection.

For Americans to grasp how Saudi Arabia and Kuwait functioned, it was useful to consider Winston Churchill's comment on how it felt to be ninety years old: "Terrible! But consider the alternative!" The Gulf Arab monarchies were puritanical oligarchies, but the alternative—to be like Iraq or Iran—was not wildly attractive to most of their citizens. The fact that the Saudi and Kuwaiti kingdoms provided peace and security for the lives and property of their people was no mean achievement by regional standards. In short, they deserved to be defended from the radicals by the United States on ethical as well as strategic grounds. Only by examining their unique societies and politics, however, can one understand how much these states differed from the American mythology about them and how U.S. policy missed opportunities to use its own leverage against them.

Up to the 1970s, Saudi Arabia and Kuwait had been among the most closed societies on earth. Some Islamic traditionalists in Saudi Arabia protested the introduction of radio and automobiles there in the 1920s and television in 1964 as dangerously anti-Islamic innovations. Now Saudi Arabia and Kuwait were being deluged by Western goods, technology, and ideas. But the Gulf states wanted to separate the importation of Western civilization's products from an imitation of its society. Bahrain's minister of development explained in 1985: "Nobody was ready for all the money that descended on us. People became confused, and they ran away to find comfort in Islam," though not in its radical fundamentalist form.[1]

Two incidents from the 1970s symbolize this fear of social disintegration in Saudi Arabia. In 1975, a young Saudi prince returned from his studies in the West to assassinate King Faisal, sparking concern that there might be some radical conspiracy against the kingdom. After a thorough investigation, it was concluded that he had acted alone, from a personal grudge: his brother had been killed a decade earlier during an anti-television demonstration. In 1978, worldwide attention was drawn to the execution of a young Saudi princess and her lover, charged with breaking the country's strict sexual code.

What was truly remarkable about Saudi Arabia—and Kuwait too—was how stable they remained in the face of such rapid change.

The regimes were too much in control, too alert to the threat, and too well endowed with money to fall easily. The Gulf Arab monarchies had much more oil income and far fewer citizens among whom to divide the benefits than did Iran, where the oil boom whetted more appetites than it satisfied. Since Iran's Islamic revolution was ethnically Persian and theologically Shia, it had only a limited appeal for the Arab and mainly Sunni Muslim majority in Saudi Arabia and Kuwait.

Wealth without hard work may not seem virtuous, but it is a very pleasurable way of life. These welfare states provided a cushion enabling the Saudi and Kuwaiti rulers to preserve enough of traditional society while giving their subjects the benefits of a higher living standard. Using their Arab identity, material benefits, and repression, these regimes kept all but a tiny number of their people from following Khomeini.[2]

Dramatic as were the changes brought by oil wealth in these societies, they were just beginning a long process, which might take many decades before it undermined the existing regimes. No cohesive revolutionary class or group existed in Saudi Arabia or Kuwait among army officers, officials, businessmen, intellectuals, or workers. The old loyalties were still strong, and these people lacked a collective political consciousness, remaining oriented instead to the divisive appeals of family, clan, and tribe.

The Saudis and Kuwaitis also defused any potential political challenge from a discontented working class by giving the menial jobs to hundreds of thousands of workers imported from Pakistan, South Korea, Yemen, and the Philippines. More educated foreigners, from Europe or Arab countries, held professional positions that the local citizens were not willing or trained to fill. Since the locals saw these guest workers as servants, not masters, the presence of so many foreigners made them content rather than angry. The imported employees were too diverse and transient to pose a political threat; besides, they considered themselves lucky to be making an income far beyond what they might have earned at home. Those instigating dissent could be easily deported. The Kuwaiti government admitted to expelling 27,000 foreigners in 1986 alone, though independent estimates were far higher.[3]

Despite their conservative anti-communism, Saudi Arabia and Kuwait practiced a kind of paternalistic socialism that made them commercial paradises. Control of the oil that furnished almost all the national income permitted the state to subsidize and protect local businesses. Saudi and Kuwaiti companies were tied to the government because most of their income came from commissions or kickbacks on its contracts. Saudi and Kuwaiti technocrats educated abroad were linked to the system because they mostly worked for the regime's bureaucracy. This bourgeoisie knew how much it had to lose if the system was overturned, for it had seen too many failures by Marxism, radical Arab nationalism, and Islamic fundamentalism to be mesmerized by such alleged panaceas.

In no Arab state were country and regime more inseparable than in Saudi Arabia, whose very name enshrined the Saud family's domination. The royal house, however, was like a political party, not an ingrown cabal. Compared to the shah's small household, there were perhaps twenty thousand members of the Saud family in all, including four thousand princes scattered in key spots throughout the country's institutions. Many of the armed forces' commanders were princes; a separate national guard under Prince Abdallah functioned, in effect, as the family's private army. Through intermarriage, subsidies, and rewards, the family's alliances extended throughout the tribes, clergy, merchants, officers, and the state's bureaucracy.

The Saudi religious establishment, too, was closely allied to the royal family and had been for more than two centuries. Even when the government had to cut spending, it kept up the clergy's subsidies. In 1986, having learned a lesson from the Shah's fate, Saudi King Fahd stressed his personal religious status as protector of Islam's most sacred sites in Mecca and Medina by taking the title "Custodian of the Two Holy Mosques."

The royal family was adept at maintaining its unity. The king was its leader but also listened to his relatives, who restrained and informed him in an ongoing private debate. The system smoothly handled each transition to a new monarch and choice of the next crown prince, a process that occurred four times between 1953 and 1982. When the throne was occupied by a weak king—as were two of the five monarchs in this century—the crown prince played a powerful role. In contrast to the system common in the West, the king's eldest son did not automatically succeed him. Instead, the selection process took into account the candidates' personal abilities and the balance of power among the family's branches.

The leading triumvirate in the 1980s and into the 1990s—King Fahd, Crown Prince Abdallah, and Minister of Defense Prince Sultan—worked well together. The six-foot-tall Fahd had long experience as interior minister and was the power behind the throne during the reign of his often ill predecessor, King Khalid. Fahd ascended the throne when Khalid died in 1982. Prince Sultan, one of the royal family's smartest and most popular members, had been Fahd's close ally for many years and was a strong advocate of modernization.

Crown Prince Abdallah, who had a special interest in inter-Arab diplomacy, preferred a slower pace of development. His frequent contacts with Damascus and his marriage to one of Syrian president Asad's relatives gave rise to rumors that he was relatively radical and anti-American. But during the Kuwait crisis, Abdallah would prove especially determined in opposing Iraq's aggression and co-operating with the United States. Even if there were some differences among its members, the family enjoyed a consensus on the great majority of issues.

Saudi development strategies were reasonably effective, and although the country spent a great deal of money on luxuries, it could afford to do so. No matter how much cash the royal family took for itself, there was plenty left to distribute as patronage to ensure popular support. Since so many people shared in the payoffs, the system's corruption was often a politically beneficial form of economic redistribution to a large portion of the population. By way of contrast, Iran's structure of corruption under the Shah had become a monopoly that enriched only a small elite and thus bred discontent.

Still, even the Saudi family's funds were not unlimited. A typical analysis during the 1970s' oil boom days claimed that Saudi Arabia "can literally buy any future." The goods purchased and investments made in the United States deepened the American stake in Saudi Arabia's sovereignty and stability. Yet riches that once seemed infinite shrank as oil prices fell and income was committed to domestic development projects and subsidies. Lower oil earnings in the 1980s pressed the Saudi and Kuwaiti rulers to slow down ambitious development plans, cut foreign aid, and borrow abroad. These governments had to consider reducing domestic subsidies, a step that could bring unrest among their spoiled citizens.

While in 1980–81 the Saudis ran a $36 billion budget surplus, by the late 1980s their annual deficit ranged between $14 and $20 billion annually. Monetary reserves fell from $150 billion at their peak in 1982 to $63 billion at the end of 1988, of which more than half was in uncollectible loans to Iraq, Egypt, and others. Kuwaiti revenue also declined, from $19 billion in 1979–80 to $9 billion in 1984.[4]

But spending less money and slowing the pace of development had advantages. The very modernization that had created jobs and raised living standards also eroded the traditional relationships, ideas, and loyalties that preserved the system. Conservatives, clerics, and tribal leaders were already complaining about un-Islamic innovations and their own reduced influence. The rulers had to be careful not to be—or let the country become—too quickly and completely modernized or Westernized. The royal family generally did find the right balance between keeping citizens happy and balancing its checkbook. For example, instead of thousands of Saudi students going abroad to college and picking up potentially dangerous Western ideas, men were encouraged and women were forced to attend newly developed universities at home.

While the Saudi royal family had domestic affairs and oil policy well under control, foreign threats were harder to manage. Unlike Egypt, Syria, and Iraq, the Saudis had no ambition to lead the Arab world. They simply wanted to be left alone in order to enjoy their wealth, preferring to avoid making enemies among the Arabs and trying to buy off potential adversaries or problems. Rather than realpolitik, a joke went, Riyadh used its currency to engage in "riyalpolitik." When Bahrain and Qatar argued over who owned a tiny Gulf island in the mid-1980s, the Saudis found the ideal solution by hiring a ship to dredge it out of existence.

In the Saudis' suspicious eyes, Arab nationalism was an excuse for others to demand their wealth. After all, if the Arabs were one people and one nation, they collectively owned, as a matter of right, all the oil and money in Saudi Arabia, not just a small portion of it doled out as Saudi charity. To keep their wealth and independence, the Saudis needed U.S. help in balancing the stronger Arab states and Iran, which wanted to take over their country.

True, a dependence on America that was too openly acknowledged would have been counterproductive, since it could expose the Saudis to accusations of consorting with an infidel power that was the Arabs' enemy. Yet the necessary adjustments were easy to make. Instead of U.S. bases in Saudi Arabia, then, there were thousands of American military technicians and advisers on Saudi bases. Saudi Arabia's tightly regulated newspapers were allowed to attack U.S. policies, but Saudi leaders rarely criticized the United States. The Saudis balanced their support for U.S. naval convoys in the Gulf by proclaiming themselves to be better and stricter Muslims than the radical fundamentalists.

Yet the Saudis always distinguished between the need to make the gestures necessary to defuse Arab or Iranian criticism and the setting of a foreign policy aimed at ensuring their own survival. The informal nature of the alliance should not have obscured the fact that the Saudis' link to the United States was a matter not of choice but of necessity for them.

When it came to internal matters, the Saudis did not hesitate to crush any threat, no matter how much it dressed itself in Islamic garb. In 1979, when a small band of armed fundamentalists took over the most hallowed mosque in Mecca—where no non-Muslims were permitted—the authorities secretly called in German commandos to wipe them out. In July 1987, Saudi police fired on demonstrating Iranian pilgrims at the Muslim shrines in Mecca, killing between four hundred and six hundred people.

Just as the Saudi regime could not become a radical opponent of the United States, it was uninterested in moving to the Soviet side in the Cold War. Riyadh knew that Moscow supported the Arab radical states, which wanted to devour the kingdom, coveted its wealth, and opposed its system. The Saudis strongly preferred capitalism, along with Western goods and living standards. They were equally convinced of the superiority of U.S. arms—ironically, from watching Israel's triumph over Soviet equipment in Arab hands— and technology. A strategic relationship with the USSR would pose the risk of Saudi officers being recruited as revolutionaries during studies in Moscow while Soviet advisers subverted the country from within. Despite some U.S. experts' fear, the Saudis and Kuwaitis never considered the USSR preferable to the United States as a protector.[5]

Similarly, the Saudis carefully avoided direct involvement in the Arab-Israeli conflict, because they had no desire to be dragged into war or to risk being the target of an Israeli attack. In its rhetoric, Riyadh was a bitter enemy of Israel second to none. The Saudis sincerely believed the most extreme anti-Jewish and anti-Israel slanders and conspiracy theories. They were known, for instance, to distribute copies of *Protocols of the Elders of Zion* and other anti-Semitic works. The Saudis barred Jews from visiting the country, a regulation they began to ease only after Secretary of State Henry Kissinger came there, accompanied by American Jewish reporters, in the mid-1970s.

Yet other than subsidizing the PLO and Syria, Saudi Arabia did little more than talk about the issue. In private meetings with Americans, Saudi officials often began with a recital of Israel's alleged sins, then, with this formality out of the way, the hosts would say, "Now let's get down to business." The Saudis' sentiments on the Arab-Israeli conflict had little practical effect on their policy.

The Saudis bought arms not to fight Israel but for self-defense against Iraq, Iran, and Syria. Arab nationalism prevented the regime from admitting that fact but did not stop it from acting in its own interest. The country became the world's largest importer, buying almost exclusively from the United States, because it had so much to protect and so many potentially dangerous neighbors from whom to safeguard itself. Knowing the purpose of these purchases, American presidents were happy to sell munitions to the Saudis.

Unable to trust or fight Iran and Iraq, incapable of even maintaining, without help, the billions of dollars' worth of U.S. arms they had purchased, Saudi leaders knew that U.S. protection was their true source of security. Consequently, Saudi officers were trained in the United States; hundreds of American technicians went to Saudi Arabia to service equipment and teach the Saudis how to use it. The United States also sold the Saudis advanced AWACS early-warning planes to protect the oil fields from air attack and provide the U.S. military with detailed intelligence about Iranian and Iraqi operations. The regime overbuilt its military facilities for the day when American forces might have to be summoned.

Certainly, the United States had a vital interest in preserving Saudi Arabia so as to keep anti-American radicals from seizing its oil and petroleum money. Yet since the Saudis had already gained U.S. protection at no political cost, they had no reason to make their foreign policy more congenial to Washington. Giving little in exchange except payments for the weapons, the Saudis understandably came to see the strategic relationship with America as a business deal rather than an alliance with mutual obligations. The Saudis still talked like militant Arab nationalists to the radicals, posed as Islamic militants to the clerics, subsidized Palestinian terrorist groups, and spoke moderately to the West, all at the same time.

By the same token, the Saudis never lifted a finger to help U.S. peacemaking efforts. Why should Saudi Arabia assist U.S. attempts to achieve Arab-Israeli peace when Washington never demanded anything as a precondition for guarding them? It refused to back the Camp David accords and instead joined the Iraqi-led front that punished Egypt for signing that 1978 treaty with Israel. The Saudis also deterred King Hussein from entering proposed peace talks in 1982 and 1985, hinting they would cut aid to Jordan, and sabotaged a 1983 U.S.-backed Israel-Lebanon peace treaty by supporting Syrian opposition to it.

This Saudi attitude created a problem for U.S. presidents trying to persuade Congress to approve massive arms sales to the kingdom. The Carter, Reagan, and Bush administrations made much of alleged Saudi moderation. "Saudi Arabia is the center of the pro-Western forces in Islam, [exerting] leadership and influence in the Arab world," Reagan administration under secretary of state James Buckley told Congress in the mid-1980s. Whether from conviction or out of expediency, Fred Ikle, Buckley's counterpart at the Pentagon, erroneously claimed that Saudi Arabia was about to make peace with Israel.[6]

While the White House took the Saudis' private pro-American rhetoric at face value, pro-Israel legislators took the Saudis' public anti-Israel rhetoric seriously. Remembering how Iran's revolution seized the Shah's arsenal, members of Congress worried that a radical regime in Saudi Arabia might use the weapons to attack U.S. forces or Israel and feared that stoking the arms race would destabilize the region. Of course, the basis for selling these arms was a correct assessment that they would be a stabilizing factor, making it less likely that belligerent neighbors or revolutionary forces would seize that arsenal—and Saudi money too—for aggressive purposes.

Congressional opposition often forced the White House to reduce planned sales to avoid defeats by the pro-Israel lobby. In the end, though, the lure of profits and jobs for U.S. companies helped push through the overwhelming majority of arms sales to Saudi Arabia. After the Iran-Iraq war ended in 1988 and Iraq's threat increased in Israel's eyes, the pro-Israel lobby became less active in fighting such deals as a $4 billion sale to Saudi Arabia proposed in the summer of 1990.[7]

Much of what was true for Saudi Arabia applied also to Kuwait. But that smaller, more vulnerable country could not even hope to defend itself by purchasing weapons. Kuwait's inherent weakness and its dangerous location between Iraq and Iran made it more eager to appease those radicals and less willing to associate itself with the United States. "He who stands too close to the blacksmith gets burned by the sparks," Kuwait's foreign minister once said of his country's geopolitical situation.[8] Nevertheless, when it came to preserving its internal security and vast wealth, Kuwait was not sentimental about Arab nationalism, Islamic solidarity, anti-Americanism, or the Palestinian cause.

Although Kuwait was young as a modern independent state, it was an old political entity whose people's strong bonds had been forged by tribal loyalty and the traditional way of life. The royal family held tightly to power to preserve this system, and as in Saudi Arabia, its many members held the key offices. To avoid having to integrate outsiders who might not be loyal to the regime, citizenship was granted only to the descendants of families that had lived there before the mid-1920s.

Limiting the number of citizens to a minority—about 800,000 people in a population of about 2 million—also maximized the share of Kuwait's wealth each of them received. Kuwait's citizens paid no income tax, while enjoying virtually free education and medical care, along with generous payments for each child. One of the country's symbols was the gigantic air-conditioned Sultan Center shopping mall, open twenty-four hours a day and featuring imported luxuries from all over the world. Many citizens had Asian servants and every modern convenience. A joke about this phenomenon recounted that an American, a German, and a Kuwaiti were discussing whether sex was work or pleasure. The American said pleasure; the German, work. "It must be pleasure," said the Kuwaiti, "or I'd have a Filipino servant do it for me."

If Kuwaitis wanted them, good jobs were available in the government bureaucracy and in state institutions. Much of the real labor, though, was done by Kuwait's roughly 1.2 million noncitizen residents, including about 400,000 Palestinians, who made up almost 80 percent of the work force. Kuwaiti banks, financial companies, and investment firms, for example, employed 15,000 Kuwaitis and 286,000 noncitizens. The latter group, many of whom had lived there for decades, made a great deal of money but could not own land and had no political standing. "I worked in Kuwait for 35 years," said a Palestinian resident, "and still we didn't get Kuwaiti passports and we are not citizens of Kuwait."[9]

Already proud of their desert pedigrees, the snobbish Kuwaitis were motivated by a narrow sense of self-interest. Lavish in their own life-styles, their charitable contributions to other states, though large in amount, were parsimonious relative to their incomes. The aid that was given fellow Arabs often came accompanied by advice to the recipients that might have been economically sound—one must work hard and live more austerely—but was resented.

Egyptians, Iraqis, Jordanians, and Palestinians did not try very hard to hide their resentment and jealousy at the Kuwaitis' good fortune, unearned wealth, and alleged laziness and greed. In private, Arab criticisms of Kuwaitis and Saudis were often harsh and petty. Visitors to Egypt and Jordan heard people ask what the Gulf Arabs had done to deserve their good fortune. Wealthy Gulf tourists who spent lots of money and bought up local real estate provoked resentment. But other Arabs restrained their feelings in the hope that they could wheedle more aid from their rich cousins.

By Western standards, Kuwait was a tightly controlled society, but it was far less totalitarian and repressive than Iraq or Iran and there was more social freedom than in puritanical Saudi Arabia. Still, the ruling family barely permitted more than the semblance of a political role for commoners. The facts that Kuwait was surrounded by dangers and that many of those clamoring for democracy were Islamic fundamentalists or radicals subsidized by Syria and Iraq made a parliamentary system seem even more destabilizing.

In 1976 and 1986, the regime suspended the National Assembly when some of its more radical members began criticizing the royal family and suggesting that its power be reduced. When the opposition began holding weekly rallies in December 1989, demanding that parliament be reopened, police used tear gas, water cannons, and stun grenades to disperse them. The regime offered a new National Council, with little power, but few people voted in the June 1990 balloting for it and dissidents continued to be arrested. On the eve of Iraq's invasion in August 1990, the Kuwaiti regime was at a low point in domestic popularity.

Kuwait thus treated noncitizens as second-class people, foreign Arabs almost as unwelcome beggars, and its own citizens as subjects who were not consulted on the country's governance. These practices made it all the more necessary for the regime to boast loudly of its Arab nationalist stance and to humor Iraq and Syria. In contrast, Kuwait was officially downright hostile to the United States. The large Palestinian community that dominated Kuwait's educational system and its press also set a tone of verbal extremism.

Kuwait's UN ambassador could speak in 1980 of a "cabal which controls and manipulates and exploits the rest of humanity by controlling the money and wealth of the world. . . . It is a well-known fact that the Zionists are the richest people in the world and control much of its destiny." In 1983, Kuwait refused to accept an American foreign service officer, Brandon Grove, as ambassador because he had technically served in Israel, though he was there as the U.S. diplomatic liaison to the Palestinians on the West Bank. In July 1985, National Assembly speaker Ahmad al-Sadun demanded that Kuwait cut off aid to the PLO and Jordan, because they were allegedly excessively moderate for even considering negotiations with Israel.[10]

Yet much of this behavior was purely for appearances. Kuwait restricted itself to symbolic and rhetorical militancy. Kuwait would announce donations to the PLO but, like other Arab states, never actually send the money. Kuwaitis mouthed standard lines about Arab brotherhood and U.S. imperialism, while putting their children in American schools and their capital in American banks. Using its funds to help the Arab world or put political pressure on the West was a low priority.

Kuwait preferred investments in the West as more secure financially and yielding the best rate of return. Sending money overseas also kept it safe from Kuwait's Arab brothers and Muslim Iranian neighbors if they ever decided to invade. By 1990, Kuwaiti private investment abroad totaled $50 to $75 billion. The state itself had about $50 billion in the United States, $30 billion in Europe (mostly England), and $20 billion elsewhere. Ten percent of its oil income went to the Reserve Fund for Future Generations, to remain untouched until after the year 2001. The Kuwaitis bought real estate, chains of gas stations, 15 percent of the Mercedes-Benz company, a share of Volkswagen, the Kiawah Island resort in South Carolina, and many other enterprises.

Yet although America was their choice for consumer products

and economic ventures, the Saudis and Kuwaitis gave ground to Iraq when it came to politics. They could take America but not Iraq for granted, and appeased Saddam not because he was friendlier but precisely because he was more threatening, closer, and readier to use force than the United States.

While the Saudis and Kuwaitis were placating Iraq, American experts urged the United States to appease Saudi Arabia and Kuwait even more, changing its policy to please them and being less friendly to Israel and more accommodating to the PLO. Although U.S. policymakers usually rejected this advice, they certainly did not ask the Gulf monarchies for concessions or support on U.S. positions. Consequently, the Saudis and Kuwaitis manipulated America, using it—like the foreign guest workers—as a mercenary, to convoy tankers or provide protection, then dismissing it with a payroll check for providing arms and technical assistance. The slogans used to keep their neighbors happy were also handy in fending off American requests for, say, help in making Arab-Israeli peace, combating international terrorism, or giving logistical assistance in helping the United States protect Gulf shipping.

Publicly taking Iraq's side in disputes with the West, the Saudis and Kuwaitis denied that Saddam threatened them, insisting he was only acting in self-defense. Their failure to build a moderate Arab coalition or urge U.S. opposition to Iraq would endanger their survival when Saddam, no longer satisfied with a large, reliable supply of golden eggs, decided to butcher the goose that laid them.

But the Saudis and Kuwaitis were not fools. Privately, they spoke of Saddam in terms of a Middle East proverb: Respect him but suspect him. They knew that the United States was the only country that could save them in their time of need, and when that moment came, neither Arab nationalist rhetoric nor Islam nor the Arab-

Israeli conflict would stand in the way of their securing its succor. Unlike their American counterparts, the Gulf monarchs were not blinded by ideological myths, toward which they had a healthy cynicism. In the end, the Saudis and Kuwaitis comprehended the United States far better than it understood them.

CHAPTER NINE

THE DESERT ROAD TO KUWAIT:
JANUARY–AUGUST 1990

> The pilgrims stood upon the shore of the lake and sent a
> frantic hail after the ship.
> "How much to take us? . . . Tell him we don't care what
> the expense is!"
> "He says two napoleons."
> "Too much! We'll give him one!"
> In a single instant . . . that ship was speeding away like a
> frightened thing.
> The two napoleons were offered—more if necessary—and
> pilgrims shouted themselves hoarse pleading to the retreating
> boatmen to come back. But they sailed serenely away and paid
> no further heed.
>
> —*Mark Twain,* The Innocents Abroad

"The post–Cold War world is arriving ahead of schedule,"
warned the *Wall Street Journal* at the end of 1989, commenting on
Iraq's military buildup.[1] Indeed, the events of 1990 would shake
the Middle East every bit as much as the fall of communism and
the Berlin Wall shook Europe. Neither the Kuwait crisis nor its
outcome was inevitable, yet Iraq's drive for power was certain to
lead to some major conflict. There were many portents: What had
the Iran-Iraq war been fought over if not who would rule the Gulf?
Why was Saddam failing to demobilize part of his wartime million-
man army and putting such a high priority on building an arsenal
of unconventional arms worthy of a regional superpower?
Changes in global politics also pushed him toward taking the

offensive. This new era was dangerous for Saddam. The Soviet bloc's collapse was ending the cold war; Mikhail Gorbachev's dramatic reforms were dismantling communism. If Communist dictators fell, so might an Iraqi regime that for over twenty years had based its state-controlled centralized economy and party-controlled society on a Soviet model that was now totally discredited. The end of Soviet emigration restrictions was allowing hundreds of thousands of Jews to go to Israel, strengthening that state. Saddam's foreign policy had been based on an alliance with the USSR and, later, on playing off the superpowers against each other. These options were also gone.

To make matters worse, the world's sole remaining superpower, the United States, was allied to his rivals or intended victims: Saudi Arabia, Egypt, Israel, and perhaps Iran again someday. Saddam told visiting Assistant Secretary of State John Kelly in February 1990 that America was the only outside power that counted in the Middle East. For him, that was more a problem than a compliment. Saddam assumed that the United States would use its overwhelming power as he would in its place: to eliminate the radical regimes and seize control of the region.

Two weeks after the meeting with Kelly, Saddam made one of the most important speeches of his career, openly launching Iraq's new radical phase. Ironically, he fired this salvo at the first-anniversary meeting of the Arab Cooperation Council, a loose grouping of Egypt, Iraq, Jordan, and Yemen, whose formation had been hailed in the West as an alliance of Arab moderates. Speaking at the Royal Cultural Center in Amman on February 24, 1990, Saddam urged a new offensive against the United States and Israel.

What could the Arabs do, Saddam asked, to save themselves from American domination? In essence, he suggested, the Arabs had three choices. They could wait until a new balance of power would be restored—perhaps allowing them to play off Europe against the Americans—but by then it could be too late. Or the Arabs could give up, arguing that there was "no choice but to submit" to America and follow its dictates on making peace with Israel and other matters. This second alternative would require that the Arabs give up forever the hope of destroying Israel or of uniting themselves.

There was, he suggested, a third possibility. Rather than revise their thinking, the Arabs might change the situation. Saddam claimed that Arab pessimism—not Arab nationalism—was the delusion. If Arabs united behind a strong leader, they could still defeat the United States and Israel, or at least hold their ground against the alleged U.S. and Zionist conspiracies to destroy them. Having earlier appointed himself the Arab world's protector from Iran, Saddam now nominated himself as leader in the war he was declaring on America and Israel. Saddam's unconventional weapons would replace the lost Soviet nuclear umbrella by making Iraq the Arabs' own superpower.

Saddam demanded the withdrawal of U.S. naval forces from the Gulf, even though the American military presence there had declined from the peak reached during the Iran-Iraq war. Behind nationalist slogans were imperialist ambitions. Just as Iran had called for a Gulf controlled by Muslims in order to remove Western forces blocking its hegemony, Iraq now wanted to remove any Western military presence so as to eliminate the outside protectors of the monarchies he wanted to dominate.[2]

Insisting that the Arabs not give up the idea of destroying Israel, Saddam claimed that Iraq's triumph over Iran "on the eastern front" and the Palestinian intifada showed the "reconquest of Palestine" to be possible. The Baghdad regime was building missile launchers in western Iraq to hit Israel. If American military experts were convinced, as the *Boston Globe* reported, that Iraq's progress meant

"Israel's supremacy in the Middle East will not continue much longer," it is not surprising that Saddam had the same idea.[3]

The United States, he claimed, was far weaker than it seemed, because it feared military confrontation and losses. America had shown "signs of fatigue, frustration, and hesitation" in Vietnam and Iran and had quickly run away from Lebanon when terrorist suicide bombers inflicted heavy losses on its marine peacekeeping force in Beirut in 1983. He believed that if Iraq acted boldly, America would not dare to confront it. The fact that the United States did not react to the threats made in Saddam's February speech only intensified his belief in this theory.

These Iraqi declarations were not merely a challenge to the United States; they were a dare to the Arab world. Would the Arab leaders and peoples heed recent history's unpleasant lessons, or would the old ideas and behavior patterns overwhelm common sense and carry them into another adventure? The apparent result was just as Saddam had hoped: The Arab masses cheered, the Arab governments—whatever their private contempt and fear of Iraq—jumped on his bandwagon or at least got out of its way. The United States stayed out of his way.

Both events and weak Western reactions confirmed Saddam's view that his strategy was working. In September 1989, Farhad Bazoft, a thirty-one-year-old, Iran-born correspondent of the British newspaper the *Observer,* arrived in Baghdad at the government's invitation. He had visited Iraq before, and apparently the regime had liked the stories he had written. But after the authorities refused to grant him permission to investigate reports of a huge explosion at an Iraqi weapons plant the previous month, Bazoft went to the site, making no secret of what he was doing. There he took pictures, collected soil samples, and drew a sketch.

A few days later, he was arrested along with a British nurse who had driven him there. Charged with espionage and probably tortured, Bazoft eventually gave a televised "confession," saying he was a spy for Israel and Britain. When the British government denied the accusation and asked mercy for Bazoft, the Iraqi regime organized massive demonstrations outside the British embassy in Baghdad. Britain recalled its ambassador and expelled six Iraqi military trainees but imposed no economic sanctions. Despite warnings from Britain that killing Bazoft would damage bilateral relations, Iraq executed him in March 1990. The nurse was released from prison in July.

To the United States and Britain, the Bazoft case was a question of human rights and press freedom. For Iraq's government, however, this was a symbolic test of wills between the Arabs and the West, by which Iraq showed itself to be defiantly independent and stronger than its foes. Iraq's information minister proudly rejoiced. British prime minister Margaret Thatcher, he declared, "wanted Bazoft alive. We gave her the body." Saddam portrayed the deed as an anti-imperialist victory. Westerners, he said, "apparently still cherish the days of the sahib." Times had changed, he warned. Iraq's dictator was proud of his defiance and, like Khomeini, saw it as proving his country's independence from the West. In response to Western coverage of Iraqi human rights violations, Baghdad television ran a program on scandals in Britain, claiming that Prince Charles danced at "cheap night clubs, frequented by drug addicts and alcoholics."[4]

King Hussein supported Saddam's claim that the West was conspiring against him. In response to its complaints about the execution, the king replied, "There has been a concentrated attack on Iraq for a long period of time without any reason to justify it." The Arab League and the Arab Cooperation Council also defended Iraq and condemned Western criticism, feeding Saddam's view that confrontation with the West was the best route to leadership over the Arabs.[5]

Now Saddam escalated the conflict another notch. On April 2, with no apparent provocation, he threatened to destroy half of Israel with chemical weapons if it attacked any Arab state. Baghdad would decide what constituted such an attack. Saddam's rabidly anti-Israel stance was partly demagoguery—since condemning that country verbally was popular in the Arab world—and partly due to the fact that Israel was the strongest local power opposing his ambition to lead and unite the Arab world. Most immediately, Israel was the only state likely to act militarily against his growing power and nonconventional arms arsenal.

In this context, Saddam claimed that U.S. and British media charges that Baghdad was developing unconventional weapons— something Iraq itself bragged about—was a plot to give Israel an excuse to attack. Whether Saddam really—and wrongly—believed that Israel was about to attack him to destroy Iraq's chemical and nuclear weapons or was simply stirring hysteria in order to rally Arab support, his threat was still another test of whether the United States would respond.

U.S. policy again failed that test, putting the emphasis on soothing rather than deterring Iraq. President Bush's only response was a routine disapproval of Saddam's statement. Later in April, with Bazoft barely in the grave and Saddam's threats still hanging in the air, five U.S. senators visited Saddam in the northern city of Mosul, presented him with a conciliatory letter from Bush, and left favorably impressed.

Iraq released a transcript of the encounter, which none of the Americans present contested, showing that not one critical word was spoken at the meeting. The group was led by Senate Republican leader Robert Dole, who had earlier called for reducing U.S. aid to

Israel while opposing sanctions against Iraq. Dole recalled his own condemnation of Israel's 1981 attack on Iraq's nuclear reactor. He joined the dictator in attacking the U.S. media, assuring him— inaccurately—that a Voice of America radio commentator had been fired for supposedly comparing Saddam's rule to that of the fallen dictator in Romania.

"I realize you are a strong and an intelligent man and that you want peace," said Senator Howard Metzenbaum, the senior Democrat there. "If a certain shift in your thinking makes you concentrate on the peace we need in the Middle East, there will be no other leader in the Middle East who can be compared with you." The senators were, of course, trying to foster good relations with Saddam, but this flattery implied that America might even support Iraq as the Gulf's dominant power.

Ignoring Saddam's threats to Israel and the United States, Dole told the Senate back in Washington, "We came away feeling that this is an intelligent man," whose long war with Iran and large debts inclined him toward seeking peace. "There might be a chance," Dole told reporters, "to bring this guy around" to a moderate, pro-American position.

Dole's stance was in line with the president's policy of avoiding friction with Iraq. Assistant Secretary of State John Kelly said the administration wanted a "trial period to see whether there's potential for improvements in their behavior and in our relationship." Another senior official said in April 1990 that Saddam "is more moderate than he was in the past and there is a good chance he will be more moderate in the future."

The other Arab states made the same error about Iraq. Saddam made a rousing anti-American speech at the May 1990 Arab summit meeting, held, appropriately, in Baghdad. Iraq's positions dominated the conference, and the final resolution supported Saddam's political line, taking a far more extreme position than the previous year's summit. It denounced U.S. Middle East policy while endorsing Iraq's "right to take all necessary measures to guarantee and defend Iraq's national security." Once again, there was no reaction by the Bush administration.

The result was a vicious circle. Intimidated and somewhat carried away by Saddam's promises, the Arab states supported Baghdad, exacerbating Iraq's already overconfident stance. Since the United States was not countering Saddam, the Arab states would not stick their necks out to confront him. At the same time, this Arab support discouraged Washington from opposing Saddam, in part because of the U.S. propensity to believe that Arabs and Muslims would unite around him against an outside threat. The Americans, Saudis, Kuwaitis, Jordanians, and Egyptians all failed to realize that appeasement was the strategy most likely to bring a dangerous confrontation.[6]

In July 1990, Iraq escalated the region's tension even further. Now, however, Saddam shifted his target from Israel, which could defend itself, to Kuwait, a far richer but a weaker victim. Saddam falsely insisted that Kuwait was demanding repayment for its wartime loans, conveniently forgetting his own regime's frequent statements of gratitude for these "gifts." For example, Subhi Frangoul, governor of Iraq's central bank, had recently thanked Saudi Arabia and Kuwait for the money as "a grant from our Arab friends."[7] The Gulf monarchies kept these transactions listed as loans on their account books only to make their own financial situation look better.

Another serious accusation was Saddam's claim that Kuwait and the United Arab Emirates were cheating on their OPEC oil export quotas, thus driving down prices. This charge was accurate, though Iraq itself exceeded these quotas when possible and Saddam's estimate that these actions cost Iraq $14 billion in lost sales and revenue was a great exaggeration. He also insisted that Kuwait was stealing oil from Iraq's Rumayla field, near their common border.

The motive for these claims was clear: Saddam wanted to make more money for reconstruction and regain Iraqi oil markets lost when production levels plummeted during the Iran-Iraq war. Iraq needed high petroleum prices to finance its military machine and its economic development. Yet the high cost of oil encouraged consumers to conserve, switch to alternative fuels, and find new sources of supply.

Saudi and Kuwaiti oil interests conflicted with those of Iraq. Their large oil and financial reserves, coupled with a smaller population, gave them an incentive to think in the long term about production and pricing. Thus the Saudis periodically raised production to keep prices lower, in order to protect their market share and discourage consumers from reducing imports.

The two monarchies were also greedy. No matter how much they earned, the Kuwaitis and the Saudis wanted more money for themselves, and they, too, were eager to make up for the profits lost during the eight-year Iran-Iraq war. Iraq's very dependency on financial support from these monarchies made Saddam nervous, and he labeled their behavior a plot to subvert him.

Saddam was also using his charges against the Gulf Arab monarchies to achieve strategic control over them. He demanded that Kuwait turn over to him Warbah and Bubiyan islands. Iraq had no particular historical claim to this territory, but possessing it would afford more access to the Gulf and a military advantage in the event of a renewed war with Iran. Unfortunately for Kuwait, handing over this land to Iraq would also let Baghdad control the approaches to Kuwait's harbor, while Iran would seek revenge against Kuwait for so strengthening its enemy. Kuwait had no intention of ceding any territory.

Arab diplomatic efforts were quickly mounted to defuse this dangerous situation. The Saudis and Kuwaitis asked for international arbitration and put their forces on alert. Egypt's president Mubarak tried to mediate. At an emergency OPEC meeting in Geneva on July 26, Kuwait and the United Arab Emirates yielded to one of Iraq's demands by accepting lower oil export quotas for themselves. When the Iraqis assured everyone they had no intention of invading Kuwait, their neighbors relaxed and demobilized. It was easy for them to conclude that—as had happened several times before—Iraq's threats were just intended to extort some money from Kuwait.

While these events were going on, the Bush administration saw its job as demonstrating to Saddam that America was not conspiring with Kuwait against him. Such behavior was in line with the American myth that the United States had relatively little leverage in the region, that U.S. criticism would make the Arabs rally behind Iraq, and that concessions would make dictators less radical. In practice, however, Saddam took the fact that no one was going to stop him as an invitation for aggression.

The State Department put its trust in an "Arab solution," merely restating the traditional U.S. position favoring freedom for navigation and oil exports in the Gulf. A Pentagon official, telling the House Foreign Affairs Committee that Saddam wanted peace and quiet to focus on economic reconstruction, blamed Israel for not making more concessions to the Arabs and thus allegedly forcing Baghdad into an "adversarial" position. The United States should move closer to Iraq, not try to isolate it, said the expert, since reducing U.S. trade and aid for Iraq would shut off their dialogue.[8]

Why didn't the United States pressure Iraq? One reason was a bureaucratic disinclination to admit that the current policy was wrong and to change course. There was some talk in the administration about reevaluating U.S. policy toward Iraq and considering whether Washington should take a tougher stand. But this never happened. Since government policy had put the United States on Iraq's "side" during the 1980s, officials identified Baghdad as a friend and sought excuses for its actions. They were convinced that Iraq would maintain a moderate course, and few were willing to revise their conceptions. Seeing their task as maintaining good, confrontation-free relations with the Arab world, they wanted to avoid friction.

The two key government officials dealing with this issue were largely amateurs in the Middle East. Assistant Secretary Kelly's only experience in the region had been to serve a short time as ambassador to Lebanon during the Reagan administration. In 1987, Secretary of State Shultz had publicly reprimanded Kelly for helping the White House implement its arms-for-hostages deal behind the State Department's back. This violation of discipline, however, made Kelly seem a White House loyalist and helped him gain the much-coveted promotion. In short, Kelly's presence in the assistant secretary post was a triumph of political influence over expertise.

His counterpart, National Security Council staffer Richard Haass, also knew relatively little about the area and was well known for his disinclination to listen to others' opinions. Haass was recognized as a strong supporter of the pro-Iraq policy and, according to other officials, rejected the idea that Iraq might invade Kuwait up until the moment when Saddam's army crossed the border. In short, the administration's team on the Gulf was slow to react and loath to rethink policy.

This, then, was the context of a meeting between U.S. ambassador April Glaspie and Saddam in Baghdad on July 25. The dictator had called in Glaspie on short notice for the purpose—unbeknownst to her at the time—of trying to determine how the United States might respond to an invasion of Kuwait. "Yours is a society that cannot accept 10,000 dead in one battle," Saddam told Glaspie. He added the veiled threat that America was vulnerable to terrorist attacks. Saddam made the remarkable claim that having conspired with Iran against Iraq, the United States was now backing Kuwait in an economic war against him, stealing Baghdad's oil income by overproduction and low prices. He warned that any U.S. opposition would be met by Iraqi "pressure and force."[9]

To placate the dictator, Glaspie correctly pointed out that the Bush administration had rejected the idea of sanctions against Iraq for violating human rights or threatening Israel or Kuwait. The U.S. government wanted good relations, not conflict. As part of her flattery, Glaspie called an ABC television program that had criticized Saddam "cheap and unjust. . . . I am pleased that you add your voice to the diplomats who stand up to the media." She praised Saddam's "extraordinary efforts" at reconstruction. "I know you need funds." She also told him that the United States would not intervene against Iraq: "We have no opinion on the Arab-Arab conflicts like your border disagreement with Kuwait. . . . [Secretary of State] James Baker has directed our official spokesman to emphasize this instruction."

The dilemma was not that Saddam disbelieved Glaspie—after all, she was merely confirming what he already believed—but that her reassurances convinced him there was nothing to fear from Washington if he went ahead and invaded Kuwait. Glaspie later defended herself by saying that she had warned Saddam the United States wanted the dispute settled peacefully and the sovereignty of all its friends in the area maintained. No one ever thought, she would explain, that Saddam would be so "stupid" as to invade Kuwait.[10]

The problem, however, was not Saddam's inadequacy as a student but the U.S. government's incompetence as his teacher. Saddam knew Kuwait could not defend itself; he doubted the United States would defend it. Although Baker and Kelly would later protect their own careers by making her the scapegoat, Glaspie had accurately conveyed U.S. policy to Saddam. Her comments were in line with all the State Department's statements and positions. In fact, the Glaspie-Saddam encounter was the culmination of all the myths that had led Americans to misunderstand the region for fifty years.

Even after this fateful meeting and on the eve of Saddam's invasion of Kuwait, the White House still opposed sanctions against Iraq. At the same moment, it was holding up a guarantee for $400 million in loan guarantees to Israel, a U.S. ally, for building homes for Soviet Jewish immigrants. In Israel's case, it tried to use aid as leverage to discourage settlements in the occupied territories.

Yet the same administration rejected any idea of pressuring Iraq over human rights or its anti-American and aggressive threats. President Bush advocated continued Commodity Credit Corporation and Export-Import Bank aid to Iraq although he knew Baghdad had broken U.S. law in regard to these programs. The administration also tried unsuccessfully to block a July 27 Senate vote to cut agricultural credits for Baghdad. Congressional calls for sanctions against Iraq angered the White House as "interference" in its prerogatives, and critics of the Iraq policy were dismissed as being part of a pro-Israel lobby. Unfortunately, the White House was the pro-Iraq lobby.

Glaspie's reports encouraged a misunderstanding of Saddam. In a secret cable to Baker on July 15, for example, she wrote: "We continue to believe that the [Iraqi government] is sending a signal to us and the Iraqi people that despite the strains in the relationship and the steady stream of harsh criticism of U.S. policies, Saddam is maintaining a dialogue with President Bush and wants good bilateral relations."[11]

Indeed, if the situation were not so tragic, Glaspie's views would furnish excellent material for satire.[12] In congressional testimony a year later, she would describe Saddam as having "felt stymied" by the meeting and claim that "he surrendered" by insisting he would not use violence to resolve the Kuwait problem. This was a clever maneuver, not a retreat. Glaspie railed at Saddam's "dishonesty," "deliberate deception on a major scale," and "zero on credibility." Yet misdirection is a vital part of international relations. It would be ridiculous, for example, to plead that the dishonesty of Germany and Japan before World War II excused those who should have doubted those governments' integrity.

Glaspie's approach, and that of the Bush administration, rejected any use of leverage on Iraq. She apologized for a Voice of America broadcast denouncing police states because Iraq found it threatening, though Baghdad was daily attacking and threatening the United States. The ambassador argued that sanctions should not be put on Iraq because keeping the dialogue open was worthwhile. Yet the only success she could claim for U.S. policy was that it helped end Iraq's use of chemical weapons against the Kurds—an assault halted because it had already served its purpose—and obtained compensation for relatives of American servicemen killed on the *Stark*, though Iraq never cooperated in the investigation of why one of its pilots attacked the ship in the first place.

This kind of argument would prompt Senator John Kerry, a Democrat from Massachusetts, to ask Glaspie whether the policy merely showed that the United States was a "paper tiger." Glaspie did not seem to understand this problem. "We tried," she said, "to show the Iraqis that there would be benefit to them if they changed their ways." But the administration did not try to show Iraq that there would be penalties if Baghdad persisted in its behavior. Communications lines were kept open at a high cost, but only a message of American pliancy was sent over them. Benefits were provided for Iraq to give the United States leverage, but then were not withdrawn lest this seem unfriendly. In the end, the United States did almost everything Iraq wanted, and Baghdad still acted in an anti-American way and invaded Kuwait.

As CIA and military intelligence reports in late July warned about the imminent danger of an Iraqi invasion of Kuwait, higher-ranking officials refused to believe them. The president did not have to know in advance that Iraq was going to commit aggression to realize that he should act to deter Baghdad. But only on July 31, after confirmed reports of an Iraqi buildup on the border of 100,000 men—five times the size of Kuwait's army—did the administration even start to react. That day, Assistant Secretary of State Kelly told the House Foreign Affairs Committee of "increasing concern" over Iraqi activities. But by then it was too late.

When Iraqi and Kuwaiti delegations met in Saudi Arabia to try to resolve their disputes that same day, the talks broke down after two hours. Saddam ordered his army across the border. On the night of August 1–2, 1990, Iraqi troops invaded Kuwait and quickly overran the country.

There was no effective resistance. Kuwait's emir and crown prince, almost all the royal family, and a large portion of the army fled into Saudi Arabia. Eventually, 400,000 Kuwaitis would be exiled temporarily from their homeland; hundreds of thousands of foreign workers fled, most of them never to return. The Iraqis closed the ports and the airport, invoked a curfew, and cut off communication to the outside world. There were mass roundups of Kuwaiti civilians, and Iraq's army pushed on toward the border with Saudi Arabia.

Almost immediately, Saddam announced that he planned to withdraw in forty-eight hours. Wishful thinking again rose among the American experts, some of whom predicted that Iraq would pull out of Kuwait rather than battle America. But they did not realize how low U.S. credibility was in Baghdad, partly as a result of their own statements and writings over the years. Saddam made no move to leave, and nothing more was heard of this supposed plan. He instead announced within a few days that the occupation was irreversible. Before the month was out, Iraq had annexed Kuwait as its nineteenth province.

Six factors had shaped Iraq's policy on this road to crisis. First, Saddam badly needed money. This was his most easily comprehensible motive in Western terms. The famed American bank robber Willie Sutton had a simple explanation for the reason he held up banks: "That's where the money is." For Saddam, Kuwait was the neighborhood vault. But the financial aspect was far from a sole or sufficient reason for invading Kuwait. If booty had been his only object, Saddam would have found it easier and safer to continue collecting tribute from that country.

Second, Iraq's leader claimed to believe that everyone was planning to undermine him: democratic enemies (the United States and Israel), Arab moderate allies (Saudi Arabia and Kuwait), and radical rivals (Syria and Iran) alike. Thus he followed the old strategy of a paranoid toward purported enemies: to get them before they got him. Yet the dictator did not entirely believe his own propaganda. On the contrary, if Saddam had felt the danger to him was greater, he would not have been so adventurous. It was the lack of Arab or American opposition—not his fear of it—that prompted the dictator to attack. Moreover, the fact that Saddam was wrong in believing himself besieged did not mean that the United States could talk him out of this delusion by appeasement.

Third, Saddam's fundamental, longer-term motive was his desire to dominate the Gulf and the Middle East, to become the savior whom Arab ideology had prophesied and Arab politics had sought for so many decades. In this context, invading Kuwait was not a violation of the Western principle of national sovereignty but a fulfillment of Arab nationalist duty. Baghdad's first priority was not to obtain money or defend itself but rather to take advantage of an obvious opportunity to fulfill its ambition.

Fourth, the Iraqi dictator expected that a desperate Arab world and its masses would rally behind him. His message was that the Arabs' accumulation of defeats meant not that they should rethink their whole worldview but rather that they should strive harder to achieve their goals. Perhaps his yes-men misinformed Saddam on the situation in the Arab world, and perhaps he, too, thoroughly believed his own ideology. But only his fellow Arab rulers had convinced Saddam that they might follow him. Once the other regimes decided to oppose Iraq they would easily hold their own subjects in line.

Fifth, at the same time that Saddam tried to wrap himself in the banner of Arab nationalism, he was continuing his policy of promoting Iraqi nationalism. Seizing Kuwait would provide booty and glory that could be shared among his subjects and would give his country increased coherence in the face of its economic and communal problems. It was no accident that Saddam appointed a Kurdish military commander and a Shia defense minister at the moment of crisis.

Sixth, the lack of opposition let Saddam conclude that an unchallenged takeover of Kuwait would be an easy, painless resolution to all his domestic problems and regional ambitions. Without this last assurance, provided by U.S. and Arab appeasement, he would not have carried out his aggression. Iraq was not afraid to invade Kuwait for the same reason it had been ready to attack Iran almost exactly ten years earlier: there was no concern about America's protecting the target.[13]

The greatest miracle of the Kuwait crisis, then, was that it became a defeat for Iraq. Under slightly different circumstances, Saddam might have succeeded in keeping Kuwait and would have gone down in history as a conqueror, not a fool. If he had handled the crisis better, his influence would have spread like wildfire in a region where popularity is ignited by power. As always, there would be those in America and the Arab world who would put a priority on avoiding trouble, rationalizing the unprovoked conquest in hope of gaining a share of the loot or avoiding the dictator's vengeance. Saddam made this hard for anyone to do. He offered so little and the material odds against him were so great as to force even those who preferred appeasement to resist.

By being more patient before launching an attack, Saddam might have first consolidated an anti-Israel Arab coalition, then waited until Iraq obtained more powerful arms—including atomic bombs—before seizing Kuwait. In that case, other local states would not have voiced any opposition. Had Saddam avoided overintimidating the Saudis—by using fewer soldiers, keeping them away from the Kuwait-Saudi border, and inviting the Saudis to inspect his forces—they would have been less likely to panic and invite in the Americans.

Saddam also neglected other steps that might have brought him success. If he had offered—even better, begun—to share the loot with other Arab states, such as Egypt or Syria, they may have hesitated to oppose him. If he had used the invasion as diplomatic leverage, quickly starting talks with the Saudis and Kuwaitis to get money or territory, he could have made a deal.

Indeed, according to the myths governing the thinking of American experts and many officials, Saddam should have won, since they expected the Arabs to unite against an infidel, pro-Israel United States. Their theories said the Arabs and Muslims would stick together, gladly allowing themselves to be looted in the name of Arab nationalism, Islam, and the Palestinian cause. Instead, most of the Arab states—except for Jordan, which hoped to share in the booty—and citizens acted like normal people and countries anywhere. They yelled for help.

Saddam made his neighbors an offer they had to refuse. If the Arab world joined America in opposing Iraq's invasion, said the Egyptian newspaper *al-Akhbar,* "it will be punishing a sister Arab state it is supposed to support. By doing nothing, it will be . . . approving the supremacy of jungle law in international and inter-Arab relations." A Kuwaiti activist, jailed earlier in 1990 by that regime, reflected this disorientation by complaining that Iraq's army "headed toward its brethren rather than its enemies. Instead of advancing nearer to Jerusalem, it headed in the opposite direction." America is our enemy, he continued, but there was no other choice. Purporting to activate Arab aspirations, Saddam simply acted as an imperialist. Kuwait did not want to be liberated by Saddam. When he held the knife to the throat of Kuwait and Saudi Arabia, the victims called the much-maligned American cop to save them.

Having protected Saudi Arabia and Kuwait from Iran in the 1980s, the United States now faced the task of saving them from Iraq. Otherwise, Saddam—as master of 20 percent of OPEC's production—might be able to dictate oil prices and production levels, use his income to build more and more weapons, subvert other Arab governments, and drive U.S. interests from the Gulf.

An Iraqi success in mobilizing and radicalizing the Arab world would also have reheated the Arab-Israeli conflict. The result might have been an Iraqi attack on Israel or a threat so serious as to precipitate a preemptive Israeli attack against the nuclear, missile, and poison gas installations with which Saddam threatened its extinction.

If the crisis over Kuwait had been "only" a major upheaval in Middle East politics, that would have been sufficient to secure its importance. Yet the issue was also the first test of what kind of world order could emerge at the end of the cold war. While the nature of U.S. interests made a strong reaction seem inescapable, it was not inevitable that the American government would fight to stop Saddam.

This was, however, the kind of crisis Americans could most easily understand, a seeming return to earlier cases where appeasement had endangered a world facing Nazi Germany or Soviet Communist aggressors. By taking leadership in this enterprise, America had a chance to establish the kind of united front that had not formed to stop German aggression before World War II. And the timing was right, since the United States was neither tied down elsewhere in the world nor facing the USSR in a superpower confrontation. Still, a president other than Bush or a slightly different chain of events might have let Saddam be the victor, leaving future historians to record Iraq's invasion of Kuwait as the start of a new era of global instability and massive bloodshed.

CHAPTER TEN

BE MY BROTHER OR I'LL KILL YOU:
AUGUST–DECEMBER 1990

*Poor hungry Hojja wanted to go to a fancy banquet but had
no invitation. So he borrowed a good cloak, making him appear
rich. Thinking him important, the guards let Hojja in. Out of
gratitude, he pushed the garment's sleeve toward the food,
saying, "Eat, my cloak, eat."*

—*Middle Eastern folktale*

Iraq's seizure of Kuwait was one of the most remarkable events
in Middle East history, equivalent to the 1941 Japanese attack on
Pearl Harbor in its shocking suddenness. Saudi King Fahd called
the invasion "the most horrible aggression the Arab nation has
known in its modern history."[1]

Within hours of the occupation, President Bush condemned the
assault and demanded immediate Iraqi withdrawal. The United
States and the European Common Market froze all Iraqi and Kuwaiti assets and imposed sanctions on Iraq. The USSR, Iraq's main
arms supplier, invoked its own embargo. The Arab League, in a
meeting Iraq refused to attend, voted 14 to 5 to condemn the invasion
and demanded that Iraq pull out.

As three Iraqi divisions armed with tanks and missiles moved toward the Kuwait-Saudi border, a U.S. mission led by Deputy National Security Adviser Robert Gates was dispatched to Saudi Arabia. The Americans showed Saudi leaders satellite photos proving that Iraq was reinforcing its army and might invade their country. In a total reversal of all previous Saudi policy, King Fahd asked for U.S. combat troops to protect his kingdom.

Iraq's own behavior made the Saudis conclude logically that they were in danger. In the occupation's opening days, there had been several small Iraqi incursions of up to five miles into Saudi territory. The government in Riyadh knew that Iraqi forces could seize its oil fields in a few hours and the whole country in a few days. Since Iraq had lied about plans to attack Kuwait, it might also be dissembling about attacking Saudi Arabia. Western intelligence analysts concluded that Saddam was not planning a further advance. Yet the Saudis would retain precious little independence if Saddam kept Kuwait, and they could expect to be next on the list when Iraq finished gobbling their neighbor.[2]

Contrary to Saddam's expectations, the immediate Saudi reaction—once U.S. support inspired courage by ensuring protection—was rage more than fear. Everyone knew, as a Saudi newspaper put it, that the United States was the only country able to counter Iraqi expansionism. The Saudi ambassador to the United States, Bandar ibn-Sultan, said that Saddam "lied to us and the world and, as a result, he has lost his credibility and we realized he has aggressive designs." Prince Khalid ibn-Sultan, commander of the Saudi armed forces, mused that Iraq must never have expected King Fahd to respond so quickly and decisively.[3]

President Bush immediately accepted Fahd's invitation to send in U.S. troops. Saudi Arabia's defense, Bush said on August 8, was a "vital U.S. interest," a diplomatic phrase meaning that the United States would go to war to preserve it. The president listed four main goals for U.S. policy: the defense of Saudi Arabia and the Gulf; the protection of American citizens there; the complete, immediate, unconditional withdrawal of all Iraqi troops from Kuwait; and the restoration of Kuwait's legitimate government. He refused to call for Saddam's overthrow, still hostage to the myth that Middle East dictators might best be convinced through compromise. Bush hoped that a deal, rather than pure intimidation, would secure Iraq's withdrawal. Later, he added that he would not be disappointed if Iraq's people got rid of the dictator, but only subsequently would it be clear how little the United States was prepared to help them do so.[4]

The president ordered a massive U.S. military airlift to Saudi Arabia, starting with F-15 fighter planes and the 82nd Airborne Division. It took months to move large numbers of troops and equipment to the Gulf, but plans that the Pentagon had been preparing for a decade were now implemented with remarkable efficiency. Within six weeks of the invasion, over 100,000 American military personnel had arrived in Saudi Arabia, to stay, said Secretary of Defense Richard Cheney, "as long as we're needed and until we are asked to leave." Bush also approved a quick $2.2 billion sale of twenty-four F-15 fighters, plus missiles, tanks, and antitank shells, to Riyadh.[5]

In addition, Saudi Arabia counterattacked Baghdad on the economic front by shutting down a large pipeline (1.5 million barrels a day) that carried Iraqi oil through Saudi territory to a Red Sea port. Turkey backed the emerging anti-Saddam coalition by closing the pipeline that took Iraq's petroleum (1.2 million barrels a day) across its land. Since 96 percent of Iraqi revenue came from oil exports—virtually all through these two routes—this was a serious blow against Baghdad's fiscal strength.[6]

Meanwhile, the Saudi position was supported at an August 10

Arab League meeting, which voted to condemn Iraq's annexation and decided to send a peacekeeping force to Saudi Arabia. Among the resolution's backers were Egypt, Syria, and the six Gulf monarchies; Iraq, Libya, the PLO, and Jordan were in the minority that refused to support it. The next day, Egyptian and Moroccan troops began landing in Saudi Arabia.

Historically, the Arab League's power had been stifled by the principle that all decisions must be unanimous. Iraq's aggression had shattered that rule, and now the Arab states adopted decisions by a majority vote. The anti-Saddam forces dominated the League and endorsed the UN-imposed sanctions against Iraq. King Hussein's pessimism reflected the division in the organization. "It could be our last summit," he said.

At the end of September, the League moved its offices back to its original headquarters in Cairo, abandoned to punish Egypt after Sadat's peace with Israel. The Arab League's secretary-general, Chadli Klibi, a Tunisian, and Ambassador to the UN Clovis Maksoud, a Lebanese national, both thought to be too sympathetic to Saddam, were forced to resign and were replaced by officials eager to carry out anti-Iraq measures.

There were now two blocs in the Arab world. Egypt, Saudi Arabia, Kuwait, the other Gulf monarchies, and Syria were in the anti-Iraq coalition; only Jordan, anti-Saudi Yemen, Sudan, and the PLO were left in the pro-Saddam camp. Saddam's Arab enemies were not eager to compromise with him. Meeting with President Bush in early September, Egyptian President Mubarak and King Fahd agreed not to negotiate with Iraq until its troops left Kuwait.

In Jordan, where many Western reporters were stationed to cover the crisis, the regime allowed and encouraged the people to cheer Iraq. Stories of tens of thousands of Jordanians "volunteering" to fight for Saddam impressed the West, but such coffeehouse heroes never turned up on the front lines of battle. An ABC journalist opined from Amman in August, "I think there is no doubt that the whole Arab population will be side to side with Saddam, even if it has to be suicide."[7] This was not a reliable indicator of Arab views, nor did it take into account the fact that in dictatorships, the rulers—not the masses—make decisions and, by repression and propaganda, shape public opinion. Iraqis questioned in Baghdad supported Saddam; Syrians queried in Damascus backed their government's anti-Iraq policy.

An average American—or a politician unfamiliar with the region—might be astonished that any Arabs at all supported Iraq, so obviously an aggressor against a fellow Arab state. But the real story was how few Arabs and Arab states supported Saddam, far fewer than Western experts predicted or Baghdad expected. In the context of Arab politics, it was much more impressive that rulers would dare call in non-Arab, non-Muslim U.S. forces and send troops of their own to fight Iraq, a fellow Arab state, under an American military commander.

Saddam tried three kinds of appeal to convince the Arabs to support him, based on what were supposedly their most firmly held, basic beliefs: Pan-Arab nationalism, Islam, and antagonism toward Israel. All of these efforts failed.

Contrary to Pan-Arab doctrine, most Arabs genuinely identified with their own "local" state. By breaking the unwritten rule of Arab politics—that Arab states might revile and subvert, but never invade, each other—Saddam freed the Kuwaitis, Saudis, and Egyptians to fight him as well. Arab commentators were quick to point out that Saddam seized Kuwait's loot for Iraq's benefit; Saudi Arabia called for U.S. help to save its own wealth; and Egypt and Syria acted in their own national interests to oppose Baghdad's aggression, since an Iraqi monopoly on Kuwait's wealth endangered their own independence and robbed them of aid. Iraq's talk about redistributing Kuwaiti oil wealth was simply not credible.

In line with the usual American myth about Arab and Islamic solidarity, former navy secretary James Webb wrongly claimed that Egypt's regime was shaky because its resistance against Iraq brought criticism from others and would trigger "an internal backlash."[8] But Egyptians saw Iraq as a rival, not a brother. Egypt's government, its main opposition party (the Wafd), and most of the public would not support Iraq in its efforts to lead the Arab world against their own country's claim to that role. Egyptian Islamic fundamentalist groups like the Muslim Brotherhood were motivated less by patriotism than by the knowledge that the Saudis would stop financial subsidies if they supported Saddam.

Egypt had needed a decade to rebuild relations with the rich Gulf Arabs who had boycotted it for making peace with Israel. Now Egyptians did not want to stand by while Iraq annexed Kuwait and dominated Saudi Arabia, which would result in a renewed cutoff of aid and investment in Egypt. There was also bad blood between Iraq and Egypt on other issues. Iraq had mistreated hundreds of thousands of Egyptian workers there during the late 1980s. To keep the funds for itself, Iraq had ordered its banks not to send their savings home. Demobilized Iraqi soldiers rioted, murdering a thousand Egyptian workers who held jobs they wanted. In contrast, by joining the anti-Iraq coalition, Egypt received huge economic benefits. The United States, Gulf monarchies, and European states canceled about half, $25 billion, of Egypt's debts. Thus Cairo's part in the struggle against Saddam was built on secure foundations in government policy and public support.

Syria, too, had ample motivation for joining the coalition. The country was in bad economic shape and had no reliable allies or aid donors. The Damascus and Baghdad regimes had been enemies for many years. In Gulf War I, Syria had supported Iran against Iraq. If Saddam won in the Kuwait crisis, Syria was high on his list as a target for revenge. Syria was bogged down in Lebanon's endless civil war, and the cold war's end cost it the Soviet backing on which it was so dependent as a source of arms and strategic support.

The Kuwait crisis brought welcome relief to this dismal situation, giving Syria a chance to escape isolation and obtain large amounts of Saudi aid by supporting the coalition, which was already in its best interest. Syria had to do little to achieve these gains. It was not asked to make peace with Israel, reduce support for terrorism, or ease its control over Lebanon. Since the Syrian regime was so unpopular—especially among the Sunni majority—there was more sympathy for Saddam in Syria than in Egypt or Saudi Arabia. But the regime had no trouble keeping it under control.

Saddam's Islamic appeal fared no better than his use of Pan-Arab slogans. He could try to portray himself as an Islamic leader fighting Western infidels in order to gain the support of the religious Arab masses and the Islamic fundamentalist forces. But as Saudi ambassador Bandar ibn-Sultan put it in August, "You cannot call for a holy war if you're not holy yourself."[9]

The Saudi government mustered its own Islamic assets by inviting Muslim clerics to observe that the Islamic holy places were not being violated by U.S. or other foreign non-Muslim soldiers in the country. The most senior Egyptian cleric, Shaikh Jadd al-Haqq, issued a decree in August denouncing Saddam: "The tyrant has to be contained lest his tyranny spread."[10] Islamic fundamentalist groups knew that the price of supporting Saddam was the loss of Saudi financial aid.

Finally, the coalition's Arab members opposed calls to link the Gulf and Arab-Israeli conflicts, totally rejecting Baghdad's attempts to wave the anti-Israel banner. They knew that it would be impossible to obtain Iraq's withdrawal if Kuwait's future was subordinated to an issue that was still unresolved after a half century. And if the Arabs did make progress in their claims against Israel, Saddam would exploit any gain by taking credit for it. "We know very well," Israeli Prime Minister Yitzhak Shamir commented, "that Iraq's intention is to present the conflict as an Israeli-Arab conflict. [Saddam] can achieve this only by attacking Israel. So we . . . will not help Iraq realize its diabolical plan."[11]

The Kuwait crisis had a paradoxical effect on U.S.-Israel relations. On the one hand, it rescued these ties from a tense period of friction over the peace process. On the other hand, the close U.S.-Arab alignment worried Israel. Shamir was well received on a trip to Washington early in the Kuwait crisis, since the United States wanted his cooperation on that issue. The success of the visit, Shamir commented, was a miracle like that commemorated by the Jewish festival of Chanukah, when the lamp at the Temple in Jerusalem burned eight days on one day's supply of oil. An opposition member of Israel's parliament replied, "and it will last about as long."

The danger Israelis feared most was a diplomatic settlement that would leave Saddam's military machine intact, with Israel as an obvious future target. Israel itself might be pressured to make concessions—as many voices in the West and Arab world were urging—to appease Saddam.

There was much irony in this situation. First, Israel had been the first to warn the West about Saddam. The United States and Europe had sharply criticized it for destroying Iraq's nuclear reactor in 1981 and ignored or ridiculed its cautions about Saddam's aggressive intentions. Second, the Kuwait crisis had very little to do with the Arab-Israel conflict. Iraq invaded Kuwait for its own gain. Even the Saudis, Syrians, and Egyptians rejected linkage to that issue as an Iraqi plot to distract attention from Kuwait. Third, the Arab turn to America for help and protection demonstrated clearly that U.S. standing in the region had not been hurt by long support for Israel.

Bush asked Israel to keep a low profile, and it agreed. But this was insufficient, some experts warned, since the Arabs would allegedly find it hard to stay in the coalition because of the U.S.-Israel alliance. Their solution was to make a deal: that Iraq make concessions on Kuwait in exchange for Israel's giving up the West Bank and Gaza. They did not see that such a prospect would send Saddam's popularity soaring in the Arab world. The Bush administration correctly rejected this idea of linkage as undermining U.S. interests. Israel, which gained nothing by an Iraqi withdrawal from Kuwait, would not have jeopardized its security on behalf of Arab states at war with it. Even Saddam gave no real indication that he would leave Kuwait under such conditions.

Aside from Israel, Turkey and Iran, the other non-Arab states in the region, also opposed Saddam's effort to lead the area. Turkey's president, Turgut Ozal, volunteered for a leading role by beginning an anti-Iraq embargo in August, though this cost Turkey its lucrative Iraqi market and revenues from the Iraqi oil pipeline, made a powerful neighbor into an enemy, and risked embroilment in a war. Ozal was seeking to ensure Western strategic and financial aid since, with the cold war over, Turkey was no longer on the front line against Soviet expansionism. But another factor was his country's yearning for acceptance as part of the Western alliance, not only for commercial advantage but as a certificate of civilization. It was a proud moment for Ozal when, in a German television interview, he reproved that country for failing the West by not sending troops to the Gulf.

Turkey's defense and foreign ministers and its army chief of staff all resigned in October, complaining that Ozal had not consulted them on the Kuwait crisis. Thus, since Ozal's stand hardly represented a national consensus, a pillar of coalition strategy rested on a very narrow base of support. Still, Turkey's cooperation was indispensable in isolating Iraq.

Iran also observed the anti-Iraq embargo and, despite its own anti-Western rhetoric, did not lift a finger against the U.S. presence in the Gulf. From the Iranians' standpoint, anything bad that happened to Saddam was good. Tehran was eager to exploit Saddam's troubles. When Iraq offered it concessions, Iran agreed to turn their cease-fire into a peace agreement, on terms favoring its interests. Iraq withdrew from disputed border areas and accepted the prewar boundaries. This accord allowed Iraqi troops to move from the Iranian border to the Kuwait front. Yet the cost to Saddam was high: the surrender of all his material gains from the Iran-Iraq war.

With such broad-based anti-Iraq support, the United Nations passed a series of resolutions that became the coalition's legal basis and operational guidelines. In August, Security Council Resolution 660 condemned the invasion, demanding immediate, unconditional Iraqi withdrawal. Resolution 661 banned trade to Iraq, and Resolution 662 rejected Iraq's annexation of Kuwait. The economic noose around Iraq was tightened in September by UN Resolutions 666 and 670. The only permissible exports to Iraq would be medical supplies or food shipments approved by the UN and distributed by international agencies. Economic sanctions were so effective and universal that even Switzerland accepted the justice of the cause and joined an embargo for the first time in its history. Iraq's imports, about 75 percent of its food calories, and exports—mainly oil—were effectively stopped.

The embargo against Iraqi and Kuwaiti oil caused a loss of four to five million barrels a day in the world market, about 9 percent of total production. OPEC, especially the Saudis, boosted exports to make up for the loss and increased its members' quotas. Combined with these steps, the already existing two- to three-million-barrel daily surplus prevented any shortfall.

For a time, though, fear sent prices steadily upward, from $18.00 a barrel on August 2 to $25.00 the day following the invasion and $28.00 on August 6. On August 24, prices hit $30.90, a nine-year high, then declined. Ironically, Saddam had achieved his goal of raising prices and income for oil-exporting states, though at Iraq's own additional expense. Saudi Arabia and others reaped a windfall profit, some of which paid for the international coalition's military expenses and economic losses.

As troops from many countries poured into Saudi Arabia, Baghdad responded with defiance, sabotaging its Arab friends' efforts to mediate an "Arab solution." Jordan was the most active of these allies, but that country was losing its standing in the West. After the invasion, Jordan trained Iraqi soldiers on U.S. equipment captured from Kuwait, repeated Iraqi propaganda, and gave Baghdad communications facilities. Despite its denials, Jordan never completely respected the embargo, as evidenced by ammunition cases later captured in Kuwait whose markings showed they were shipped from Amman during the crisis.

King Hussein went to America in mid-August to try to improve his worsening image and resolve the conflict, which threatened to crush Jordan between stronger powers. He came straight from seeing Saddam and others—Arafat and the presidents of Tunisia and Yemen—who opposed sanctions and the U.S. military presence. Shortly before King Hussein's meeting with President Bush in Maine, Saddam made such a strong personal attack on the president as to put Jordan's monarch in an embarrassing position. The king desperately tried to play on his relationship with Bush, whom he called "an old friend." Instead, an angry Bush demanded that Jordan close its ports to cargo bound for Iraq. To lock Amman into this position, Bush quickly announced the king's personal—and not altogether sincere—promise to enforce UN sanctions.

The UN had endorsed the stopping of ships by force if necessary to inspect them for contraband. The U.S. Navy and coalition forces began intercepting hundreds of ships in the Gulf and the Red Sea and looking for goods transported to or from Iraq. This procedure was called "interdiction" rather than a "blockade," since the latter was an act of war.[12]

The situation was rich in irony. To avoid war and secure Iraq's withdrawal, the United States had to convince Iraq of its readiness to attack. To keep Kuwait, Iraq had to convince the Americans of its fearlessness and the futility of fighting. It was a recipe for confrontation.

Nonetheless, many Americans—and an even higher proportion of Middle East experts—believed Saddam would decide to withdraw. Their political culture told them that problems were solvable and that leaders inevitably become moderate through experience. The same reasoning had convinced people that Iran wanted good relations with the United States in 1979, Syria sought a face-saving way out of Lebanon in 1983, Iran would quickly end its unwinnable war with Iraq in 1984, King Hussein was eager to enter peace talks with Israel in the mid-1980s, the PLO was ready to abandon terrorism and make a deal for a West Bank/Gaza state in 1988, and, most recently, Iraq wanted to rebuild from war and would not invade Kuwait in 1990.

In fact, Iraq felt that threatened confrontation was its best weapon to make the Americans back down, as Baghdad thought they had done in Vietnam, Iran, and Lebanon. If the Americans fought Iraq, said Saddam in August, "it will be a greater tragedy for you than

Vietnam. . . . The United States would no longer be number-one in the world. . . . God is on our side and Satan is on the side of America. Can Satan win over God?" An Iraqi newspaper extended the analogy: "The U.S. military establishment lost in Vietnam thousands of victims and the army's military reputation against local forces who were less in power and ability." Americans could not bear the desert climate or accept the heavy losses that would be inflicted by Iraqi forces, better armed and more experienced than the Vietnamese. Iraqi newspapers frequently cited articles in American publications, like *Time* magazine, that reported their country was powerful and feared by the West.[13]

Thus, by stalling long enough, Iraq would make the Saudis lose heart, seek a deal, and ask the Americans to leave. By the spring of 1991, the melting mountain snows would cause flooding downriver, making it harder to fight in southern Iraq. The Saudis would prefer not to have a huge U.S. military presence in their country during the Muslim holy month of Ramadan and the concurrent pilgrimage to Mecca, a sensitive time that brings heightened religious fervor and hundreds of thousands of foreign Muslim visitors.

In a speech broadcast on Iraqi television in September, President Bush had explained to Iraq's people, "The pain you are now suffering from is a direct result of the course of action chosen by your leadership." He assured them, "It is impossible for Iraq to succeed."[14] Unfortunately, Bush never convinced Saddam.

Meanwhile, to gain additional leverage against the West, Saddam kept thousands of Western residents in Kuwait as unwilling "guests," taking several hundred into custody and refusing to let the rest leave. These people could go, Saddam said, only if Bush withdrew U.S. troops from the Gulf and dropped the boycott against Iraq. Otherwise, they would be held as "shields" at Iraqi industrial and other facilities, to ensure that the coalition did not bomb them.

Iran's seemingly successful use of hostages a decade earlier in its conflict with America played some role in inspiring Iraq's move. This was also the kind of act, in its use of force and intimidation, that Saddam had often employed against domestic opponents and neighbors. Now, for the first time, he was employing it directly against the West.

There were initially some superficial signs that the ploy might work in undermining the anti-Saddam forces. Many ex-politicians and other figures who sought the public eye journeyed to Baghdad to free hostages from their respective countries: ex–West German chancellor Willy Brandt, former Japanese prime minister Yasuhiro Nakasone, Austrian president Kurt Waldheim, ex–Nicaraguan leader Daniel Ortega, ex-boxer Muhammad Ali, rightist French leader Jean-Marie Le Pen, leftist British politician Tony Benn, and former U.S. attorney general Ramsey Clark. Each supplicant strengthened Saddam's conviction that he was in the driver's seat, splitting the coalition and magnanimously handing out favors to those who pleased him.

But these were largely marginal or discredited people. The taking of hostages had no effect whatsoever on the coalition's growing pressure against Saddam. The most memorable symbol of the attempt to show Saddam's humane side at this time was a broadcast in which he met some hostages and patted the head of a small, terrified British boy. Dictators or terrorists may maneuver Western television into showing their pictures, but seeing such images can make viewers hate them more.

Saddam soon realized that rather than weakening the coalition and dissuading it from fighting Iraq, his holding their citizens was increasing his enemies' anger and further uniting them against him. Since Saddam was trying to forestall a Western military assault, the scheme had become counterproductive. By raising tensions, it made war more likely; keeping civilian prisoners who might need to be rescued could escalate rather than postpone the timing for an assault on Iraq.

Consequently, having proved his strength by seizing the foreigners, the Iraqi dictator tried to show his magnanimity by releasing most of the Western women and children in September and the remaining hostages in November and December. In a sense, Saddam's handling of this matter paralleled what he was trying to communicate in his broader handling of the Kuwait crisis: that he was a remorseless foe who would go to any lengths to win. By letting the hostages go, he thought to demonstrate his flexibility, a readiness to make a deal over Kuwait.

One reason Saddam's hostage taking did not bring him Western concessions was an important change in American public opinion. Popular disgust with the Reagan administration's covert arms-for-hostages deals in 1985 and 1986 had altered the mainstream view; Americans had begun to believe that the personal tragedy of such prisoners and their families should not dictate U.S. policy.

Saddam similarly miscalculated with his second effort to pressure his enemies: shutting down embassies in Kuwait. Since Baghdad claimed that Kuwait no longer existed as a country, it ordered all foreign missions there to close. Iraqi troops surrounded the offices and cut off their power and water. At the Scandinavian embassies, the Iraqis arrested Kuwaiti workers and threatened to kill them until the ambassadors agreed to leave.

The United States insisted that its embassy in Kuwait would stay open and retaliated by reducing the number of Iraqi diplomats in Washington from fifty-five to nineteen. There was worldwide condemnation when Iraqi soldiers escalated the battle by briefly invading the grounds of the Canadian, Belgian, and French missions in September. The French, sensitive on points of national honor,

responded by sending more troops to Saudi Arabia. The U.S. mission
held out as long as possible, using its swimming pool as a water
reservoir. Gradually, all foreign diplomats left Kuwait, but the coalition members still officially considered their missions to Kuwait
open. Western embassies continued to function in Baghdad until
the eve of the war, when most were closed. Again, the Iraqi hard-
line style, which had worked well between 1988 and 1991, brought
Western defiance rather than acquiescence.

Iraq's main effort in September and October was to split European
powers—especially the USSR and France—and Arab states from
the coalition. In the end, Paris and Moscow both cooperated with
U.S. policy, though their steadfastness may have owed as much to
Saddam's intransigence as to their own constancy. France's President
Mitterrand made occasional statements, including a major speech
at the UN, that seemed to undercut the U.S. position by suggesting
the coalition should offer Saddam a deal in which he could keep
part of Kuwait. Nonetheless, France sent one of the largest contin-
gents of troops into Saudi Arabia and stayed loyal to the coalition.

Moscow followed a similar pattern of hinting at a willingness to
appease Iraq. Yevgeny Primakov, the top Soviet diplomat on Middle
East issues, visited Baghdad and returned to Moscow claiming that
Iraq was softening its position. The USSR wanted to avoid war,
since thousands of Soviet technicians were still in Iraq and a U.S.
military victory so near its southern border would seem to swing
the balance of power too much in Washington's direction.[15]

Still, Gorbachev played an extremely useful role on behalf of
the coalition. He and Soviet foreign minister Eduard Shevardnadze
urged Iraq to come to its senses or face disaster. Shevardnadze preferred improving relations with the West and Israel to backing
radical Arab clients whom the faltering Soviet economy could no
longer afford to subsidize. Iraq already owed the USSR more than

$6 billion. It seemed far wiser to gain lucrative ties with Saudi Arabia, which reestablished relations as a reward for Moscow's support for the coalition.

U.S.-Soviet competition in the Middle East came to an end when, in September, Gorbachev met Bush to coordinate their stands. The Soviet leader quoted the American president as telling him that during the cold war, the United States thought the USSR had "no business" being in the region. Now Washington was accepting a Soviet role. But the United States had changed policy largely because it knew Moscow could do little to threaten U.S. interests there.

Reinforced by Western support, the Arab states also stood their ground, ignoring Saddam's threats. By mid-November, there was little interest when King Hassan of Morocco proposed an Arab summit to work out a compromise. The Arab coalition members condemned those who were supporting Saddam. A Kuwaiti writer asked the PLO and Jordan, "Why do you interfere in a matter that does not concern you?" The Saudi newspaper al-Yom castigated the coalition's critics for echoing Iraq's argument that its victims had "no right to seek the assistance of [their] friends when we decide to occupy you." In retaliation for Jordan's pro-Iraq stance, the Saudis expelled Jordanian diplomats, stopped oil supplies, and closed its borders to Jordan's trucks and products.[16]

The Palestinians were the only group displaying outright enthusiasm for Saddam. The intifada and its own diplomatic initiatives had given the PLO an opportunity to seek better relations with the United States and a negotiated settlement with Israel. Instead, the PLO began shifting from Egyptian to Iraqi patronage; escaping pressure from Cairo to be more moderate and make peace with Israel, it sided with a strongman who brandished missiles and chemical weapons and threatened to attack Israel. As part of this change, PLO offices were quietly transferred from Tunis to Baghdad, and most top-level PLO meetings were held in the Iraqi capital. An Iraq-sponsored PLO member group narrowed Arafat's options by launching a terrorist attack on Israel in May 1990. When Arafat refused to denounce the raid, Washington suspended the U.S.-PLO diplomatic dialogue.[17]

Frustrated at the intifada's inability to make any substantial political gains through militancy or negotiations, West Bank Palestinians issued statements, leaflets, and newspaper articles calling on Saddam to attack Israel. Even the most moderate leaders in the occupied territory succumbed to the temptation to hail Saddam as their idol. A thousand Palestinians marched in the West Bank town of Jenin, chanting, "Saddam, you hero, attack Israel with chemical weapons!" A few PLO leaders were horrified at the cost of their pro-Iraq stance, but Arafat firmly kept his boat steered toward the rocks. As an Arab writer put it, "God save this nation from its heroes!"

The Palestinians had not learned from their misplaced faith in Egypt's dictator Nasser in the 1950s and 1960s. Disappointed by Arafat's record in the 1970s and 1980s, they again sought a more stalwart defender. The PLO believed in Baghdad, said the Israeli dovish politician Yossi Sarid, as it once expected Moscow or Pan-Arab nationalism to be its savior, moving "from bed to bed," never comprehending that Arab leaders would merely use it, then toss it aside.[18]

In the Kuwait crisis, as during the Iran-Iraq war, the Arabs shoved the Palestinians to the back burner, contradicting in practice the claim that the Arab-Israel conflict was the central issue around which all else in the Middle East revolved. The PLO, said a Saudi newspaper in October, needed a new leadership, "who can speak to the world in a more civilized way and who oppose any kind of aggression and occupation, if it is by Israel, Iraq, Palestinian terrorists or others." A columnist for the Egyptian newspaper *al-Ahram* described Arafat as looking toward Saddam like "a child pleading for chocolate" or a "worshipper before his deity."[19]

The Gulf monarchies cut off aid to the PLO. In anger, Abbas Zaki, a leader of al-Fatah, the largest PLO member group, called the loss of Saudi contributions the price of "Palestinian dignity." "The presence of foreign forces has overshadowed, indeed wiped out, the justice of Kuwaiti demands," he said in September. The multinational forces had "2800 Jewish rabbis in their ranks," and Kuwait was now in Israel's camp. Arafat himself claimed in speeches and interviews that the United States was trying "to take control of the world's sources of oil" and said Israel was about to invade Jordan. Many, though by no means all, Palestinians in Kuwait collaborated with Iraq.

By November, the United States and the coalition could no longer postpone their own fateful decision. At this point, they had three options: to wait in hope that economic and diplomatic sanctions would force Iraq to yield, to make a deal with Saddam, or to fight a war.

The counsel of wishful thinking opted for a long siege. The embargo and boycott, wrote *New York Times* columnist Tom Wicker in November, were "squeezing Iraq" into a resolution, whereas war "would shatter the anti-Iraq coalition," since it was uncertain that Arab states could "lead their populations into full-scale war against a brother Arab nation."[20]

The facts pointed in the opposite direction: waiting was a greater danger to the coalition. Iraq produced enough food and possessed sufficient spare parts—coupled with some smuggling through Jordan—to let it survive easily for well over a year without being starved by the embargo. The economic shutdown was hurting Kuwaitis more than Iraqis, who had seized their food reserves. Kuwait was also suffering under an intense reign of terror. Iraq's policy was to plunder the country for loot and to destroy Kuwait so thoroughly that it could never be reconstituted. Thousands of Kuwaitis fled; many of those who remained were arrested, tortured, or killed. Anything movable, from money to cars to zoo animals, was carted off to Iraq.[21]

Domestic factors in both Saudi Arabia and the United States also gave the coalition a time limit. Within a few months, continued inaction would steadily weaken the coalition's hand. Saudi Arabia would conclude that the United States was bluffing, make its own peace with Baghdad, and ask the expeditionary force to leave. The war must start before March 1991, explained an Egyptian magazine, because once the Muslim holidays and the hot summer made military operations difficult, Iraq would stay in Kuwait for over a year and perhaps forever. In America too, the longer the crisis, the more anxious complaints there would be for the return of loved ones on military duty in the Gulf. There would surely be a growing insistence by the public, the media, and the Congress that the issue be quickly resolved.

The second option, to negotiate with Iraq, was a mixed blessing at best. As long as talks were being held, there would be tremendous pressure against the coalition's taking any military action, and Iraq could spin out talks endlessly. If Iraq was compelled to withdraw from Kuwait without gaining any advantage, it would be a defeat for Saddam. But if inducements were added to entice Saddam— like money, border changes, an Iraqi protectorate over Kuwait— the adventure would have seemed a triumph.

Iraq was not bargaining toughly; it was simply not bargaining at all. Baghdad could have used diplomacy to give U.S. public opinion and the allies hope for a peaceful solution, thus postponing war, dividing the coalition, and throwing U.S. policy into confusion. Instead, Saddam moved to blot out any memory of Kuwait: he renamed Kuwait City Qadhima; divided Iraq's new province into three sections; and split off part of the country into Iraq's Basra district, naming this new area after himself.[22]

In November, Iraqi information minister Latif Nassif al-Jassim announced that Kuwait no longer existed and therefore the world should forget about it. Hussein Kamil, Saddam's brother-in-law and right-hand man, added, "We have nothing to worry about from a war with the United States. The Americans are not prepared to pay the price of a war with Iraq." Saddam himself said Iraq would no more leave Kuwait than America or Britain might give up one of its cities.[23]

Clearly, these were not the actions of a man who intended to pull out soon. Contrary to the way Americans played the game, Iraq saw concessions as a prelude to more U.S. pressure, not as a way to achieve compromise. Saddam felt that surrendering would lose him more face at home and among the Arabs than would being defeated. Since the regime's legitimacy rested on intimidating its own subjects, an appearance of cowardice by Saddam could shatter the Iraqi public's awe and fear of the ruling elite, and hence its obedience. Such a loss of credibility could produce an internal revolt (as would happen after Iraq lost the war). Besides, Saddam believed that if he withdrew, America would be all the more likely to attack, not only to liberate Kuwait but to remove him from power entirely. This is what Saddam would have done if he had been Bush.

Why should Saddam accept a total defeat in advance of a battle he had some reason to hope would never take place? The cost of war in lives and resources did not frighten Saddam. He was a revolutionary, not an accountant. "When men offer their blood,"

Saddam said, "they want men to lead them, men who are also ready to offer their own blood." In this light, his blunder to stand firm becomes comprehensible.[24]

The coalition's only real alternative, then, was to prepare to use the troops from two dozen countries that were arriving in Saudi Arabia. These included the Egyptian 3d Armored Division; the U.S. 3d Armored Cavalry Regiment and 1st Cavalry Division, with some units of the 2d Armored Division; and the British 7th Armored Brigade. In early November, the United States and Saudi Arabia agreed that the U.S. commander, Lieutenant General Norman Schwarzkopf, would direct any offensive, while Saudi Lieutenant General Prince Khalid ibn-Sultan was in overall command of the joint forces. Both countries would have to approve an attack on Iraq. The Saudis were ready to do so. Saudi diplomats commented, "A mere Iraqi withdrawal is not enough." Since no one could guarantee that Iraq would not try again someday, the only solution was "a military strike that will close the page on Saddam Hussein's regime in its entirety."[25]

Meanwhile, President Bush had to mobilize four constituencies whose support he needed to take military action: his own administration, U.S. public opinion, Congress, and the international coalition. Saddam made this effort easier by offering no attractive compromise that might have split these groups.

Every president, of course, is the leader of his government. There is a story that John Kennedy, once a minority in his own cabinet, proclaimed after a vote, "One for and ten against—the ayes have it." Nonetheless, a chief executive must muster support throughout the government to ensure that his policy is implemented. When the Kuwait crisis began, Bush's lieutenants were divided over whether the United States should fight if Iraq did not withdraw. Defense Secretary Cheney was Bush's closest ally in urging a tough policy.

The other three top officials playing a leading role on the issue— Secretary of State James Baker, National Security Adviser Brent Scowcroft, and General Colin Powell, chairman of the Joint Chiefs of Staff—were far more doubtful.

Baker, an old associate of the president who lacked foreign policy experience, worried about European and Arab reluctance to be steadfast. A veteran dealmaker, he preferred a compromise even if it meant making concessions to Baghdad regarding the Gulf or the Arab-Israeli conflict. Scowcroft, a career military officer who had held many high-level foreign policy posts, had been an architect of the pro-Iraq policy before the invasion and also favored making a deal with Saddam. Within less than two months after the crisis started, though, both men concluded that there was no alternative.

Powell, the fifty-three-year-old son of Caribbean immigrants, was the first black and the youngest officer ever to be chairman of the Joint Chiefs. He had run the NSC for a time during the Reagan administration and served two tours of duty in Vietnam. To him, as to many American officers, Vietnam's lesson was a warning that the U.S. military should not go to war without the civilian leadership guaranteeing the necessary forces and the public providing strong support. No one expressed the army's view of the Vietnam factor better than General Schwarzkopf: "I *hate* what Vietnam has done to our country! I *hate* what Vietnam has done to our Army! The government sends you off to fight its war. It's not *your* war, it's the government's war. . . . And suddenly, a decision is made, 'Well, look, you guys were all wrong.'" After almost two decades devoted to rebuilding its reputation, the U.S. military did not want this to happen again.[26]

Thus, before committing themselves, Powell and the Pentagon wanted Bush to assure them of the tools, freedom of action, and forces they deemed necessary. The President's early-November decision to raise U.S. troop levels in the Gulf to over 400,000 was a turning point. The military then enthusiastically focused on fulfilling its mission of defeating Saddam in battle.

Bush's subordinates were bound to follow his orders, but events—and news of atrocities in Kuwait—also persuaded them that the president was right. Saddam's behavior indicated no willingness to compromise; and intelligence reports predicted that the embargo could not succeed by itself.

Bush's greater difficulty in winning popular and congressional support at home was partly his own fault. His speeches failed to arouse the American people, many of whom professed in polls and conversation not to understand the issues at stake. Being weak at formulating a political vision, he never quite succeeded in explaining what the crisis was all about.

Baker made a better case for the war. Iraq's aggression was threatening to destroy "one of those rare transforming moments in history" when there was a chance for a better world, he explained in an October 29 speech to the Los Angeles World Affairs Council. America was acting on "hard and terrible experience." Appeasement would only postpone and deepen the crisis as Iraq grew stronger and built biological, chemical, and nuclear weapons. By controlling so much oil, Saddam could plunge the world into deep recession. "If his way of doing business prevails, there will be no hope for peace in this area." Saddam would not stop until he was stopped.

The coalition was "exhausting every diplomatic avenue to achieve a solution without further bloodshed," continued Baker, and it was winning: "Every day as the sun sets, Iraq gets weaker. Every day as the sun rises, the international community remains firmly committed to implementation of the Security Council resolutions." But force must be used if need be to ensure that Iraq reaped no reward for aggression: "Let no nation think it can devour another nation and that the United States will somehow turn a blind eye. Let no dictator believe that we are deaf to the tolling of the bell as our fundamental principles are attacked. And let no one believe that because the Cold War is over, the United States is somehow going to abdicate its international leadership."[27]

These arguments, along with Republican partisan support and patriotic sentiments, were persuasive. There was also genuine popular outrage over Saddam's brutality and Kuwait's suffering. It was hard for liberal politicians or leftist and pacifist demonstrators to portray the issue as a new Vietnam or Nicaragua. Iraq was a ruthless aggressor; Kuwait was an undemocratic but genuine victim. The strategic stakes were undeniably high. The United States could not be said to be acting unilaterally, given the broad supportive coalition and the extensive UN role. In this case, force and morality, American leadership and multilateralism, were closely linked. Before the end of 1990, Bush had won support from most of the American public.

There were a number of problems in Congress, however, and the President had a harder time obtaining a political mandate to conduct a military attack.[28] After so many battles over Vietnam, Nicaragua, and other issues, members of Congress wanted to defend their institution's own prerogatives to help set foreign policy. Democrats were suspicious about what seemed to be the White House's propensity to do anything it wanted without Congress's approval. A number of them argued that Bush had no legal authority to commit U.S. troops to war.

No politician wanted to be held responsible for a long, bloody, or disastrous war. Even Senator Sam Nunn, a Georgia Democrat generally seen as a hard-liner on defense matters, preferred waiting for sanctions to work. Republicans supported Bush but were nervous about the potential for a political catastrophe if the war went wrong. Faced with an almost hopeless task of getting back into the White

House, the Democrats were eager to gain some partisan advantage from Bush's mistakes.

The administration pushed for a deadline. On November 29, the UN Security Council passed Resolution 678, demanding that Iraq withdraw by midnight on January 15, 1991 or face war. Iraq rejected it. Bush offered to invite Foreign Minister Tariq Aziz to Washington and send Baker to Baghdad to negotiate. Iraq proposed December 17 as the date for the first visit and January 12 for the second, a schedule the United States saw as a stalling tactic. The United States responded by suggesting fifteen dates between December 20 and January 3, 1991; all were refused by Iraq.

As a last-ditch effort to avoid war, Bush offered Iraq one more chance. When it was announced that Baker would meet Tariq Aziz on January 7, 1991, Iraq claimed victory, since the United States had earlier rejected talks before Iraq left Kuwait. Iraqi officials, persuaded that their analysis had been correct all along, hinted that a deal was in the making. Now that war was imminent, Baghdad believed, Washington was flinching. Misunderstanding had reached an all-time high.

Thus, in the seven-hour meeting at the Intercontinental Hotel in Geneva, a delighted Aziz exuded confidence, telling Baker that everything could be resolved. "If the American administration changes its position and works with us," he announced, Iraq "would love to be partners" in a new world order. Baker's assessment was different. He was there not to negotiate but to give a warning. Clearly, Baker did not communicate it persuasively enough to overcome the Iraqis' stubborn preconceptions. Western intelligence reported that Saddam's personal emissary at the meeting, his brother Barzun Tikriti, told Iraq's dictator that the United States would not go to war.

In London, Iraqi officials approached bankers to arrange future ventures. "But," asked the British financiers, "what about the crisis and the sanctions?"

"Oh," replied the Iraqis. "The crisis is already over, and we won."

Bizarre as this dialogue seemed, it reflected Baghdad's expectations. Saddam believed that time was on his side, that America could not fight and lacked the stamina to continue the confrontation for very long. For him, the fact that the United States had more airplanes than Iraq was irrelevant; the real question was whether America would use them. Thus he played for time, reasoning that Bush would be unable to hold together his international alliance and hold off domestic criticism. Surrounded by yes-men and profoundly ignorant of the outside world, Saddam was walking into a trap of his own making.

Ironically, every antiwar speech or demonstration in the United States fed Saddam's belief that the Americans would not fight and, hence, made war more likely. Iraqis, living in a dictatorship where no dissent was permitted and democracy was poorly understood, interpreted open dissent as a sign that a government was weak. To them, Bush seemed to be facing a virtual domestic revolt. The United States had retreated from Vietnam and Lebanon and deserted the Shah, Iraqi officials told Western journalists and diplomats, while Saddam was ready to sacrifice tens of thousands of lives. The Iraqis asked, "Do you really believe that Bush is ready to do the same?" They shook their heads. "No, this is unlikely."

All the techniques that had served Saddam so well in the past—intimidate your enemy, force him to surrender by giving no quarter, make clear that the alternative would be costly—were used yet again. The United States, too, had followed its own patterns, believing that moderation and compromise would prevail. This policy also increased Saddam's confidence that he had won and that Bush merely wanted a face-saving way out.

Five days after Baker and Aziz met in Geneva on January 7, 1991, Congress passed a joint resolution, following a sharp debate—in the Senate, 52 to 47; in the House, 250 to 183—that authorized the president to use force. The deadline came on January 15. With no Iraqi pullback, the United States and the coalition implemented the UN ultimatum and attacked at dawn on January 17, 1991.

CHAPTER ELEVEN

THE MOTHER OF DEBACLES—GULF WAR II: 1991

"Fear only the person who sets no limits on his bad behavior."

—*Arab proverb cited by Saddam Hussein*

Like some sequel to the American western film *High Noon,* the two combatants advanced slowly toward each other up the long main street, fingering their triggers as the January 15 deadline approached. The United States would not back down after sending more than 500,000 soldiers to the Gulf; Saddam gave it no peaceful alternative.

In *High Noon,* however, the townspeople ran away, leaving the brave lawman alone to face a gang of bandits. The Gulf crisis went the opposite way: Everyone rallied around the United States; Iraq was deserted. Most Arab regimes had joined the side that seemed the obvious winner; the others watched, ready to accede to whoever proved stronger.

Saddam had badly misread America and the Arab world. Bush had the coalition's green light and the American people's strong support. Yet Iraq's leaders ignored all the danger signs: the U.S. troop buildup, the public scheduling of a coalition attack for January, Soviet warnings that it would support the use of force, more troops sent by Egypt and Syria, the coalition's continued solidity, and a lack of sanctions-busting activity.

Yet it is easier to comprehend Saddam's misplaced confidence when one listens to those American politicians and Middle East experts who also misunderstood the situation in terms of all the wrong, traditional myths about the region. Once again, although many argued otherwise, there was no shortage of those who claimed that the Arabs and the Muslims, galvanized by an obsession with the Arab-Israeli conflict, would unite around Saddam and against the West. They predicted that war would set off a wave of anti-Americanism from Morocco to Oman, and they overestimated Iraq's military strength.

"Within six months," said Senator Ernest Hollings, a Democrat from South Carolina, "every fundamentalist mullah, every Arab nationalist, will say, 'the United States came here and invaded this Third World country for oil.' . . . And, face it, they will be speaking the truth!" Former under secretary of state George Ball, a veteran Arabist, commented, "There will be bitter talk of the Crusades and Western colonialism, and all the occasions in history where the Western world has appeared to intervene in what the Arabs regard as [their] own affairs."[1]

New York Times columnist Tom Wicker had proclaimed, "Bush stands warned—Congress is unlikely to support a war." Opposition continued during the last-minute congressional debate in January. Senate Democratic leader George Mitchell cautioned, "There has been no clear rationale, no convincing explanation for shifting American policy from one of sanctions to one of war." The risks included high casualties, "billions of dollars spent, a greatly disrupted oil supply and oil price increases, a war possibly widened to Israel, Turkey or other allies, the possible long-term American occupation of Iraq, increased instability in the Persian Gulf region, long-lasting Arab enmity against the United States, a possible return to isolationism at home."[2]

In the words of the Brookings Institution fellow Judith Kipper, a Middle East expert who made frequent appearances on American television, "We will be seen as the big bullies, no matter how many Arabs we have around us." Professor Michael Hudson of Georgetown University declared that Saddam was "going over the heads of the Arab leaders and appealing directly to the people. And he seems to be having some success." Professor L. Carl Brown of Princeton, who had earlier opined that Europe was replacing the United States as the area's chief power, warned, "A crushing military defeat of Saddam Hussein will convert the bully of Baghdad into a martyr."[3]

In fact, the United States had been invited in the first place by a majority of Arab rulers, and most Arabs did not blame the United States for the crisis. Saddam, explained an Egyptian writer, "talks about holy war to purge Arab land of the foreign forces that but for his foolishness would not have come here." Arabs would follow Saddam only if he became a proved winner by succeeding in his aggression. In that case, the 1990s would have made the previous thirty years of Middle Eastern history seem a picnic in comparison. And given the way Arab conspiracy theories were invented, if the United States had not countered Iraq's invasion, it would soon have been taken for granted that Saddam was America's designated agent to rule the region. But since the United States was challenging Iraq, the tide went in the opposite direction, and those who otherwise might have ignored sanctions abided by them.

The terrorist factor, like the innate Arab support for Saddam, was overestimated. Representative Lee Hamilton, a Democrat from Indiana, considered the congressman most knowledgeable on the Middle East, said, "If war comes, it will be difficult to imagine where Americans will be safe in the Middle East for some time to come." Senator John Kerry, a Democrat from Massachusetts, former defense secretary James Schlesinger, the columnists Evans and Novak, and many others agreed that terrorism would be widespread and effective.[4]

Such predictions missed two important points: the United States should not allow terrorists to set its foreign policy; and those countries sponsoring terrorism were intimidated by the United States. Other than Iraq itself, the terrorists' patrons—Syria, Iran, and Libya—were anti-Saddam or neutral and had no interest in ordering attacks on the coalition. The collapse of the Communist regimes eliminated the terrorists' best non-Arab friends, making their operations, especially in Europe, more difficult. Even Iraq refrained from using its terrorist assets—the Palestine Liberation Front and the Arab Liberation Front, among PLO member groups, as well as its own intelligence services—since it wanted to avoid, not provoke, a U.S. attack.

The most effective operation was carried out by Abu Nidal's pro-Saddam Palestinian terrorists against the PLO's main critic of Iraq, though it was not clear whether this was a personal vendetta or a mission undertaken on Iraq's behalf. On January 15, Abu Iyad and two other al-Fatah officials were shot by their own bodyguard in Tunis.

Abu Iyad, a comrade of Arafat since they entered politics in the

1950s, was a leading figure in PLO intelligence and terrorism operations. An austere man who saw himself as an intellectual warrior, he had smiled at me in a 1989 interview only when enthusiastically affirming his claim to be the PLO's number two man. In fact, Abu Iyad was a poor politician and a loner who was ultimately loyal to Arafat though he often questioned Arafat's positions from a more hard-line perspective. Distrustful of the PLO's subordination to any Arab state, Abu Iyad had criticized Arafat's subordinate attitude toward Saddam.

The killer, a member of Abu Nidal's anti-Arafat Palestinian group, had pretended to defect to the PLO. Abu Nidal had his own motive to kill Abu Iyad, arising from a long struggle with the PLO, but he usually acted as a "hired gun" and was said to be working for Saddam at the time. Had Iraq's dictator eliminated a PLO leader who opposed him, or did anti-Saddam Arab states order the killing as a strike against their enemy's PLO ally? Whatever the answer, it was—like the PLO's support for Saddam—another in a long series of self-inflicted Arab and Palestinian wounds.

The mercurial Libyan dictator, Muammar Qaddafi, proved cagier than Yasir Arafat in this crisis and did nothing to help Iraq. As usual, rivalry, not Arab solidarity, prevailed. On one hand, Qaddafi considered himself—not Saddam—the rightful Arab leader. On the other hand, he wanted to escape his own isolation from the West, Egypt, and Saudi Arabia. Despite all his Arab nationalist, anti-imperialist, anti-American rhetoric, Qaddafi watched passively while his "brothers" fought the United States. Further, he possessed a respect for U.S. power, which had been reinforced by the American air attack against him several years earlier. In the end, Saddam was left only with Yasir and Yemen, the weakest forces in the Arab world, with little to offer him.

Yet many American politicians and experts still doubted that the coalition would be able to sustain itself in battle as it had in peace. A few days before the war began, Hamilton said, "Support for the United States from coalition partners will be questionable in the case of hostilities." War, he added, would "split the coalition; estrange us from our closest allies; make us the object of Arab hostility; endanger friendly governments in the region; and not be easy to end, once started." Ball claimed that "the coalition would almost fall apart overnight" and the United States would be left "with not a single friend except Israel" in the region.[5]

Iraq's biggest boosters in earlier days were now among the most ardent defeatists regarding America's chances. Evans and Novak published assertions that almost all Arab leaders agreed that the death of a single Iraqi soldier would make them desert the coalition. They insisted that Iraq's conquest of Kuwait "cannot now be undone from outside," proclaimed that Syria and Iran would do nothing against Saddam, and virtually rejoiced in claiming that Bush's policy was losing domestic and international support.[6]

Former national security adviser Zbigniew Brzezinski, originator in the 1970s of the idea that the United States could make Iraq an ally, warned that an attack would lead to a split with European allies, Arab anti-American hostility, financial disaster, and the loss of any gains from the U.S. victory in the cold war. He forecast "a global wave of sympathy for Iraq" and reflected the most extreme Arab propaganda in claiming that Israel might "take advantage of an expanded war to effect the expulsion of all Palestinians" from the West Bank."[7]

In fact, the coalition's Arab members knew that the Americans would hand them a quick, total victory. Kuwait and Saudi Arabia sought vengeance and vindication, confident that only Saddam's defeat could preserve their sovereignty. Iran and Syria wanted Iraq weakened and Saddam eliminated as a rival who would be all the more threatening if he made himself master of Kuwait and victor over America.

After Bush obtained congressional support to attack, Senator Joseph Biden, Democrat from Delaware, warned the president on the Senate floor, "The Senate and the nation are divided on this issue. You have no mandate for war." Senator Ted Kennedy, Democrat from Massachusetts, added in his speech, "There is still time to save the president from himself—and save thousands of American soldiers in the Persian Gulf from dying in the desert in a war whose cruelty will be exceeded only by the lack of any rational necessity for waging it." If these powerful Americans inveighed against war, why should Saddam expect the United States to fight?

In one sense, however, Saddam was totally correct. American eagerness to bring U.S. troops home from Vietnam and retreat from foreign responsibility had made it fumble the diplomatic outcome there. The Vietnam War and the Iran hostage crisis became political disasters because, win or lose, they could not be concluded rapidly enough. Saddam understood that the United States could not fight a war if it could not win fast, keep casualties low, and get out quickly. The dictator's mistake was his disbelief that Bush could fulfill these conditions in defeating Iraq. Saddam reasoned that the same need to keep the war short, restrict losses, and bring the troops home soon also meant that the United States lacked the willpower and the staying power to bring him down.

Still, in the days up to January 15, this congenital American impatience operated against Iraq. Bush's eagerness to end the crisis made him want to attack Iraq rather than wait longer. There were already constant media stories about low morale in the forces, frictions in the coalition, problems of repairing equipment, and the troops' longing for alcohol, not to mention the presence of female military personnel. If Bush retreated, he would appear a fool and an appeaser at the next election; if he procrastinated, he would have to face the rising expenses and domestic complaints entailed in keeping several hundred thousand soldiers marooned in the Saudi desert.

Wishful thinking also prevailed in Iraq when it came to the nation's own military preparations. If the Bush administration's lack of credibility with Baghdad made war inevitable, it also brought a huge U.S. military advantage. Saddam would never believe that the real U.S. war plan could be so freely published in American newspapers. Thus Iraq was unprepared to fight despite five months of threats to spill rivers of American blood.

The dictator was too accustomed to defining reality at home to take seriously the probability of intense aerial attacks and a consequent need for civil defense. The country's oil minister had been fired in late October for imposing strict rationing. Putting such restrictions on Iraqis would seem like an admission of the sanctions' effectiveness. "Rambo films will not be played out on the land of Iraq," said Saddam on November 29, the day the UN gave him six weeks to get out or be thrown out of Kuwait. Few Iraqis believed there would be a war; even fewer believed American air attacks would get through. In Baghdad, windows were not taped and there were no blackout regulations, air raid drills, or plans to evacuate civilians. "It is almost," commented the British magazine *The Economist*, "as though President Saddam Hussein had always planned to take his country to the brink of war—but not beyond."[8] Indeed, that was true, but the decision was no longer in his hands.

On the morning of January 17 in the Middle East, a full twenty-four hours after the UN deadline, U.S. and allied planes took off from aircraft carriers or airfields in Saudi Arabia and Turkey. They hit their targets in Iraq with devastating effectiveness. Still, Saddam brimmed with confidence. "You may be capable of starting aggression and war," he told Bush through an interviewer. "But after taking the first step along this path, you will not be able to define the battlefield, the kinds of weapons that will be used in the showdown, or its duration. . . . The battle will be prolonged, and much blood will be shed in it. Israel, offspring of American wickedness . . . will come under the hammer." General Schwarzkopf was more accurate than Saddam in his own assessment that day: "The Iraqis have no concept of what they were getting involved in."[9]

The U.S. strategy played to its own high-technology strength, which Iraq had no way to counter. Contrary to Saddam's claim, the United States could define the battlefield, the weapons, and the duration of the conflict. Most Arabs appeared awed by the initial attack and Iraq's seeming inability to retaliate. Even Qaddafi spoke in press interviews of Saddam's "irresponsible actions." Completely outclassed in the air and attacked on the ground, Iraqi pilots soon began flying to Iran to escape the fighting. Baghdad ordered most of the air force to join the stampede, in an admittedly slim hope of saving it. Iran gladly confiscated the 147 arriving planes as "reparations" for the Iran-Iraq war.

The U.S., British, and French air forces pounded Iraq in thousands of sorties, using relatively accurate bombs and missiles to destroy military installations, factories, and communication centers, with few losses to themselves. The sky over Baghdad lit up in the deadly fireworks of Iraqi antiaircraft fire and American cruise missiles. The planes moved on to smash Iraqi army units at the front, pinpointed by satellites and reconnaissance planes. The Iraqis had no aerial defense to stop the rain of bombs, no reliable intelligence to tell them about the coalition's troop movements.

Baghdad had only one way of retaliating. Near Jerusalem's Damascus Gate, Palestinian youths sold plastic sheets to cover windows against Iraqi chemical attacks, excitedly shouting, "Saddam is coming! Saddam is coming!" Indeed, his Scud-missile messengers were about to arrive in Israel and in Saudi Arabia. Foreigners fled Israel; well-intentioned relatives and friends called from abroad, urging people to go.

Just before January 15, a delegation of American journalists and experts met Prime Minister Shamir. At the meeting's end, the group's leader said, "Thank you for seeing us. We're leaving tonight, because we don't want to be around on January 15." He laughed at his own tasteless joke. "I guess you don't have a choice."

"Oh, yes," said one of the prime minister's aides. "We do have a choice. We just happen to like it here."

Few Israelis went to work those days. Schools were closed for what children called the "Saddam holiday." Food-stand owners sat by their radios all day, waiting for a code word that would call them up to the army. Social workers found that psychologically disturbed people often took the actual outbreak of war in stride: external reality overpowered personal problems. Customers besieged hardware stores, seeking plastic sheets and tape for sealing their windows.

Everyone, everywhere, carried the gas mask boxes that resembled large Chinese take-out food containers, which many soon covered in bright wrapping paper. Comedy was called into service to combat fear. The popular comedian Doron Nesher transformed his box into a nest for a dove. One joke asked, "Why is land near the Iraqi Scud sites so expensive?" The answer: "It's only five minutes from downtown Tel Aviv!" Tel Aviv Mayor Shlomo Lahat commented that the Iraqi Scuds might take only five minutes to reach the city but would then need at least ninety minutes to find a parking space. In the unintentional-black-humor department, Israel television cheerily showed *War and Remembrance,* a television drama about World War II, full of bombing scenes and air raid sirens.

After news of the U.S. air strike on Iraq, Israeli radio instructed people to stay inside and prepare for an Iraqi reprisal raid. A special program for new Russian immigrants explained the use of gas masks and anti–chemical war equipment. Water and food were taken to rooms; windows and doors were sealed with tape, glass crisscrossed by adhesive to keep it from fragmenting into deadly projectiles. Gas masks were tried on, the dark, rubbery smell nauseating one at first, drying the throat and making it sore. Everyone was hoping that the war would be an anticlimax.

At 2:00 A.M. on January 18, I was getting ready to sleep, listening to music on the radio. The phone rang and, to my surprise, it was Ralph Begleiter of CNN News in Washington. "Barry," he said, "there's a report that Iraqi missiles have hit Tel Aviv." Perhaps he had some source in the U.S. military, which was watching by satellite for Iraqi Scud launchings.

"That's ridiculous," I replied. "It's perfectly quiet here." I held up the phone to confirm this fact. That very second, there were seven loud explosions outside, bright flashes of light came through the window, and the building shook. Immediately, though belatedly, air raid sirens began their chilling up-and-down wave of sound, and the radio broadcast a warning to take shelter and put on gas masks right away.

My first thought was that I did not want to be the one who announced to the world—and Saddam's gunners—that Iraqi Scuds had hit the city, earning an ignominious place in history as Iraqis continued to fire salvos to the right coordinates.

"Um, Ralph, I have to go," I said calmly and politely.

"Don't hang up! Don't hang up!" he insisted.

"No, really, I'm sorry. I can't talk now. Bye."

Later, when I recounted the story, someone asked, "What was more important, your life or the story?"

"If you can't guess that the answer is the second one," I answered jokingly, "you haven't known many journalists."

At the moment, though, there were other concerns. I had to break the two seals on the gas mask filter and screw it into the mask, seal the door with tape, shove a wet towel against the bottom, and huddle down to wait while I watched the television and listened to Israel's radio station for instructions and the BBC for news. I sat quietly to control my heartbeat and breathing. On my nightstand was food, water in a covered container, and the special gauze, powder, and emergency syringe to be used if any chemical mist landed on one's skin. Only later did I realize that since I was sitting opposite the taped window, any nearby hit would have riddled me with flying glass. From then on, I sat on the floor.

For the next four hours, five million people waited until told they could take off their masks. Even then, they were instructed to stay inside their sealed rooms for several hours more. Few had much sleep that night. Only months later was it revealed that one Scud had landed near a textile plant. When monitors picked up substances used in the cloth processing, a chemical weapon was suspected.

The U.S. and Israeli intelligence assessments that doubted whether Iraq did not have usable chemical warheads were kept secret. After all, nobody wanted to be the one who confidently predicted Saddam could not possibly use such arms, only to see scores of people die a horrible death from them. Of course, Saddam did not fire these unconventional weapons. On top of the technical shortcomings, he must have been restrained by the fear that a single chemical warhead could bring Israeli nuclear retaliation.

Slowly, one learned the essentials of this strange type of warfare. The sirens gave exactly five minutes' warning, and a remarkable amount of a lifetime could be packed into that space of time. The real danger point was the next sixty seconds, when the missiles hit.

As old war movies taught, being able to hear the blast meant you were still alive and safe. Meanwhile, millions of people in Saddam's targets—Saudi Arabia and Israel—lived in fear every night.

The country was split into areas, with Tel Aviv—Region A—usually the last to receive an all-clear, since it was the main Iraqi target. Boredom and anxiety competed as car alarms, the noise of buses, and especially motorcycles in the night sounded chillingly like the start of a siren's wail. For each real alert, false ones set off the nervous system a dozen times. Very late at night, there was a more soothing sound: the engines of El Al planes flying in thousands of Soviet Jewish immigrants despite the crisis.

The greatest burden was borne by those caring for frightened children, who had to be put in special cribs or masks, and elderly relatives. At the gloomiest moment, a huge Israeli flag was strung across a whole wall of Habimah, the national theater, and like the image in "The Star-Spangled Banner," it was still there after each perilous night.

Everyone claimed to know where each missile struck, dropping hints over the telephone (". . . near the third stop of the bus you used to take to school"). Despite the efforts of Israel's government to keep the exact locations out of the media, U.S. State Department spokeswoman Margaret Tutwiler announced during Defense Minister Moshe Arens's visit to Washington that one had fallen near his house, giving Iraq potentially priceless intelligence. It was fortunate that the missiles were so inaccurate, the warheads so small, and the Iraqi gunners so negligent and so harried by air attack. If Israel had not destroyed Iraq's nuclear reactor in 1981—an act condemned by America and the world—Iraq would have had weapons a thousand times more devastating and death-dealing.

Under Secretary of State Lawrence Eagleburger had come to Israel just before the war to urge patience and to promise that the

American air force would knock out the missile launchers. At the end of December 1990, the United States had offered two batteries of Patriot defensive missiles. When the fighting began, Israeli crews were still training at Fort Bliss, Texas, and the United States rushed American-crewed batteries to defend Israeli cities, the first time in the country's history that foreign troops had come to help it fight. At America's request, Israel waited for the coalition's bombing and secret commando raids to knock out the Scud launchers.

The U.S. government was trying to forestall Israeli retaliation against the missile sites in western Iraq, arguing that any Israeli action might make Arab members drop out of the coalition. Yet the Arab states were in the coalition not as a favor to the United States but in pursuit of their own vital interests. The Kuwaitis wanted to recover their country, the Saudis needed America to defend them, Egypt could not accept Saddam as the Arabs' leader, and even Syria openly said it would do nothing if Israel attacked. If Israel had hit their common Iraqi enemy and Syria and Saudi Arabia acquiesced, the taboo against making peace with Israel would have been invalidated.

According to an old pattern, the siege of Israel was occasion for temporary sympathy from the West. As the French writer Pascal Bruckner noted, "The Jews . . . were adored as long as they were persecuted, wandering, and uprooted but were detested as soon as they obtained a land, a State, and an army. . . . What was loved was a depersonalized, suffering victim."[10] Israelis hoped—and the Bush administration promised—that after the war the world would remember their sacrifices, that restraint would bring political credit and economic support later. But they doubted, wisely, that this memory would linger long.

In contrast, virtually every Palestinian leader, even the most moderate of the West Bank middle class, let himself be carried away by wishful thinking in repeating Iraq's claims—conveyed by Amman's radio and television—that it had shot down many allied planes and was winning the war.

The atmosphere of illusion was heightened by wild rumors that Israel would expel massive numbers of Palestinians, invade Jordan, or even hit West Bank towns with chemical weapons and then blame Iraq. The PLO accused the United States of "cowardly aggression" against Iraq: "We are all exposed to aggression when [Baghdad] is bombed." It warned that "blood, catastrophe and destruction will sweep the world." The preacher at East Jerusalem's al-Aqsa mosque, Shaikh Daoud Atallah, told worshipers, "God destroy Israel! God destroy the United States! God give victory to Saddam!" Another Palestinian said, "Our fate now is in the hands of Iraq," precisely the kind of intransigent, fatalist thinking that had so long crippled their cause.[11]

Palestinians in the West Bank—living under a tight curfew—and in Jordan were heartened by the fact that Iraqi rockets had struck Tel Aviv. Palestinians not only cheered from rooftops but held parades with floats carrying mock-ups of Scuds. Trying to convince Arabs to bolt the coalition, the PLO claimed that Israeli planes were operating out of Turkey or even Saudi Arabia. Arafat asserted that U.S. cruise missiles were being fired at Baghdad from Israel's Negev desert. In south Lebanon, the PLO tried to start its own war by firing rockets and sending terrorist squads into northern Israel.

Elsewhere, the coalition's military success discouraged Saddam's supporters, for whom wishful thinking jostled with a fatalistic pessimism that, once again, the Arabs would be humiliated. No one wanted to sacrifice himself for a loser. This, too, was Jordan's situation.

King Hussein had faced many problems in his long rule, but

never had he seemed so pessimistic and passive; he looked far older than his fifty-four years. His Palestinian subjects naively thought Saddam would destroy Israel for them; the Islamic fundamentalists, who controlled thirty-four of eighty seats in parliament, cynically wanted to use Iraq to put themselves into power. The king played to the mob, condemning the coalition's attack on Iraq, claiming it was waging war on all Muslims and trying to take over the area.

This political game was played at a frightful price. Although Amman unilaterally wrote off its debt to Kuwait after Iraq's invasion, it was by far a net loser. The coalition's embargo cut revenue from the port of Aqaba and the profitable transit trade to Iraq and the Gulf. Unemployment rose and, ultimately, 300,000 Jordanian citizens, mostly Palestinians, returned from Kuwait or from other Gulf states where they had been fired as potential fifth columnists. Yet aside from militant talk, Jordan's government and people did little to help Saddam.

Some non-Arab members of the anti-Saddam coalition tried harder to save Iraq as the bombing continued through January and February. The USSR, Iran, and European leaders urged a quick end to the war, so that Saddam could save face and preserve his army from destruction.

Once again, though, Saddam hardened his heart, like Pharaoh faced with the ten plagues. He refused to take advantage of various offers, if only for the purpose of manipulating their sponsors into pressuring Washington to stop military operations. He still did not assume that Iraq would be defeated, expecting that the coalition's ground forces could be pinned down in a protracted war with heavy casualties. Saddam was a great believer in the eventual victory of the side willing to suffer most. The United States could damage but not defeat Iraq, he had told an American diplomat. Though the enemy may occupy some territory, Saddam said, "we have staying power in battle."[12]

But Iraq's military proved more a facade than an effective foe. Though a million strong, the army was composed of soldiers who were largely untrained and poorly led. An officer corps selected for political loyalty had made the regime more secure from coups but less able to fight wars. Saddam and his inner circle did not trust the army to make its own decisions but themselves lacked military know-how. While Saddam loved to wear a field marshal's uniform, he had no real experience as a soldier. Mubarak and Asad, professional officers before they were political leaders, had a more realistic understanding of warfare. Perhaps this explains the difference between Saddam's recklessness and their relative caution in waging war.

Some could not understand why Iraq's professional officers did not talk sense to the dictator. "Saddam's military leaders are not fools," said Senator Sam Nunn in January, arguing that Iraq would make a political compromise rather than go to war.[13] But precisely because they were not fools, Iraq's generals had no wish to tell Saddam the unpleasant truth and risk execution.

Facing U.S. maneuver warfare and bombs was quite different from the war with Iran, when Iraq's army sat securely in trenches, facing an enemy that lacked air power. The Iraqi soldiers' spirit was shattered. In one intercepted radio message, an officer under bombardment could be heard screaming hysterically, begging for supplies and crying for his mother. The regime's rigid control and the officers' fear of taking initiatives—the classic bane of Arab armies—was disastrous once air attacks broke communication lines between headquarters and the front. As soon as defeat seemed likely, morale collapsed; the officers fled and the soldiers surrendered.

The coalition's aerial battering of Iraq was just a prelude to the ground attack. With Iraq's army disorganized and demoralized, the coalition's tanks and troops advanced northward into Kuwait and Iraq on February 24. The ground war lasted one hundred hours. Tens of thousands of Iraqis gave up without firing a shot. Iraq had already poured millions of barrels of Kuwait's oil into the Gulf; now the retreating Iraqi army set Kuwait's oil wells on fire and destroyed public buildings in Kuwait City. The coalition captured all of Kuwait and much of southern Iraq, then U.S. forces wheeled eastward to cut off the enemy columns.

Once again, Saddam resisted making concessions to end the war, while, out of humanitarian and political considerations, others tried to save him. Some of the Europeans feared that defeating Iraq completely would be too costly in casualties and might lead to an Arab backlash against the West. The Soviets put forward a cease-fire plan for a gradual Iraqi withdrawal from Kuwait in tandem with the lifting of sanctions, an accord that would allow Saddam to claim victory and delay implementation.

President Bush refused. Eager as he was to end the war, nothing short of a clear Iraqi defeat was acceptable. Finally, with coalition armies surrounding Iraq's remaining forces and penetrating closer to his cities, Saddam accepted all the UN resolutions. Bush quickly agreed to a cease-fire. Otherwise, he feared, a march on Baghdad would be necessary to unseat Saddam, entailing heavier casualties, a protracted war, and a long-term U.S. military presence in Iraq. The problem was that Saddam could not be trusted to keep to the terms. Schwarzkopf later stated publicly that he had wanted to fight a little longer to destroy Iraq's forces, which might have inspired the regime's breakdown or Iraqi generals to revolt. Instead, the president ordered Schwarzkopf to stop.

On February 26, Baghdad cheered the news that still another

war was about to end. "You have faced the whole world, you great Iraqis," said the government radio. "You have won." Such an illusion could barely be maintained even within Iraq. American casualties totaled 148 killed and 467 wounded, many of them from friendly fire. Perhaps 200,000 Iraqi soldiers and several hundred civilians had died.[14]

Arab supporters of the coalition were jubilant; Iraq's friends were stunned into silence. In Tel Aviv, I tore down the plastic sheets and tape from the window and flung open the wooden shutter. It was spring, and birds were singing in the trees. An old man walked down the street carrying his gas mask box. Bystanders tried to assure him that he didn't have to carry it anymore. He smiled and opened it: he was using it to carry home eggs from the store.

For Iraqis, life was far grimmer. Much of the country's infrastructure was in ruins. Yet while the dictator had lost everything he seized on August 2, 1990, he kept all he had before. Unwilling to let Saddam have Kuwait, the United States would let him stay in power in Iraq. This policy corresponded to the original U.S. war aims but, given the magnitude of the coalition's victory, was a case of foolish consistency. Bush left the dictator in place to wreak vengeance at home and plan revenge against his enemies abroad. A large part—though by no means all—of the victory had been thrown away.

"Our policy," said an NSC staffer, "is to get rid of Saddam Hussein, not his regime."[15] The president overestimated the likelihood that Saddam's colleagues and generals would throw him out. They were too dependent on their leader and too fearful of his excellent intelligence system to act against him. In the Middle Eastern fashion, they were waiting for the Americans to present Saddam's head on a platter or at least give them the signal for starting a coup that would receive U.S. support.

Iraq's Kurds and Shia thought Bush's earlier speeches expressing hope that Saddam would be overthrown by his own people gave them the go-ahead. On March 2, the Shia rebelled in Basra. Fighting spread to other southern cities and then to the Kurdish north. Although Bush had urged Iraqis to get rid of Saddam, he disclaimed all responsibility for the upheaval and denied any intention of helping the rebels.

The Iraqi army units that Bush had not allowed Schwarzkopf to destroy—due to the allies' squeamishness and a desire to spare the Iraqis more suffering—now fired on their own people. They started by surrounding and shelling the southern cities. Hundreds of Shia civilians were killed; tens of thousands fled across the American lines or the Iranian border.

The situation in the north was even worse. In earlier years, the regime had destroyed hundreds of Kurdish mountain villages and forced people into closely controlled towns. Now Baghdad's Kurdish militia defected in revolt. Nationalist guerrillas seized army equipment and took over; Kurdish warriors briefly danced in the streets. Then Iraq's army marched north. The coalition did not interfere. Fearing Saddam's wrath, over two million Kurds fled over the frontier to Turkey and Iran. The whole region was emptied. As March ended, Saddam again controlled Iraq, except for the coalition's dwindling occupation zone in the south and a small safe haven it established for the Kurds in the north.

Bush had let Saddam survive because he accepted arguments rooted in the old myths about American weakness, Arab unity, and the radicals' strength in the Middle East. The first assumption was that Arabs and Iraqis would hate America for winning too big a victory. As regional history and the local revolts had shown, though, once Saddam fell, the Iraqi people would have thanked America for helping rid them of a bloodthirsty tyrant. Iran, Syria, and other regional states would have been even more eager to propitiate a superpower capable of such domination. Instead, millions of Iraqis paid the price for America's last-minute trepidation.

The second argument was that the fall of Iraq's regime would lead to that country's dissolution and a severe power vacuum in the Gulf. In fact, the United States was now the dominant regional power, and everyone in the Gulf—if not in Washington—knew it. Neither Syria nor Iran was about to challenge this hegemony or risk huge losses after seeing the outcome of Gulf Wars I and II.

The likelihood of Iraq's disappearance was also wildly overstated. Whoever its ruler might be, Iraq's geopolitical weight would always be considerable, since it was the sole Arab state combining a large population with enormous oil wealth. The Gulf Arab monarchies had riches but no manpower for large armies; Egypt and Syria were populous but poor. In truth, there was no one left to take advantage of Iraq's weakness. The USSR was impotent; Iran had not obtained new planes, ships, or tanks since 1977 nor even begun to recover from its defeat in the war with Iraq. Syria was too distant as well as economically weak, and militarily preoccupied in Lebanon and against Israel.

Iraq's partition was also extremely unlikely. None of its neighbors had any major claims to ownership of Iraq's territory. Turkey never challenged Baghdad's post–World War I border in the north, whose revision would only give Ankara a larger, unwanted Kurdish minority. Iran, which had failed to conquer Iraq at the height of its power, hardly wanted a rematch that would also bring confrontation with the United States. Iraq's own Kurds and Shia, as their failed revolt showed, were far from being able to secede. Their goals were not to create a new state but, respectively, to gain autonomy and to take over Iraq.

The third wrong notion was the customary myth that the way

for the United States to win influence was to make concessions to Arab regimes, particularly its enemies among them. Actually, the United States' standing rested on exactly the opposite ability: to demonstrate overwhelming power in order to persuade regional states that confrontation was futile and cooperation was beneficial.

Making an example of Saddam would have achieved this end, deterring future aggressors and letting Washington broker new arrangements on Gulf security, arms control, and Arab-Israeli peace-making. A few Arab and Iranian newspapers might grumble that the United States was an imperialist bully—which they would do anyway—but the regional governments would compete to have the United States as an ally or at least to avoid having it as an active enemy.

To achieve this real, full victory would not have required an American march on Baghdad or additional casualties. A few more days of continuing operations against Iraq's military would have eliminated the troops needed to put down the popular rebellions. The specter of destruction would have given Iraqi officers and officials a far greater incentive to move against the dictator.

In fact, the U.S. interest was the exact opposite of the Bush administration's interpretation in March 1991. The best outcome of the war would have been to weaken Iraq's central government so as to render it less able to threaten the Gulf or anyone else. Supporting Kurdish autonomy was an easy way to do that. Bush was wrong on strategic as well as moral grounds to do nothing as the rebellions were crushed and hundreds of thousands of people were turned into refugees. But those Americans who had opposed the war altogether—who in effect were prepared to see Saddam go on ruling both Iraq and Kuwait—were in no reasonable position to criticize the president for not having gone further.

Having successfully survived by using his brutality, Saddam was ready to wait patiently for alliances to rearrange themselves, as they always did in the region, for the coalition army to leave, and for the sanctions to erode. Iraq hid as many of its missiles as possible, and as much of its nuclear technology and chemical-warfare capacity as it could. Saddam hoped that in a few years, he would rebuild his strength and changes in Arab politics would allow him to pursue his ambitions again.

The experience had not changed Saddam's ideas, even as it reduced his ability to implement them. As soon as the United States let Saddam survive, its plan for a postwar new world order was badly subverted, though not altogether ruined. Still, the other Arabs and the Americans had learned from the Kuwait crisis and from their own mistakes.

CHAPTER TWELVE

THE EMPEROR'S NEW ORDER

*To chase away some noisy children, Hojja told them there
was a free banquet at the mayor's house. When they ran to
see, he was pleased with his cleverness, then thought: I'd better
go see if it's true!*

—*Middle Eastern folktale*

"U.S.A.! U.S.A.!" chanted joyful Kuwaitis who had once cheered
anti-American Arab leaders. Americans, too, were swept away by
a wave of pride and patriotism. It seemed to be the start of a new
era in U.S. history. Within nine months—much faster than
expected—the oil-field fires were out, the refugee citizens were back
home, and Kuwait was back in business. But the region's psycho-
logical and political dislocations could not be so easily restored.

The parades and celebrations did not eradicate the fact that the
Arabs and the United States could not simply blame what had
occurred on an evil dictator's deceit. The Arabs in general, Saudi
Arabia and Kuwait in particular, Europe, and the United States
were also responsible for the crisis, having led Saddam on and built

him up. A Kuwaiti poet, Souad al-Sabah, who had once cheered Saddam, wrote:

> *He who killed Kuwait is our own flesh and blood,*
> *He is the embodiment of all our ways.*
> *We made him in accord with our own measurements. . . .*
> *We all applauded the tyrants and tyranny,*
> *We can't complain about our idols.*[1]

Saddam had too faithfully heeded the lessons taught him by experience. No wonder he expected that U.S. vacillation, European cowardice, Arab nationalism, Islamic radicalism, Saudi appeasement, and anti-Israel passion would allow him an easy victory. Before August 1990, the Bush administration had been pusillanimous as long as it could avoid trouble. Between 1985 and 1990, U.S. companies sold Iraq items with military applications worth $1.5 billion, a figure that would have been higher if Baghdad could have financed additional deals. West Germany and France helped Saddam far more.[2]

Even after Iraq seized Kuwait and the U.S. government awoke, many in the West were ready to accept Saddam's aggression. Part of the intelligentsia was still obsessed by the idea that America— not communism, dictators, or terrorism—was the world's cancer. Bush's domestic critics—Democrats, liberals, and isolationist conservatives alike—complained that he was being too tough, urging patience and a deal with a tyrant they should have been the first to oppose. From them came dangerous bad counsel: bribe Iraq to withdraw; expect Arab states to leave the coalition; refuse to destroy Saddam or help the Kurds.

If Iraq had given these faint-hearted Americans some encouragement, it might still own part or the whole of Kuwait. "All of the so-called diplomatic options," Henry Kissinger explained, "would have made matters worse. Each would have left Iraq in a militarily dominant position."[3] The Kuwait crisis showed how much the United States could achieve when it was willing to shed—at least temporarily—the myths so often promulgated by experts and sometimes swallowed by politicians. To its credit, the White House rejected defeatist advice. Drawing on experience with other dictators, it insisted that aggression be thwarted.

Could these same leaders, experts, and journalists learn something from experience? The immediate postwar prognosis was inauspicious. Wishful thinking and all the ideas that had helped produce the crisis in the first place took control again in Washington. Bush refused to fight a few more days to destroy the remaining half of Saddam's army trapped in southern Iraq, and thus ensure the dictator's fall. His rationale for this ill-considered mercy was wrong on all counts. Instead of defusing domestic criticism by ending the war quickly, he was blamed for letting Saddam survive.

The proper American task had been not to occupy Baghdad and set up a new regime but to destroy enough of Iraq's army to let officers know they must oust the dictator to survive or to ensure that a revolt overwhelmed the tyrant. The only way to break the cycle of Arab politics was to prove to the regimes that aggression and demagoguery were suicidal, that they must change their ways or disappear.

As usually happened, America was far better at having a vision than at implementing a strategy. It resolved the immediate problem of the Kuwait crisis but missed part of the chance to change the region's underlying structure and create a real new order there. Like outposts that did not yet know the battle was over and lost, American Middle East experts fought on for the old myths. They spoke as if the United States had been defeated or would have been better off if Iraq had won the war in the Gulf. Too complete a U.S. triumph, they warned, would surely make Arabs consider America an imperialist bully. The United States did not need to eliminate Saddam, wrote former State Department official James Akins, since he would "soon be dead at the hands of his own countrymen" or in exile. Nonetheless, Americans would be seen as the "destroyers," not the saviors, of Arabs or Islam. There would be growing anti-American demonstrations and terrorism; U.S. allies in Egypt, Syria, and Morocco would "be shaken and could be overthrown"; and the Saudi regime would last only a few years longer. There might be some hope, Akins suggested, if the United States gave in to all the Arab demands on the Arab-Israeli conflict and other issues.[4]

Such people still did not comprehend that power was more important than popularity and that the United States had in fact saved the Arabs from Saddam's unwelcome embrace. Those Arab leaders who already doubted U.S. staying power would be less, not more, cooperative with Saddam still in power and looking over their shoulder.

Though he dissented from the president's order to stop fighting, even General Schwarzkopf was something of an innocent in the bazaar on these matters. Iraq "suckered" him by breaking promises it made at the truce talks, he would tell interviewer David Frost a few weeks later. When Iraq's delegates asked to be trusted, Schwarzkopf recalled, "You almost feel like coming back and saying 'Why?'" But why just "almost"? Because despite all that had happened, even this tough, worldly American commander could not quite believe that they would look him in the eye and lie. Schwarzkopf also believed in fair play. If Iraq's rulers "broke the rules," he asserted, "they would pay for it." The men who ran Iraq knew better: by lying and cheating, they had always made others do the paying. And now the United States again did not retaliate when they breached those rules.

Bush's denial that there was any formal U.S. commitment to the Kurdish or Shia Iraqis was technically true. But the rebels understandably interpreted the American president's clear, oft-voiced wish that the dictator be deposed as a call to action and an offer to help. Both for realpolitik and for humanitarian reasons, U.S. policy should have backed Kurdish autonomy to weaken Iraq's central government so it would not again be a threat. Instead, America spared Saddam's soldiers and weapons so they could kill Iraqis and reestablish control. Saddam quickly returned to his old tricks: hiding chemical, nuclear, and other weapons; finding ways around the embargo; and stalling for time to outwait the coalition's patience in maintaining it.

Some observers felt that little had changed. The Washington correspondent of the British newspaper *Financial Times* summarized the case against Bush—and U.S. policy—in June 1991: "The Middle East looks as confused and chaotic as ever." There was no peace conference, much less a solution, for the Arab-Israeli conflict. "Plans for a new security system in the Gulf appear to be in disarray." There were "widespread reports of human rights violations" instead of elections in Kuwait. The White House had to concede that much of Iraq's arsenal remained intact—U.S. military claims of destruction had been greatly exaggerated—and that Baghdad was continuing to build missiles. In exchange, it could only offer wishful thinking that Saddam would fall without being pushed too hard.[5]

A lot of this critique was valid. But the region's system had undergone significant changes, even if they were less substantial than might otherwise have been achieved. Undermined by the events of the 1970s and 1980s, any chance for Arab unity, Islamic revolution, the destruction of Israel, joining the Soviet camp, or expelling Western influence—the mainstays of Arab rhetoric for almost four decades—was gone. Actually, it was already too late; the ideas were obsolete before Saddam, Khomeini, and their friends made their last-ditch effort. It was left only to admit that fact and act accordingly.

Of course, the old ways would continue to close minds and shape behavior. As Fouad Ajami put it, "Cultures often stubbornly refuse to look into themselves. They retreat into the nooks and crannies of their received history, offer up the standard evasions, fall back on the consolations they know."[6] Societies first react to change by revising rhetoric and tactics in order to preserve their substance. In politics, having one's cake and eating it too is the optimal solution.

New trends, however, developing for years, had now culminated in a crisis that pushed the Arabs toward moderation, the West, and the first real prospect of resolving the Arab-Israeli conflict. The main factors included Egypt's return to Arab preeminence; the political failure of Arab nationalism and radical Islam; a stronger Israel and the Arab states' reluctance to go to battle with it; Moscow's collapse and the cold war's end; America's emergence as the Gulf's protector; and a maturity arising from the Arab world's own experience and development.

First, after a decade's isolation for the "crime" of advocating a new approach that favored moderation, alliance with the United States, and a diplomatic settlement with Israel, Egypt had returned to the Arab ranks as an advocate of these very principles. Arab embassies reopened there in 1987; Asad and Qaddafi visited to concede Egypt's absolution. Cairo dominated the 1989 Arab summit with a call to jettison radicalism, work with the United States, and recognize Israel.[7] Saddam had understood that without a radical alternative, Egypt's influence would shift the direction of Arab politics.

Second, behind a smoke screen of Pan-Arabism, Arab states had become viable entities on their own. Since Nasser's death in 1970, no charismatic figure appeared to unite the Arabs or even to enjoy any real following outside his own borders. Qaddafi's always unsuccessful bid to do so was a farce that revealed the hollowness of the enterprise. It meant far more to be an Iraqi, a Jordanian, or a Syrian in the 1990s than before, when many of their citizens could remember a time before these independent states existed. Each country diverged more and more from other Arab states in its political and economic structure, its history, and its geopolitical situation.

Although Saddam first seemed a throwback to earlier times and previous despots, his isolation would prove how much things had changed. Saddam acted so selfishly and unilaterally as to show himself to be a thoroughgoing Iraqi nationalist; Saudi Arabia's rulers acted like Saudi nationalists by inviting U.S. troops. What a strange, ultimately unworkable system it was that required the Saudis and Kuwaitis to donate the instruments of their own destruction, to praise those who would murder them, and to celebrate policies that produced only defeat and humiliation.

For a time, at least, radicalism was discredited. Terrorism and revolutionary Islamic fundamentalism succeeded nowhere in the Arab world, despite all the noise they made. In Lebanon, fundamentalist groups did not even win hegemony in their own Shia community, much less in the country as a whole. Tehran was not a highly attractive model to emulate, and its revolution was not exported. Fundamentalist movements formed the main opposition in several countries but did not—certainly in their more extreme forms—seem poised for victory.

Third, Arab states were less able to afford radicalism or fight the United States or Israel because they could no longer look to Moscow for help. Communism's collapse destroyed the Arabs' alternative arms supplier and diplomatic champion, forcing them to be on better terms with and more dependent on the United States. Syria, for example, was plagued by high inflation, population growth, and foreign debt. "As time went by," said Muhammad Aziz Shukri, dean of Damascus University's law school, "our defeats were repeated and we realized that Israel is not alone." Many Syrians were "sick and tired" of fighting and were more concerned about the price of gasoline than about calls to battle.[8]

Fourth, the United States was now the area's sole superpower. Overall U.S. engagement in the world might diminish, but the Middle East would remain a very high priority. While much of U.S. involvement there had derived from the Cold War, Moscow's decline did not eliminate the conflict with local extremists. After all, the United States opposed Iranian and Iraqi aggression in the Gulf though neither was acting as a Soviet client.

The Arab states' and Iran's need for good relations with Washington gave it an opportunity to use power as leverage for resolving the Arab-Israeli and Gulf security problems. Now leaders had to worry more about pleasing America than about keeping Arab or Iranian demagogues happy. Even Iran acted to settle old quarrels, helping to release the American hostages held by its Lebanese clients before 1991 ended.

There were, of course, limits on U.S. influence. The local states wanted to concede as little as possible, and America often gave its favors too cheaply. Bush quickly pardoned King Hussein's scandalously pro-Iraq behavior. And while Saddam's case proved that U.S. help for radical dictators would not stop them from turning on its benefactor later, Bush forgave Syria's anti-American terrorism and human rights abuses, gave it a free hand in Lebanon, and let the Saudis pay Syria $2 billion in aid to spend on new Soviet-made arms.

Fifth, it was easier to make progress toward solving the Arab-Israeli conflict, though there were still many barriers to a negotiated solution. Arab states had already been gradually disengaging, learning from the defeats suffered in 1948, 1956, 1967, 1973, and 1982.

The Arabs saw that time was clearly not on their side. Israel was getting stronger, tightening its hold over the captured West Bank and Gaza Strip by building more Jewish settlements. The Palestinian uprising had failed to dislodge Israel from that land. The immigration of several hundred thousand Soviet Jews underlined Israel's staying power.

The new era brought by the Kuwait war further altered these circumstances. Saddam's Scud offensive was, politically, an anticlimax; direct U.S. military intervention in the Gulf forced each Arab leader to wonder if an attack on Israel might bring similar retaliation. For Arab regimes, the Israeli-Palestinian conflict had become too dangerous to toy with anymore.

Instead of appeasing the most radical forces and the PLO, Arab states needed better relations with Washington and had to show some interest in making peace. For the Palestinians, diplomacy seemed the only way to end their suffering. Palestinians had been isolated by their support for Saddam. Over 300,000 of them were expelled from Kuwait and other Gulf states. Americans showed more interest in these deportees' rights than did their supposed Arab brothers. A Kuwaiti banner hung outside al-Fatah's offices there read: "Anyone who is a Palestinian is a traitor. This is the home of the enemy collaborators against Kuwait." In Lebanon, the reviving government disarmed most of the remaining PLO forces.[9]

Syria, Jordan, and the West Bank/Gaza Palestinians had said they would never negotiate directly with Israel, go to the conference table without the PLO, or accept the Camp David framework with its plan for an interim stage of autonomy in the occupied territories. Now they accepted all three and more. Yet the new regional situation also brought peace closer than ever before.

The historic October–November 1991 Madrid peace conference, the ensuing follow-up bilateral talks in Washington, and the January 1992 regional meeting in Moscow—though boycotted by Syria, Lebanon, and the Palestinians—were genuine breakthroughs. In Madrid, the Jordanian, Lebanese, Syrian, and Palestinian delegations talked face-to-face with Israel in a way that was unthinkable before the Kuwait crisis. At the Moscow meeting, Saudi Arabia, Kuwait, Morocco, and Tunisia sat down with Israel for the first time.

Israel itself remained split after so many years of Arab threats, terrorism, and wars. The conservative Shamir government was concerned that a smaller state would be more vulnerable to Syrian or Iraqi aggression, Jordanian instability, and PLO irredentism. Compared to these dangers, conservatives argued, the status quo was not so bad.

The liberal opposition argued that things could be far better. It was willing to cede some of the captured land for solid security guarantees and peace agreements. Maintaining good relations with the United States was a priority, as was successfully integrating hundreds of thousands of Russian Jewish immigrants. While conscious of the continuing threats, the Labor Party and its allies felt more confident in Israel's ability to handle them. In June 1992, Israeli voters elected a government headed by Yitzhak Rabin that pledged to accelerate negotiations and freeze most settlements—those he defined as politically rather than strategically necessary—in the West Bank and Gaza Strip.

Still, while belligerency had turned into passivity by the 1980s and then into a willingness to negotiate after the Kuwait crisis, it would still be a while before talking turned into agreeing. Arab states were not eager to risk abandoning their most fundamental policies. They knew that political conditions could soon change again and hoped that it would be possible to build a good image in Washington without making real concessions.

The fact that Arab-Israeli peace was more possible than ever before did not mean it would be easy to achieve. Americans assume that countries always want to resolve conflicts. In the past, though, many factors—ideology, hope of victory, neighbors' opposition, and fear of instability—made Arab regimes consider peace with Israel as unnecessary and dangerous. The more effective the arrangements to avoid another war—a condition of "no war, no peace" or, more properly, "no fighting, no treaty"—the more acceptable became the status quo.

Jordan had shunned talks, fearing that Arab radical states would subvert it, oil producers would stop subsidies, and its own people might revolt. Even success at the negotiating table was problematic: regaining the West Bank would bring Jordan more potentially rebellious Palestinian citizens; an independent PLO-led state could destabilize Jordan by subverting its own Palestinian majority. For Syria, peace would eliminate its role as the most militant anti-Israel state along with the Soviet help and Arab financial rewards that policy once brought. If Israel became an accepted regional power, it would align with Jordan and Egypt against Syrian interests in Lebanon and elsewhere. Syria's only gain from a settlement—the Golan Heights—was an economically inconsequential place whose main use was as a base for attacking Israel.

The area's new situation mitigated but did not eliminate many of these historic problems. Every likely solution also posed considerable drawbacks for Syria and Jordan. Many Palestinians were loath to make necessary concessions that would split their ranks and to forsake the goal of destroying Israel. The PLO refused to commit itself clearly to recognizing Israel and stopping terrorism; Palestinian Islamic fundamentalist groups took an even harder line.

Saudi Arabia and Kuwait had an easy way out, telling other Arab states to make peace while they stayed mainly on the sidelines. Syria already had Lebanon and did not see the need for any concessions. Other Arabs hoped that the United States would force Israel to hand them the West Bank, Gaza, and Golan without their giving up anything directly. Both sides often acted as if the United States was the party that most needed peace. Syria's government newspaper *Tishrin* greeted visiting Secretary of State James Baker in May 1991 by claiming that diplomatic failure damaged countries directly engaged in the conflict less than "it jeopardized American credibility."[10]

The transition would be complex and hesitant, with the possibility for deadlock at every turn and on dozens of issues. For both sides, the status quo had real attractions. A peace process would be measured in years, not months. Yet despite all the frustrations, circumstances were gradually moving forward, each year and each round of negotiations coming closer to some resolution.

The sixth new regional reality was that the United States had become the guarantor of Gulf stability and security even without troops on the scene or formal defense treaties with the local states. This was quite sufficient for U.S. purposes, since the aim was never to seize the Gulf's oil but merely to keep it out of the hands of enemies. After the demonstration of U.S. power against Iran and Iraq, there would be no challengers for some time. The Saudis wanted to keep arrangements informal. Paradoxically, the overwhelming U.S. advantage rendered all the more unnecessary the formal Gulf security structure Washington advocated, secured by treaties and guarded by the permanent presence of outside troops. The Saudis' very need to invite U.S. troops induced them to show independence by not having them stay.

Sensitive to the myth of Arab solidarity, the United States had favored an "Arab solution" to Gulf security in a March 1991 agreement to station Egyptian and Syrian troops there. The Saudis themselves rejected this idea of accommodating politically correct—but potentially subversive—foreign Arab units. After all, the Saudis felt they had the U.S. army, the world's best, on retainer. The Kuwaitis also had little interest in Arab protection, having signed an agreement to position American military equipment in their country, where a relatively small U.S. force remained behind.

Just as the region preferred American protection to mutual agreements, it had a similar attitude toward arms limitations. After all, explained *The Economist,* the lessons of the Kuwait crisis "point in the other direction. Iraq's neighbors have learnt that it was a mistake to let their own power fall so far behind Saddam Hussein's. Israelis will conclude that, but for their country's undeclared nuclear deterrent, Iraq would already have doused them in toxic chemicals. And Mr. Hussein has been taught to acquire nuclear arms, if he has the chance, before next pouncing on a weaker neighbor."[11]

Thus the U.S. victory in the Gulf eased the pressure for a slower arms race by lowering the risk of local war. Only U.S. preeminence could handle the threat of proliferating missiles and nuclear weapons, by leading international efforts to limit their influx. Since there were enough greedy companies and indigenous scientists to ensure that such arms could be smuggled or locally produced, U.S. deterrence would have to block their use. The fact that this pressure would be applied unequally was simply a recognition of the differences among the parties involved: The United States sold conventional arms to Egypt, Israel, and Saudi Arabia while trying to block the spread of nuclear arms to Syria, Libya, and Iraq—and while tacitly accepting Israel's possession of them.

Political ideas had often been powerful weapons in the Middle East. Democracy was the new buzzword in the Arab soul-searching that followed the Kuwait crisis. Too many other ideological gods had failed. The heirs of revolutions once hailed as fulfilling the masses' aspirations—in Algeria, Egypt, and elsewhere—were now seen as corrupt, inefficient establishments.

Certainly, the proportionately huge new Arab generation, growing up at a more advanced stage of modernization and Westernization, had less respect for the status quo. Development and science, education and communications, urbanization and travel, along with other factors, might eventually create a stable, democratic society. Yet this was no sure thing. During the 1950s and 1960s, many Western scholars had identified dictators like Nasser as agents of modernization who would dissolve traditional society and bring progress.

Might the dictators and monarchs be swept away altogether? This seemed as doubtful to happen quickly as it was pleasant to contemplate. The kind of social development and cultural change necessary to produce democracy was neither a fast nor a certain process. France had taken a century to advance from bloody revolution to ingrained democracy. The road to stable representative government in Germany, Italy, Russia, and Japan had been even rockier.

The Middle East was far from being the American Midwest. In contrast to Eastern Europe, there was no democratic tradition or independent-minded middle class to demand reforms. There were serious barriers to the spread of multiparty parliamentary democracy, an import into the Arab and Islamic world that—whatever cultural, historical, sociological, or other factors are blamed—had not done well or survived long there. Far more than much of Africa and Asia, the Middle East had strong alternative traditions, hostile to many Western ways and institutions.

The Middle East situation of rapid change, discredited rulers, and economic downturns constituted a recipe for antidemocratic instability. Reforms often brought crises; extremists tried to use democracy to seize power themselves; opportunists posed as noble democrats to persuade foreigners to help them gain power. The parliamentary regimes of the new independent states in the 1920s, 1930s, and 1940s had been discredited and were overthrown by populist military coups in the 1950s. The Shah's limited efforts to open up his political system spun out of control and led to the Islamic revolution.

Khomeini's rise to power, Lebanon's civil war, Syria's repression, Iraq's treatment of the Kurds, and the role of radical Islamic fundamentalists as the main opposition show that moderate, nonviolent forces were not the most likely heirs to power. Tough dictators armed with advanced weapons and ready to use force were not easily displaced.

Nor were the self-proclaimed democrats themselves necessarily forces for moderation. In Kuwait, the most outspoken of these before Saddam's invasion had been backed by Iran, Iraq, or Syria. In Algeria and Jordan, those claiming to support civil rights were mainly anti-American fundamentalists, who were Saddam's most enthusiastic supporters and bitterly opposed peace with Israel.

A political culture favoring extremism and demagoguery can turn pluralism into its own enemy. If the public itself supports antidemocratic values, elections and free speech may merely bring new dictators to power. The Arab world could see more internal upheavals, fueled by the friction between social mutations and rigid political systems, with pro-democratic revolts being the least likely outcomes.

As they had done with nationalism and Islam, regimes in Egypt, Jordan, Kuwait, Iran, Lebanon, and Tunisia manipulated parliaments, elections, and multiple parties as a safety valve. At the same time, they used control over the state, the media, and ballot boxes to guarantee their own victory. The opposition accepted its permanent status in exchange for being allowed to function and share some privileges. When Algeria's and Jordan's experiments with democracy looked as if they might let Islamic fundamentalist oppositions gain power, the regimes changed the rules.

Only in the future will it be possible to know if the Middle East finally moved toward convergence with the West or took a path of its own in the twentieth century. One of history's great questions is whether technology will make societies more homogeneous or make it easier for them to preserve their distinct traditions. Does an industrial society inevitably create an educated middle class that demands more freedom, or can technology just as easily be used to reinforce the existing way of life?

People do not simply walk away from their own history and political culture; they always carry some of it along as baggage. The Gulf crisis and the events before it shook but did not break the region's system. Some regimes would continue hitting their heads against the wall, albeit less hard.

Iraq, Libya, Syria, Iran, and the PLO were still led by extremists who accepted a temporary, tactical need to make some compromises with U.S. power while considering it antithetical to their ambitions and looking for a way out. On a regional level, though, they could not dictate the future for others. As so often happened in Middle East history, the barking of the dogs did not interrupt the caravan's progress. Middle East dictators and extremists paid for miscalculating America's peculiar combination of naïveté and great power when they provoked that country, which could not have been less inclined to fight them.

Still, since the Middle East never lacked the capacity to astonish, it should not have lost the ability to surprise the United States. The likelihood was that the region would remain a cauldron of turmoil, though the temperature would be somewhat reduced. Equally, the United States, as its responsibility grew, was learning more about the area, while retaining a large measure of miscomprehension. Perhaps the best metaphor for this situation was a story told by Muhammad Mossadegh, who himself had been a victim of American gullibility. A moderate Iranian prime minister, Mossadegh was misperceived as pro-Communist by the United States and was overthrown by the CIA in 1953.

As a young student in Switzerland, Mossadegh wanted a driver's license for his motorcycle. The test required that he drive around on the vehicle for an hour. A Swiss policeman at the starting point noted the time. Off went Mossadegh. A few feet beyond the first street corner, out of the official's sight, he crashed into a vegetable stand, sending produce flying in all directions. The vendor started screaming at Mossadegh; Mossadegh yelled back. A crowd gathered, taking sides in the dispute. Finally, Mossadegh and the merchant agreed on a price for the damage. Mossadegh mounted his motorcycle and rode back around the corner. The Swiss policeman looked at his watch. "Congratulations," he said. "You passed."

The U.S. experience in the Middle East was not so different from Mossadegh's ride—the road to success was paved with miscalculations and disasters—but, like Mossadegh, America passed the test. The course of U.S. policy was like that of a roller coaster, which weathers all the bumps and dips to arrive safely. Yet the U.S.

comprehension of what had happened often more closely approximated the policeman's viewpoint, misinterpreting the course of events.

Each time there had been a life-or-death confrontation, the United States acted as a preserver of relative liberty. In a fashion that was always better late than never, it saved the globe in World War II; endured a long, costly struggle against Soviet communism; and helped stop Iran from exporting revolution and Iraq from expansionism. In the end, the United States arrived at the finish line, achieving its goals. But it failed to understand what had happened along the way.

NOTES

CHAPTER ONE: Innocents in the Bazaar

1. U.S. Department of State, *Foreign Relations of the United States, Paris Peace Conference 1919*, vol. XI (Washington, 1945), p. 133.
2. For telling me this story, recounted in Crane's unpublished memoirs, I am deeply indebted to Professor Martin Kramer.
3. Just as he was a patron for the author of Pan-Islam, in the 1930s Crane financially sustained George Antonius, a Palestinian Christian who worked with the British and wrote *The Arab Awakening*, the book most responsible for formulating the myth of Arab nationalism as the centerpiece and inevitable future of Middle East history.
4. Pascal Bruckner, *Tears of the White Man* (New York, 1986), pp. 117, 121, 122–24. This can lead to effects bordering on the comical. More than one commentator claimed that Americans in Lebanon were targeted as retribution for U.S. shelling of rebel artillery, which accidentally hit villages in 1983, failing to realize that those places were Druze, while anti-American terrorism emanated from the Shia Muslims.
5. Intellectual iconoclasts have never fared well in the Arab-Islamic world. An Egyptian scholar, Ali abd al-Raziq, became a pariah after writing a book in 1925 suggesting that Muhammad was only a religious, not a political authority. Sadiq al-Azm, scion of a famous Damascus family, was persecuted by Lebanese Muslim clerics in the 1970s and lost his Lebanese university teaching position for writing a book suggesting that Islam should be excluded from politics. Author Salman Rushdie found that he could not write freely about Islam even from the sanctity of London, when the Iranian government threatened to kill him and he had to go into hiding.
6. Personal conversations.
7. Bruckner, op. cit., p. 213. On the history of British Arabism, see Elie Kedourie, *The Chatham House Version* (London, 1970).
8. Seth Tillman, *The United States in the Middle East: Interests and Obstacles* (Bloomington, Ind., 1982), p. 276; Malcolm Kerr, "American Middle East Policy: Kissinger, Carter and the Future," Institute for Palestine Studies Paper #14, 1980, p. 8. See also Thomas C. Sorensen, "U.S. Foreign Policy and the

Middle East: Origins and Limitations," *Journal of Arab Affairs*, vol. 2, no. 1, (October 1982), pp. 1–27.

9. For a survey of these textbooks, see the author's article in Josh Muravchik, *Global Education* (Washington, 1992). None of the texts examined mentioned, for example, that Iraq invaded Iran in 1980, that Iraq's government was repressive, or that it used chemical weapons against its own citizens.

10. Fouad Ajami, "The Arab Road," *Foreign Policy*, Summer 1982, pp. 23–24; Fouad Ajami, "Stress in the Arab Triangle," *Foreign Policy*, Winter 1977–78, p. 106.

CHAPTER TWO: American Graffiti

1. Kerr, op. cit., p. 7. He was assassinated by Lebanese terrorists in 1984. For examples of overestimating Soviet success, see Dev Muraka, "Moscow's Comeback to Center Stage," *Middle East*, August 1981; Sulayman al-Furzuli, "Soviet Peace Gives Kremlin Strategic Gains at U.S. Expense," *al-Hawadith*, June 11, 1982. Muhammad Salim al-Sayyid, "The USSR and the Palestinian-Israeli War," *al-Siyasah al-Duwaliyya*, October 1982. Ghassan Bayram, "Moscow Has Won the Lebanese War," *al-Mustaqbal*, April 28, 1984; Larry Napper, "The Arab Autumn of 1984: A Case Study of Soviet Middle East Policy," *Middle East Journal*, Autumn 1985.

2. Edward Said, *The Palestine Question and the American Context*, Institute for Palestine Studies (Beirut, 1979).

3. Kerr, op. cit., p. 11.

4. Robert Lacey, "Saudi Arabia: A More Visible Role," *The World Today*, January 1982, p. 11.

5. See, for example, *Gallup Report*, "Americans Sanction More Raids if Libyan Terrorism Continues," no. 247 (April 1986); *Washington Post*, April 30, 1986.

6. *U.S. News & World Report*, April 28, 1986. Robert Satloff, "The Arab World Is Sitting It Out," *New York Times*, May 9, 1986; Laurie Mylroie, "Arab World's Silence Refutes the 'Experts,' " *Los Angeles Times*, April 18, 1986.

7. Kerr, op. cit., pp. 17, 7–8.

8. John Campbell, "The Middle East: A House of Containment Built on Shifting Sands," *Foreign Affairs*, vol. 60, no. 3 (1981), p. 626.

9. Ibid.; *Time*, June 16, 1986, p. 19.

10. Charles MacDonald, *U.S. Policy and Gulf Security* (Stanford, 1984); Elmo

Zumwalt and Worth Bagley, *Washington Times*, June 22, 1987; *Wall Street Journal*, November 4, 1980; Udo Steinbach, "The Iranian-Iraqi Conflict and Its Impact Upon the 'Arc of Crisis,'" *Journal of South Asian and Middle East Studies*, Summer 1983, p. 15. See also Faisal al-Salem, "The U.S. and the Gulf: What Do the Arabs Want?" *Journal of South Asian and Middle East Studies*, Fall 1982, pp. 24–25.

11. Kerr, op. cit., p. 9.
12. Assistant Secretary of State Richard W. Murphy, Testimony to the House of Representatives Foreign Affairs Committee, March 6, 1986.
13. Said, op. cit., pp. 13–15.
14. Ibid.

CHAPTER THREE: The Discreet Charm of Saddam

1. Fuad Rikabi, *al-Hal al-Awhad* (Cairo, 1963), pp. 81–84.
2. Speech to Arab trade unions, November 3, 1990, U.S. Department of Commerce, Foreign Broadcast Information Service, *Daily Report*—hereafter *FBIS*—November 5, 1990, p. 15.
3. Ofra Bengio, "Ba'thi Iraq in Search of Identity," *Orient*, December 1987, p. 515; Amatzia Baram, *Culture, History & Ideology in the Formation of the Ba'thist Iraq*.
4. Tawfiq al-Hakim, *The Return of Consciousness* (New York, 1985), pp. 20–21, 28.
5. Ibid.
6. Amatzia Baram, "Qawmiyya and Wataniyya in Ba'thi Iraq: The Search for a New Balance," *Middle Eastern Studies*, vol. 19, no. 2 (April 1983), pp. 194, 196, 198.
7. Ibid.
8. Ibid., pp. 190–91.
9. *Al-Thawra*, May 5, 1986, cited in Bengio, op. cit., p. 512.
10. Baram, op. cit., p. 193.
11. Ian Black, "Iraqi Intelligence Colonel Led Terrorists in Bid to Kill Envoy," *Guardian*, March 7, 1983.
12. Amnesty International, *Iraq: Evidence of Torture*, April 28, 1981.
13. *Al-Thawra*, January 3, 1980, *FBIS*, January 4, 1980, E-1–2.
14. *Business Week*, August 4, 1975 and June 6, 1977; *Newsweek*, July 4, 1977.

15. *Washington Post*, June 12, 1977.
16. Uday Saddam Hussein, "The Other Face of Saddam Hussein," *al-Qadisiyya*, August 14, 1990 (*FBIS*, August 28, 1990, p. 31).
17. *Le Monde*, August 5–6, 1979; *New York Times*, July 30 and August 9, 1979. Among those executed were former deputy prime minister Adnan Hussein, the leader of the trade union federation, former education and industry ministers, and the commander of a Baghdad garrison.

CHAPTER FOUR: Iran's Revolution and Gulf War I

1. Uriel Dann, "The Iraqi Invasion of Kuwait: Historical Observations," Dayan Center, August 1990.
2. *New York Times*, January 12, 1972.
3. Throughout this book, the phrase "Gulf Arab monarchies" will be used to refer collectively to Saudi Arabia, Kuwait, the United Arab Emirates, Qatar, Bahrain, and Oman.
4. All these issues are described in more detail in Barry Rubin, *Paved with Good Intentions: The American Experience and Iran* (New York, 1980).
5. Quotations are from Khomeini's last testament.
6. Speech of February 11, 1986, in *FBIS—South Asia*, February 12, 1986.
7. *Kayhan International*, November 3, 1985; Said Raja'i Khorasani, *Iran Times*, January 24, 1983; Asghar Musavi Khoini, *New York Times*, November 5, 1982; *Wall Street Journal*, April 26, 1982.
8. Bengio, op. cit.
9. Statement of January 1981, cited in Adeed Dawisha, "Iraq and the Arab World: The Gulf War and After," *The World Today*, May 1981, p. 189.
10. Bruce Maddy-Weitzman, "Islam and Arabism: The Iran-Iraq War," *Washington Quarterly*, vol. 5, no. 4 (Autumn 1982), pp. 181–88; Tehran International Radio, August 4, 1985 (*FBIS*, August 7, 1985, pp. I-4–5).
11. Ibid., p. 194.
12. Foreign Affairs, *Year in Review 1981*, p. 557.
13 Amos Perlmutter, "The Courtship of Iraq," *New Republic*, May 3, 1980; "MacNeil/Lehrer Report," April 19, 1980, transcript, pp. 19–22; *Wall Street Journal*, April 29, 1981.
14. Ibid.; Amatzia Baram, "Saddam Hussein: A Political Profile," *Jerusalem Quarterly*, no. 17 (Fall 1980).

15. August 19, 1980 (*FBIS*, August 20, 1980, pp. E-1–2).
16. *New York Times*, June 17, 1981.
17. Maddy-Weitzman, op. cit.; Tehran International Radio, August 4, 1985 (*FBIS*, August 7, 1985, pp. I-4–5).
18. Three billion dollars went directly to Iran, $1.4 billion was returned after being held a few additional months to ensure U.S bank loans were repaid, and $4 billion was eventually remitted after arbitration of other claims. Iran used an additional $3.7 billion of assets to pay off U.S. bank loans. All this money, of course, belonged to Iran in the first place. Tehran was paid no ransom.
19. Mohammed Ayoob, "Between Khomeini and Begin: The Arab Dilemma," *The World Today*, July 1983, pp. 254–63; *The Economist*, "Black Tuesday for the Arabs," May 29, 1982; Jamal Ismail, "Khomeini and Zionism Are Two Bayonets in Conflict with Arab Nationalism," *al-Dustur*, November 29, 1982; Abd al-Wahhab al-Qaysi, "Anybody Who Does Not Side with Iraq in Its War Is a Traitor to Arabism," *al-Dustur*, April 14, 1986; "The Debris of Arab Unity," *South*, September 1982.
20. See, for example, *FBIS-SA*, December 27, 1985, p. I-1 and December 30, 1985, pp. I-1–2; and *Kayhan*, December 21, 1985 (*FBIS-SA*, January 2, 1986, p. I-1).
21. Prime Minister Mir-Hussein Musavi, *Iran Times*, March 14, 1986.

CHAPTER FIVE: Iraq's Victory

1. *The Economist*, October 3, 1987; *Iran Times*, March 29, 1985.
2. *Washington Post*, April 11, 1981.
3. Joseph Kostiner, "Counterproductive Mediation: Saudi Arabia and the Iran Arms Deal," *Middle East Review*, Summer 1987; *The Economist*, August 16, 1986.
4. On Montazeri, see *Iran Times*, May 17 and November 29, 1985. Both Montazeri and Khamenehi were Khomeini's former students. During the shah's regime, Montazeri was in prison or internal exile for twelve years and was reportedly tortured. He was released in late 1978, and Khomeini gave him a series of high-level posts.
5. *Newsweek* and *Time*, March 25, 1985.
6. Israeli prime minister Shimon Peres picked as negotiators David Kimche,

director-general of the Foreign Ministry; Jacob Nimrodi, former Israeli defense attaché in Tehran; and Al Schwimmer, founder of Israel Aircraft Industries.

7. *Iran Times*, July 12, 1985.

8. This issue is discussed in Barry Rubin, "The Iranian Revolution and Gulf Instability," in Shirin Tahir-Kheli et al., *The Iran-Iraq War: Old Conflict, New Weapons* (Praeger, 1982).

9. President's Special Review Board, *The Tower Commission Report*, (New York, 1987), p. 73. Members of the commission were former senator John Tower, former secretary of state Edmund Muskie, and former national security adviser Brent Scowcroft.

10. The role of U.S. politics in the affair is not entirely clear. Israeli officials say that North sought to transfer the Hawks faster so that hostages might be released as a public relations gimmick for the November 1985 U.S.-Soviet summit meeting. Hakim testified that North pressed hard to have the hostages freed to help Republicans in the November 1986 elections. The contra diversion scheme and the plan to obtain funds for other covert operations added to Casey's and North's incentive to sell arms.

11. *The Tower Commission Report*, op. cit., pp. 18–19, 63. Actually, the possibilities for a rescue were higher than the administration realized, and it rejected proposals to try for fear of failing. For a firsthand account, see William Cowan, "Intelligence, Rescue, Retaliation, and Decision Making," in Barry Rubin, *Terrorism and Politics* (New York, 1991).

12. The story was broken by an article in *al-Shira*, November 3, 1986 (*FBIS*, November 6, 1986, pp. I-1–3). See also *FBIS*, November 5, 1986, p. 16.

13. *Report of the Congressional Committees Investigating the Iran-Contra Affair* (Washington, 1987), p. 12.

14. *New York Times*, May 26, 1985.

15. See, for example, *New York Times*, October 5, 1984; "The Tuesday Fires," *al-Dustur* (Amman), June 30, 1986; *Arab Times* (Kuwait), July 18, 1987.

16. *FBIS*, June 30, 1987, p. J-2.

17. *Washington Post*, June 17 and 29, 1987.

18. *Washington Post*, June 3, June 30, and September 19, 1987.

19. Christopher Madison, "A Reflagged Policy," *National Journal*, November 28, 1987.

20. Henry Kissinger, "Wandering in the Gulf," *Washington Post*, June 21, 1987.

21. Prime Minister Hussein Mussavi, *Washington Post*, September 7, 1987; *Washington Post*, August 13, 1987.
22. *The Economist*, August 29, 1987.
23. *Washington Post*, August 13, 1987.
24. *New York Times*, September 23 and 26, 1987.
25. *Washington Post*, October 18, 1987.
26. *Washington Post*, June 6, June 26, and October 11, 1987; Kuwait News Agency, October 26, 1987 (*FBIS*, October 27, 1987, p. 16); *New York Times*, October 16, 1987.
27. *FBIS*, May 20, 1987, p. C-6. See also *Washington Post*, June 26, 1987. Ambassador Saud Nasir al-Sabah, Kuwait News Agency, October 26, 1987 (*FBIS*, October 27, 1987, pp. 16–17); see also *FBIS*, June 23, 1987, p. J-1.
28. *Washington Post*, December 1, 1987.
29. *Al-Jumhuriyya*, August 23, 1988.

CHAPTER SIX: THE EVIL GENIES OF HISTORY

1. Hassan Nafan, "Arab Nationalism: A Response to Ajami's Thesis on the 'End of Pan-Arabism,' " *Journal of Arab Affairs*, vol. 2, no. 2 (Spring 1983), pp. 173–74, 182.
2. Hisham Sharabi, *Arab Intellectuals and the West* (Baltimore, 1970), see pp. 98–101, 130–36. The title of a 1930s article was "Why Are Moslems Lagging Behind the Christians?" Its author, Shakib Arslan, urged Islam unity. His brother, Adil, favored Pan-Arab nationalism and later became a Nazi collaborator.
3. Hilmi al-Qa'ud, "Relaxation . . . Then What?" *al-Da'wa*, July 1979, in *Joint Publications Research Service*, no. 201 (August 29, 1979), pp. 28–30.
4. The notion of an Arab nation had occurred to no one before the 1880s and only to a tiny group of intellectuals or army officers before 1920. Nonetheless, Arab writers never tired of claiming that Arab identity has always been the central theme of Middle East history and that Arabs would inevitably form a single state, owing to their common language, territory, and culture. See, for example, Awni Farsakh, "History and Identity in the Arab Homeland," *al-Mustaqbal al-Arabi*, May 1983, pp. 24–53, and Sabri Ismail Abdallah, "The Arab Nation: The Scientific Truth Versus Error and Confusion," *al-Mustaqbal al-Arabi*, December 1985, pp. 4–19. Radical movements in Lebanon played a

major role in the civil war. Other groups included the region-wide Arab National Movement, the Popular Front for the Liberation of Palestine, and the Democratic Front for the Liberation of Palestine.

5. Sharabi, op. cit., pp. 130–36.

6. Fouad Ajami, "The End of Arab Nationalism," *New Republic*, August 12, 1991, p. 23.

7. See, for example, Martin Kramer, "Azoury: A Further Episode," *Middle Eastern Studies*, vol. 18, no. 4 (October 1982), pp. 351–58.

8. *Al-Mustaqbal al-Arabi*, July 1984, cited in Elie Kedourie, "Critics in Despair," *New Republic*, March 24, 1986, p. 33. This is not meant to understate the historical basis for such attitudes. The fact that apparent rivals Britain and Russia divided Iran into spheres of influence in 1907 and the Anglo-Soviet accord forcing abdication of the shah in 1941 reverberated in Khomeini's view of the Cold War as a facade behind which Washington and Moscow were united in exploiting the rest of the world. The return of Shah Mohammad Pahlavi to power in 1953 with the CIA's help was a basis for the idea that the United States controlled the country.

9. Constantine Zurayk, *The Meaning of the Disaster* (Beirut, 1956), p. 2.

10. Ajami, "The End of Arab Nationalism," loc. cit., p. 25.

11. Ibid.

12. Adeed Dawisha, "Comprehensive Peace in the Middle East and the Comprehension of Arab Politics," *Middle East Journal*, Winter 1983, pp. 44–45.

13. Ibid.

14. Cited in Anouar Abdelmalek, *Contemporary Arab Political Thought* (London, 1983), p. 40.

15. Al-Hakim, op. cit., pp. 50, 55. See also Hasan Madiyah Salim, "The Fostering of the Arab Child's Political Consciousness," *al-Mustaqbal al-Arabi*, May 1983; Tawfiq Abu Bakr, "The Flourishing of Arab Regionalism: Between Truth and Exaggeration," *al-Arabi*, September 1984; and Stewart Reiser, "Pan-Arabism Revisited," *Middle East Journal*, vol. 37, no. 2 (Spring 1983).

16. The same rule applied among competing political movements. Thus, despite its name, Lebanon's leftist Progressive Socialist party was led by a feudal clan chief and consisted of his Druze followers.

17. Adeed Dawisha, "Arab Regimes, Legitimacy and Foreign Policy." Paper presented at the American Political Science Association meeting, November 1984.

18. Ibid. See also Hasan Hanafi, "Arab National Thought in the Balance," *Jerusalem Quarterly*, no. 25 (Fall 1982), pp. 54–67.

19. Ibid.

20. Cited in Emanuel Sivan, *Radical Islam* (New Haven, 1985), p. 74.

21. Lewis Awad, "The Arab Society: Possibility of Dialogue, The Egyptian Experience," in Edward Said, *The Arabs Today: Alternatives for Tomorrow* (Columbus, Ohio, 1973), pp. 62ff. In the same book (p. 42), Arab sociologist Sadiq al-Azm writes that "Reactionary anthropologists have declared showmanship and emotionality as constant traits of the Arab. These are in reality ill symptoms of a backward society." But these traits exist even if they are only "symptoms."

22. Ajami, "The End of Arab Nationalism," loc. cit., p. 26.

23. *Iran Times*, November 29, 1985.

24. Al-Hakim, op. cit., pp. 49–50.

25. Fouad Ajami, "The End of Pan-Arabism," *Foreign Affairs*, Winter 1978–79, p. 357.

26. Fouad Ajami, "Between Cairo and Damascus," *Foreign Affairs*, vol. 54, no. 2 (April 1976), p. 444.

27. Fouad Ajami, "Stress in the Arab Triangle," op. cit., pp. 91–92.

28. Mohammed Anis Salem, *The World Today*, May 1982, pp. 175–77, 184. See also Sidqi Ahmad al-Dajani et al., "The Arab-Arab Dialogue," *al-Mustaqbal al-Arabi*, December 1982, pp. 134–46; Hasan abu-Talib, "The Crisis of Arab Solidarity," *al-Siyasa al-Duwaliyya*, April 1982, pp. 119–21; Hafiz al-Jamali, "What to Do?" *al-Ma'rifa*, December 1982, pp. 22–37; Awni Fursakh, "The Imperialistic Idea and the Plan for Disunity," *al-Mustaqbal al-Arabi*, April 1982, pp. 123–30.

29. *The Economist*, May 15, 1982, p. 60; Arnold Hottinger, *Swiss Review of World Affairs*, July 1983. See also the series in *al-Dustur* (Amman): "Inferno Swallows an Arab City," August 22, 1983; "The Day of Looting," September 5, 1983; "An Arab City Drowns in a Pool of Blood," September 12, 1983.

30. Ajami, "The End of Arab Nationalism," loc. cit., p. 25.

31. Barry Rubin, *Islamic Fundamentalists in Egyptian Politics* (New York, 1991).

32. To hear this message's flavor and power, listen to a sermon by Khomeini: Islam "has answers for the needs of men from the beginning to the end . . . for daily life and for issues that might arise in the future and about which we know nothing now. . . . [It] satisfies all the material, spiritual, philosophical,

and mystical needs of all humanity at all times until Judgement Day." It was
a duty to fight to put this regime into authority everywhere. If Muhammad
had stayed home and preached, said Khomeini, "we would have followed
his example." Instead, he launched "an armed struggle and established a
government. He then sent missionaries and representatives everywhere. . . .
He brought the glad tidings that we are going to conquer the entire world
and destroy everybody." Muslims today should imitate the prophet: "He set
up a government, we should do the same. He participated in various wars,
we should do the same. He defended Islam, we should also defend it." Even
the occasion of Khomeini's sermon, Muhammad's birthday, showed divisions
within Islam: Sunni Moslems generally don't celebrate it; Sunnis and Shias
do not even agree on the date. Thus Iran's call for an Islamic "unity week"
for the anniversary set off heated criticism from abroad. Speech on Tehran
radio, November 10, 1987, in *FBIS-SA*, November 12, 1987. See also *Kayhan
International*, May 19, 1985.

33. *Iran Times*, December 22 and 27, 1985. The amounts from Western countries
and Turkey exceeded 78 percent.

34. See above, note 32. Islamic fundamentalism, he notes, is not against "new
inventions, innovations, and industries." It merely rejects "freedom to do all
that is forbidden and corrupt." He advocated a capitalist system with some
state direction, emphasizing restraint and social justice. "Islam is not in favor
of amassing great wealth at the expense of depriving the meek and oppressed
masses."

35. Hisham Sharabi, "Unity, Disunity, and Fragmentation in the Arab World,"
in Edward Said, *The Arabs Today: Alternatives for Tomorrow* (Columbus, Oh.,
1973) pp. 137–38.

36. King Hussein, "Unity, Disunity and Fragmentation in the Arab World,"
speech of November 15, 1985 (*FBIS*, November 15, 1985, p. D-11); Mubarak,
Qatar News Agency, March 6, 1986 (*FBIS*, March 7, 1986, p. A-1). In the
words of Edward Said, "An enthusiasm for distant generality thus covers up
particular experiences and with them immediate failure." The struggle to
obtain the unattainable leaves the Arab "embittered or apathetic, his leaders
have as little regard for him as he has vague passion for them." Said, op. cit.,
pp. 5–6, 137–38.

37. Ajami, "Stress in the Arab Triangle," loc. cit., pp. 100–1.

38. Ajami, "The End of Arab Nationalism" loc. cit., p. 26.

CHAPTER SEVEN: AMERICA'S FRIEND SADDAM

1. Fuad Mattar, *al-Tadamun* (London), July 10, 1989 (*FBIS*, July 26, 1989, pp. 19–23).
2. Ibid.
3. Susan Epstein, "The World Embargo on Food Exports to Iraq," Congressional Research Service, September 25, 1990; *Washington Post*, August 8 and 13, September 16 and 17, 1990; *Los Angeles Times*, August 7, 1990. See also Paul Gigot, "A Great American Screw-Up," *The National Interest*, Winter 1990–91.
4. *Washington Post*, February 25, 1992.
5. Henry B. Gonzalez, "BNL, Iraq and the CCC Program." Numerous internal government documents on these matters were provided by the House of Representatives Banking, Finance and Urban Affairs Committee. See, for example, State Department memo "The Iraqi CCC Program," October 26, 1989.
6. Ibid., *Washington Post*, April 29, 1992.
7. Ibid. In a cable to Baker, Glaspie wrote, "From a foreign policy perspective the [Corporation's] decision is difficult to justify. . . . Turning down the CCC credits would send the signal that the administration had decided to join forces with those in the Congress who had already reached the conclusion that the US had no option but to pursue a policy of sanctions and containment." The Agriculture Department investigation, she added, had found no wrong-doing on the part of Iraq.
8. *The Economist*, October 27, 1990; State Department report, "Unauthorized BNL Lending to Iraq," August 1989; *Washington Post*, March 22, 1992. The Justice Department did not indict, however, a Jordanian businessman involved in the conspiracy who was also well connected to King Hussein of Jordan. *Washington Post*, March 31, 1992.
9. Report of House Banking, Finance and Urban Affairs Committee, February 3, 1992; Rep. Henry Gonzalez letter to President George Bush, January 31, 1992. See also House of Representatives Committee on Banking, Finance and Urban Affairs, *Banca Nazionale del Laboro (BNL)*, April 9, 1991; *Iraqi and Banca Nazionale del Laboro Participation in Export-Import Programs*, April 17, 1991; *Banca Nazionale del Laboro Affair and Regulation and Supervision of U.S. Branches and Agencies of Foreign Banks*, October 16, 1990. See also, *Washington Post*, March 17, 1992.

10. In fairness, it should be added that the administration criticized Iraq's human rights violations and some of its other acts, but these statements were never linked to actions. Iraqi authorities naturally expected this practice to continue, with formal complaints merely providing a cover for practical acquiescence. From all indications, this is what Saddam thought would happen when he invaded Kuwait.

11. *Washington Post*, May 9, 1992.

12. *Washington Post*, October 6, 1988; see the Defense Intelligence Agency's submission on the Helmy case, September 19, 1989.

13. *Arab Times*, February 15, 1989 (*FBIS*, February 17, 1989, pp. 28–29); speech to international meeting of Arab lawyers, November 28, 1988 (*FBIS*, November 30, 1988, pp. 20–28).

14. Bashir al-Alak, "Iraq Economy Said to Be Strong Despite War," *Baghdad Observer*, November 18, 1980.

15. *New York Times*, November 3, 1988; June 8 and November 25, 1989.

16. A few articles were published detailing corruption, for example in *al-Iraq*, March 7, 1989; *Christian Science Monitor*, April 17, 1989; *Arab Times*, February 15, 1989 (*FBIS*, February 17, 1989, pp. 28–29).

17. *Financial Times*, April 18, 1989; *The Economist*, December 16, 1989, p. 16.

18. My thanks to Dr. Patrick Clawson for this list of projects.

19. November 14, 1988 (*FBIS*, November 16, 1988, pp. 27–29).

20. *Los Angeles Times*, July 12, 1989; *Washington Times*, August 16, 1989; *New York Times* and *Washington Post*, March 1, 1989; February 8, 1989, briefing transcript; *Le Monde*, November 10, 1988.

21. *Washington Times*, October 17, 1988; *Washington Post*, October 12, 1988; *New York Times*, May 23, 1990; letter from Marshall Wiley, *Washington Post*, October 20, 1988.

22. *Washington Post*, October 4, 6, and 12, 1988; Taha Yasin Ramadan, *al-Anba*, October 8, 1988 (*FBIS*, October 12, 1988, pp. 27–30).

23. Nizar Hamdoon, "The U.S.-Iran Arms Deal: An Iraqi Critique," *Middle East Review*, Summer 1982, pp. 35–36.

24. *Kayhan*, October 20, 1987 (*FBIS*, November 4, 1987, p. 54).

25. Speech to Arab lawyers, November 28, 1988 (*FBIS*, November 30, 1988, pp. 21–26); *Financial Times*, April 18, 1989; *Christian Science Monitor*, April 17, 1989. Iraq shipped tanks, rocket launchers, and ammunition to Lebanese militias and the anti-Syria Lebanon government. David Butter, "Iraq Chal-

lenges Syria for Centre Stage," *Middle East Economic Digest*, October 28, 1988. *Al-Thawra*, April 23, 1989 (*FBIS*, April 25, 1989, p. 29), called on Syrians to overthrow their rulers.

26. Laurie Mylroie, *Boston Globe*, October 14, 1990; *al-Sharq al-Awsat*, March 8, 1989 (*FBIS*, March 14, 1989).

27. Kuwait News Agency, February 15, 1989 (*FBIS*, February 15, 1989); *FBIS*, April 3, 1989. See also Iraq News Agency, June 7, 1989 (*FBIS*, June 7, 1989, pp. 21–22).

28. *Al-Thawra*, April 9, 1989 (*FBIS*, April 10, 1989).

29. *Al-Thawra*, April 21, 1989 (*FBIS*, April 25, 1989, p. 28).

30. *Al-Tadamun*, December 4, 1989 (*FBIS*, December 7, 1989, p. 22).

31. See, for example, *New York Times*, January 17, 18, 29, and 31, 1989; *Washington Post*, January 14 and 19, 1989; *Washington Times*, January 19, 1989. Publicity about a new Libyan factory for making chemical weapons heightened attention on the issue. *Washington Times*, March 8, 1989.

32. Iraq News Agency, May 1, 1989 (*FBIS*, May 2, 1989, p. 19). See also *FBIS*, May 9, 1989, pp. 18–21. Iraq News Agency, *FBIS*, May 1, 1989, p. 20.

33. *FBIS*, March 20, 1989, p. 33; *Middle East Mirror*, December 21, 1989, pp. 7–8; *al-Jumhuriyya* (Baghdad), December 19, 1988 (*FBIS*, December 27, 1988; pp. 21–23). *Washington Times* and *Washington Post*, January 19, 1989; *New York Times*, January 29, 1989.

34. James Bruce, "Assessing Iraq's Missile Technology," *Jane's Defence Weekly*, December 23, 1989, pp. 1371, 1374. *Washington Post*, May 3, 1989. Seth Carus, *The Genie Unleashed: Iraq's Chemical and Biological Weapons Program* (Washington, 1989).

35. *Washington Times*, December 14, 1989. For a tour of an Iraqi nuclear facility, *Alif-Ba*, July 26, 1989 (*FBIS*, August 7, 1989, pp. 18–20).

36. *Al-Jumhuriyya* (Baghdad), December 19, 1988 (*FBIS*, December 27, 1988, pp. 21–23); *FBIS*, March 20, 1989, p. 33.

37. *Los Angeles Times*, March 9, 1990. An unusually foresighted *Los Angeles Times* editorial of March 10, 1990, was entitled "Why Israel Needs Those Missiles," pointing to the threat of an Iraqi attack.

38. Not all American politicians understood the importance of nonproliferation. Former president Jimmy Carter announced, "It may be that the very knowledge that there are chemical, biological and nuclear weapons in the Middle East will cause these leaders to be cautious in what they do."

39. *Washington Post*, September 13, 1990.
40. *Alif-Ba*, April 4 and July 2, 1990; *al-Jumhuriyya*, May 19 and 27, 1990; *al-Qabas* (Kuwait), May 13, 1990; *New York Times*, October 17, 1988.
41. *Christian Science Monitor*, April 21, 1989.
42. *The Economist*, May 12, 1990.
43. *Christian Science Monitor*, April 21, 1989.
44. *Middle East Mirror*, February 19, 1990, p. 2.
45. *New York Times*, *Washington Post*, and *Washington Times*, June 23, 1989; *Defense Week*, February 13, 1989; *New York Times*, February 3, 1989.
46. House Foreign Affairs Committee hearings, November 7, 1989, Federal Transcripts; *Middle East Mirror*, November 15, 1989, p. 25.
47. Interviews with U.S. officials; *Washington Post*, February 9, 1990.

CHAPTER EIGHT: Brave New Gulf

1. Bahrain's minister of development Youssef Shirawi, quoted in *Los Angeles Times*, July 14, 1985.
2. About 30 percent of Kuwaitis and 10 percent of Saudis were Shia Muslims.
3. *Washington Post*, January 12, 1990; *The Economist*, April 18, 1987.
4. *The Economist*, June 27, 1987, p. 14; Hobart Rowan, "Reassessing Saudi Arabia's Economic Vitality," *Washington Post*, July 19, 1986.
5. See Chapter Two.
6. Barton Gellman, "Romancing the Saud," *New Republic*, August 4, 1986.
7. *New York Times*, March 1, 1986; *Wall Street Journal*, July 9, 1990.
8. Cited in *FBIS*, April 12, 1988, p. 27.
9. *Ha'aretz*, August 17, 1990.
10. Speech of December 1980, cited in Daniel Pipes, "The Politics of Muslim Anti-Semitism," *Commentary*, August 1981, vol. 72, no. 3, p. 39. See also Rushdi Abbas al-Amara, "The Historical and Religious Influences on Israel's Behavior," *al-Siyasah al-Duwaliyyah*, no. 70 (October 1982), pp. 64–85.

CHAPTER NINE: The Desert Road to Kuwait

1. *Wall Street Journal*, December 13, 1989.
2. Text *FBIS*, February 27, 1990, pp. 1–5. In a January speech in Cairo, Saddam also blamed the United States for the immigration of Soviet Jews to Israel. *Washington Times*, January 30, 1990.

3. *New York Times*, March 30 and April 9, 1990; *Washington Post*, March 30, 1990; *Boston Globe*, January 15, 1990.

4. Lee Stokes, UPI, March 20, 1990; *The Economist*, March 17, 1990, p. 40.

5. Iraq News Agency, October 31, 1989 (*FBIS*, November 1, 1989, pp. 19–20); *New York Times*, March 15 and 18, 1990.

6. *Washington Post*, May 29, 1990; speech, *FBIS*, May 31, 1990.

7. *Christian Science Monitor*, January 10, 1990.

8. Phebe Marr, House Foreign Affairs Committee hearing, July 17, 1990.

9. Quotes from text in *Washington Post*, September 13, 1990.

10. *Washington Post*, September 23, 1990. Glaspie's testimony to the Senate Foreign Relations Committee, March 20, 1991.

11. Glaspie to Baker, July 15, 1990. A good sense of the administration's view is conveyed in Assistant Secretary of State Kelly's May 25, 1990, testimony to the House of Representatives Foreign Affairs Committee: "The fundamental goal of responsible U.S. policy towards Iraq is to influence Iraq to play the responsible regional role that its new power requires." Kelly highlighted Iraq's "legitimate security concerns" and called Saddam's belligerent statements "an attempt to deter what he genuinely fears is an imminent Israeli attack. . . . We believe Iraq has clearly received the important message of unanimous U.S. Government concern over its recent actions." Baghdad "is signalling that it wants to bring U.S.-Iraq relations back to a more positive level. . . . Instead of isolating Iraq we will only wind up isolating ourselves" by imposing sanctions.

12. The following quotes come from her testimony to the U.S. Senate Committee on Foreign Relations. See also House Foreign Affairs Committee, *United States–Iraqi Relations*, March 21, 1991. For a critique of administration policy toward Iraq's unconventional weapons programs, see *United States Policy Toward Iraq: Human Rights, Weapons Proliferation, and International Law*, June 15, 1990.

13. *Arab Times*, February 15, 1989 (*FBIS*, February 17, 1989, p. 29); *al-Sharq al-Awsat*, March 8, 1989 (*FBIS*, March 14, 1989, p. 37).

CHAPTER TEN: Be My Brother or I'll Kill You

1. David Pike, "Testing Times for the Saudi Rulers," *Middle East Economic Digest*, August 24, 1990.

2. *New York Times*, October 4, 1990.

3. *Saudi Gazette*, October 2, 1990; *Le Monde*, August 30, 1990; Pike, op. cit.

4. *New York Times*, August 29, 1990; Baker testimony to Senate, September 5, 1990.

5. *International Herald Tribune*, September 12, 1990.

6. The other two Iraqi export routes—a pipeline across Syria and by tanker through the Gulf—had been sealed off during the Iran-Iraq war. The naval embargo would keep the sea route closed.

7. Rhonda Habib, Amman bureau chief of Agence France-Presse and ABC news consultant, "Nightline," August 16, 1990. Middle East News Agency, September 17, 1990, and *FBIS*, October 23, 1990; *New York Times*, November 2, 1990.

8. January 31, 1991, cited in *Washington Times*, March 12, 1991. On Egyptian fundamentalists, see Barry Rubin, *Islamic Fundamentalists in Egyptian Politics* (New York, 1991).

9. Bandar ibn-Sultan, "MacNeil/Lehrer Newshour," August 13, 1990; *Le Monde*, August 30, 1990.

10. *Al-Hayat*, August 22, 1990.

11. Reuters, August 29, 1990.

12. *New York Times*, August 17, 1990.

13. See, for example, *al-Thawra*, October 1, 1990. Other Iraqi propaganda themes—as in *al-Thawra*, October 10, and *al-Qadisiyya*, October 16—included the spread of corruption in Saudi Arabia by Western troops and Iraq's use of disinformation to fool the enemy. Baghdad radio, November 7, 1990 (*FBIS*, November 8, 1990). *Al-Jumhuriyya*, September 26, 1990; Saddam, interview with CBS, *Middle East Mirror*, August 30, 1990, p. 3; *Al-Jumhuriyya*, August 14, 1990.

14. *New York Times*, September 12, 1990; speech of September 16 (*FBIS*, September 17, 1990). See also Baker's testimony to the Senate Foreign Relations Committee, September 4, 1990.

15. *The Economist*, November 3, 1990; *New York Times*, September 19, 1990.

16. *Al-Sharq al-Awsat*, cited in *Middle East Mirror*, August 30, 1990, p. 21; *al-Yom*, August 30, 1990. See also *FBIS*, September 11, 1990, p. 16.

17. Israel refused to negotiate with the PLO but was willing to meet with pro-PLO Palestinians from the West Bank and Gaza Strip, a framework the PLO accepted after the 1991 Gulf war. The PLO's refusal to make clear its willingness to recognize Israel and renounce terrorism also kept it from being accepted as an interlocutor. The point is not that the failure of diplomacy

was completely the PLO's fault but that the organization could have done more to make progress. The PLO and the Palestinians, of course, were the biggest losers from Arafat's failure to do so.

18. *Ha'aretz*, August 17, 1990.
19. *Al-Nadwa*, October 1, 1990.
20. On pro-administration groups, see the Committee for Peace and Security in the Gulf press release, December 12, 1990, and "The Stakes in the Gulf," *New Republic*, January 7–14, 1991. The critical remarks are from Tom Wicker, "The Wrong Strategy," *New York Times*, November 14, 1990.
21. UN Resolution 674 (October 29) condemned Iraqi human rights abuses, while Resolution 677 (November 28) criticized the demographic changes.
22. My thanks to Dr. Amatzia Baram for suggesting some of these points.
23. *Wall Street Journal*, November 2, 1990; *New York Times*, November 4, 1990; Text of CNN Interview, *FBIS*, November 1, 1990, pp. 16–22.
24. November 28, 1988 (*FBIS*, November 30, 1988, pp. 21–26).
25. *Al-Sharq al-Awsat*, December 2, 1990, (*FBIS*, December 5, 1990); *al-Masa'a*, November 25, 1990.
26. C. D. B. Bryan, "Operation Desert Norm," *New Republic*, March 11, 1991.
27. Transcript.
28. *New York Times*, August 28, 1990.

CHAPTER ELEVEN: The Mother of Debacles

1. Morton Kondracke, "Party Pooper," *New Republic*, March 25, 1991, p. 10; Jacob Weisberg, "Gulfballs," *New Republic*, March 25, 1991, p. 19.
2. *New York Times*, December 2, 1990; *Washington Post*, January 11, 1991.
3. October 11 and December 13, 1990, cited in *Washington Times*, March 22, 1991; Weisberg, op. cit. On Kipper's background, see David Segal, "Shrink Rap," *New Republic*, March 25, 1991, p. 18.
4. January 11, 1991, cited in *Washington Times*, March 20 and 21, 1991; November 27, 1990, and January 7, 1991, cited in *Washington Times*, March 11 and 12, 1991.
5. January 11 and 12, 1991, cited in *Washington Times*, March 21, 1991.
6. Columns of August 13, 29, 30, and 31; September 21; October 22; November 7, 12, 16, and 30; December 28, 1990; and January 7, 1991.
7. *Washington Times*, March 22, 1991; Weisberg, op. cit.
8. *The Economist*, December 8, 1990.

9. *Middle East Mirror*, January 18, 1991, p. 14; *New York Times*, January 18, 1991; Reuters, January 18, 1991.

10. Bruckner, op. cit., p. 216.

11. Karen Laub, "Palestinians Fearful of Attack, but Proud of Iraq for Targeting Israel," Reuters, January 18, 1991.

12. *Al-Safir*, September 29, 1990.

13. *Washington Times*, March 25, 1991.

14. According to Pentagon figures, 35 of the American dead and 72 of the wounded were hit by their own side.

15. Senate Foreign Relations Committee, *Civil War in Iraq* (Washington, 1991), p. 15.

CHAPTER TWELVE: The Emperor's New Order

1. Souad al-Sabah, "Who Killed Kuwait?" translated and cited by Fouad Ajami, "The End of Arab Nationalism," loc. cit., p. 27.

2. *New York Times*, April 10, 1991. For a detailed assessment of the Iraqi buildup, see Kenneth Timmerman, *The Death Lobby: How the West Armed Iraq* (New York, 1991).

3. Henry Kissinger, "A Postwar Agenda," *Newsweek*, January 28, 1991.

4. James Akins, *International Herald Tribune*, March 4, 1991.

5. Lionel Barber, *Financial Times*, June 17, 1991.

6. Ajami, "The End of Arab Nationalism," loc. cit., p. 26.

7. Interview, Middle East News Agency, January 24, 1989 (*FBIS*, January 25, 1989, p. 15).

8. Nolan Strong, "Flexibility and Fears," *Jerusalem Report*, December 12, 1991, pp. 32, 34.

9. *New York Times*, March 4 and 8, 1991.

10. *Los Angeles Times*, May 17, 1991.

11. *The Economist*, October 6, 1990, p. 45.

INDEX